Against the New Politics of Identity

Against the New Politics of Identity

How the Left's Dogmas on Race and Equity Harm Liberal Democracy —and Invigorate Christian Nationalism

Ronald A. Lindsay

PITCHSTONE PUBLISHING
DURHAM, NORTH CAROLINA

Pitchstone Publishing
Durham, North Carolina
www.pitchstonebooks.com

Library of Congress Cataloging-in-Publication Data

Names: Lindsay, Ronald A. (Ronald Alan), author.
Title: Against the new politics of identity : how the Left's dogmas on race
    and equity harm liberal democracy-and invigorate Christian nationalism /
    Ronald A. Lindsay.
Description: Durham, North Carolina : Pitchstone Publishing, [2023] |
    Includes bibliographical references. | Summary: "Philosopher Ronald A.
    Lindsay offers a sustained criticism of the far-reaching cultural
    transformation occurring across much of the West by which individuals
    are defined primarily by their group identity, such as race, ethnicity,
    gender identity, and sexual orientation"— Provided by publisher.
Identifiers: LCCN 2023013657 (print) | LCCN 2023013658 (ebook) | ISBN
    9781634312448 (paperback) | ISBN 9781634312455 (ebook)
Subjects: LCSH: Democracy—United States. | Right and left (Political
    science)—United States. | Identity politics—United States. |
    Nationalism—Religious aspects—Christianity.
Classification: LCC JK1726 .L565 2023 (print) | LCC JK1726 (ebook) |
DDC
    324.273—dc23/eng/20230403
LC record available at https://lccn.loc.gov/2023013657
LC ebook record available at https://lccn.loc.gov/2023013658

For Debra
Still my west wind

[A]s we are philosophers or lovers of wisdom, [although] both are dear, piety requires us to honor truth above our friends.

Aristotle, *Nicomachean Ethics*, Book I, Chap. 6, 1096a 14–15
(trans. W.D. Ross)

CONTENTS

INTRODUCTION

The Motivation for This Book

In the past several years, the United States, along with some other Western democracies, has undergone a far-reaching cultural transformation. There are many different aspects to this transformation, for example, constant references to "white privilege" and "white supremacy," denunciations of "cultural appropriation," entry into our discourse of such terms as "intersectionality," the special insight granted to the "lived experience" of those who are allegedly oppressed, ubiquitous commands to indicate one's chosen pronouns, and the pervasiveness of race as a touchstone for nearly every social policy. These indicia of cultural transformation, however, are the consequence of three more fundamental, serious, and portentous changes, namely the following: the growing acceptance of the tenets of standpoint theory, that is, the claim that those who are allegedly oppressed or marginalized have some epistemic advantage over others—with "others" typically meaning white males—and everyone should defer to their wisdom; the nearly universal embrace by universities, corporations, and government institutions of the doctrine of systemic racism, that is, racism is embedded in the laws, regulations, and institutions of the United States, making racism pervasive; and the view that equity, understood as the elimination of racial, ethnic, and other group identity disparities in all areas of life, must take precedence over other selection criteria, such as individual merit, achievement, or need.

These three inter-related social and political phenomena also fuel the menacing growth of social censorship. There are continual efforts to silence those who question the new orthodoxy, such as by "de-platforming" those with opposing views, firing employees who take issue with corporate pronouncements, and intimidating anyone who does not fall in line by classifying them as sexist, transphobic, or racist and then enlisting a social media dogpile. After all, if a white person does not have the lived experience necessary to understand racism, why let him address it? And if anything that might sustain racial disparity is, by definition, racist, why allow racists to give their arguments against equity-driven social policy? And, of course, one must always be vigilant with respect to micro-aggressions. Identity politics and speech restrictions go hand-in-hand. One must control the debate while simultaneously impugning one's critics.

The new trinity of standpoint theory, the doctrine of systemic racism, and the equity mandate is bringing about radical and extensive changes in education, healthcare, employment, entertainment, law enforcement, and government policy. Merit-based admission to schools and universities is rapidly becoming a thing of the past. Academics and bureaucrats demand that distribution of vaccines be based on race, not need.[1] The American Medical Association's 2021 strategic plan for health equity calls on physicians to become social activists and to give priority to combatting "white supremacy" and "intersecting systems of oppression," while advising them that meritocracy is a "malignant narrative."[2] Businesses whose profile of higher-level employees doesn't match the statistical mix of blacks or Hispanics in the population are leaving themselves open to accusations of racism, no matter how objective their selection criteria may be. Every category of awards for film, television, and music is scrutinized to see whether appropriate percentages of people of color are recognized, and book publishers and agents increasingly want "own voices" only. Defunding of the police is coupled with zero-bail policies and altering of prosecutorial priorities. The American federal government has committed itself to "an ambitious whole-of-government equity agenda."[3] The sweeping transformation underway can properly be considered a cultural revolution.

In using the term "cultural revolution," some may think I am inviting comparison to the most notorious cultural revolution of the last century, namely the Maoist cultural revolution that gripped and crippled China for about a decade beginning in 1966. Yes and no.

Certainly, there are similarities. The initial locus of China's revolution was its schools and universities, with indoctrinated students turning into self-righteous mobs attacking teachers and others perceived as "bourgeois," "capitalist roaders," or "counter-revolutionaries." Exams were abolished as a tool of class division. Egged on by the regime, the students became Red Guards and set about overthrowing the "Four Olds," namely old ideas, culture, habits, and customs. In the course of their endeavors, the Red Guards destroyed statues and other historical sites, renamed streets, and rid libraries of dangerous texts. They relentlessly promoted the set of dogmas they wholeheartedly embraced, conveniently summarized in Mao's Little Red Book, and woe to anyone who failed to show sufficient obeisance to these dogmas. If one were lucky, one could escape with no more than public humiliation and ritualized self-denunciation. Many were not so fortunate.[4]

If one substitutes "racist" for "capitalist roader," Columbus and Jefferson statues for Confucius statues, the self-criticism of American faculty (such as the chilling spectacle of ritual confessions of racism at Northwestern University)[5] for the self-abasement of Chinese scholars, and Ibram Kendi's *How To Be An Antiracist*—a book bought in bulk by school districts, universities, and corporations—for the Little Red Book, the parallels are striking and informative.

But, of course, there are critical differences as well. The Chinese Cultural Revolution was initiated by Mao himself, for his own purposes, which appear to have been a mix of concern for consolidating his own power and his own confused ideas about the need for continuous revolution. Students were the tinder, but Mao lit the flame. By contrast, in the United States, our cultural revolution was not driven by any government official but rather was fostered over time by academics, beginning in the 1970s and 1980s with the first formulations of standpoint theory and critical race theory. But although initially confined to the university setting, these theories, though their influence on a couple of generations of students, affected the perceptions and thinking of a large number of people. When the time came for an event to trigger the implementation of these theories, millions of people, especially in the younger generations, were ready. That triggering event was, of course, the video of the death of George Floyd, which overnight resulted in a cascade of pledges from schools, businesses, and local, state, and federal governments to join the antiracist struggle—as well as a series of riots in several cities.[6]

These riots, violent as they were in some cases, highlight another fundamental difference between America's cultural revolution and China's. China's revolution had as an integral part the torture and killing of tens of thousands of individuals and, eventually, the exiling to the countryside of millions, where they were subjected to back-breaking labor and "re-education." Despite the Floyd riots, nothing like that has happened in the United States. Although some American employees forced to sit through hours-long diversity training where they are encouraged to engage in self-criticism may consider this psychological torture, the reality is that America's cultural revolution is nowhere near as violent or destructive as China's.

One important reason for this is that the United States is a liberal democracy, with fairly firm foundations and, until recently, a consensus regarding fundamental rights for individuals, including the right to due process and equal treatment under the law. Furthermore, beyond the First Amendment's prohibition of government regulation of free speech, the United States enjoyed a culture of free speech, in particular in the university context. As long as this culture prevailed, the United States was resistant to dogmatic ideologies. Open debate provided a framework for airing differences and conflict resolution.

Unfortunately, support for the values of liberal democracy is eroding, both on the Right and the Left. From the Left, the driving force behind this erosion is the new politics of identity. If someone not in your racial, ethnic, or gender identity group cannot challenge your claim on a particular issue without committing "epistemic injustice," meaningful political dialogue is severely inhibited. Indeed, if someone opposing your view is automatically a racist, it suggests there is little reason for debate and no prospect or need for compromise. And equal treatment under the law is being replaced by equitable treatment. It is a fundamental tenet of the doctrine of systemic racism that discrimination against whites is not only permissible but required. "The only remedy to racist discrimination is antiracist discrimination."[7]

Group identity is replacing the individual as the unit of moral, legal, and social concern. Group identity determines when one can speak and when one must remain silent. Public policy is now guided by the imperative of eliminating statistical disparities between identity groups, whatever the cost to individual rights. And if some of those disparities persist, it cannot be the aggregate result of decisions by individuals; no, the ideology of group identity insists the cause must be racism or sexism or some other "ism" deeply embedded within some occult system.

These implications of the new politics of identity distinguish it from what, in more halcyon days, was sometimes referred to as identity politics. The old identity politics referred to individuals with perceived common interests forming groups to work together to promote and protect those interests. So, we have the NAACP, the American Jewish Congress, the Catholic League, the American Legion, and so forth. Nothing wrong with that. The old politics of identity was principally a way of ensuring one's interests were not ignored, one's voice was heard. The new politics of identity demands that the group's interests receive priority and that only the group's voice is heard. If obtaining a seat at the table was the metaphor for the old identity politics, excluding "oppressors" (usually meaning whites) from the table is the metaphor for the new politics of identity.

Not unexpectedly, the intolerance of the Left is calling forth a sharp, and equally concerning, reaction from the Right. Manipulating legitimate grievances that many have about being categorized as racists, having their schools prioritize indoctrination over academics, and having their job opportunities limited by tacit quotas, demagogues on the Right have created a reactionary constituency. Too many, frustrated and insulted by the daily drumbeat of mainstream news stories describing how racism is baked into our society, seek alternative sources of news, which, unfortunately, in some cases can be little more than purveyors of falsehoods and fantasy. Collectivist thinking and group identity on the Left is matched by populism and communitarianism on the Right, with a yearning for some mythical past where America was once unqualifiedly "great." In pursuit of this vision, some are willing to resort to violence, as confirmed by the events of January 6, 2021.

So liberal democracy is threatened from both sides of the ideological spectrum. In this book, I will analyze both sets of threats, exposing the flaws in the dogmas on both sides. Most of my focus will be on the dogmas of the Left for a few reasons. First, few have ventured any sustained criticism of them. Indeed, they are currently the prevailing dogmas of the American establishment. One would be hard-pressed to find a university, major corporation, or mainstream media outlet that does not accept as unassailable truth the doctrine of systemic racism. Second, I consider the threat from the Right to be, in part, a reaction to the prevalence of left-wing dogmas. Part of Donald Trump's attraction has been that he is seen by some as the most prominent politician willing to push back, however inarticulately and clumsily, against identity politics. For that reason, many—too many—are willing to overlook his troubled relationship with facts and the obvious flaws in his temperament. Were identity politics to recede, the threat from the Right would also.[8] Finally, as someone who is a liberal, albeit a classical liberal in the John Stuart Mill sense, I am especially concerned and dismayed by the ways in which prevailing views on the Left have betrayed key principles of liberalism: identity groups have replaced the individual as the fundamental unit of moral concern, censorship of "offensive" speech is championed, and race-based discrimination is openly advocated. Weirdly, these very illiberal positions are usually characterized as liberal positions by the media. They are not. If anything, they share similarities with positions held by those on the authoritarian Right. Regarding the suppression of speech, the only difference between the identity Left and the authoritarian Right is the type of speech considered intolerable.

Accordingly, in the first three chapters, I concentrate on dogmas of the Left. I will argue that standpoint theory is fundamentally flawed and self-contradictory and that it is ultimately inconsistent with liberal democracy, where no individual or group can claim special authority; that the case for systemic racism has not been proven and that it rests on an improper use of the concept of disparate impact; and that the push for equity sacrifices individual rights and, at best, will only mask the problems it sets out to remedy.

I will then pivot to address a dogma that appeals to many on the Right. Interestingly, this dogma is, in some ways, a reflection of the Left's identity politics; it is the belief that the United States has a distinct identity as a Christian nation. This belief exerts a strong attraction for many in part because it provides a patina of legitimacy to policy positions Christian nationalists advocate: they are not trying to impose their values on others; rather, they are trying to restore the country to its Christian roots. I will show that the Christian nationalists' historical claims are groundless, leaving aside the impracticality of asserting a Christian identity for the United States in light of the country's increasing diversity.

Throughout my examination of dogmas on both the Left and Right, I will rely on empirical evidence and reasoning, with the hope that the underlying principles of debate in a liberal democracy still have some purchase: that the identity of a person who makes a claim ultimately has no bearing on its truth or falsity; that truth is not determined by majority vote or emotionally appealing rhetoric; and that no assertion has any more validity than the evidence and reasoning offered in support of it.

What's Not Covered and Why

As noted above, many of the cultural changes that have swept across the United States in recent years have also affected other Western countries, especially after the death of George Floyd. These changes include the increasing prominence of identity politics, the growing acceptance of restrictions on allegedly offensive speech, and the ever-expanding re-evaluation of aspects of Western culture, such as classical music, which are often deemed too "white."[9] It was tempting to expand this book accordingly to encompass discussion of these trends in other countries, but it would not be possible to provide detailed analysis of the dogmas underlying these trends while keeping this book at a manageable length. This is especially true with respect to the claim of systemic racism. The claim of systemic racism has been made in several different countries.[10] This claim is based on policies, past and present, of a particular country. One would have to study and analyze the history and current policies of each country to do justice to this claim. The history and policies of the United States are not the history and policies of the United Kingdom, let alone that of France or Germany. An enterprise of such breadth is beyond the scope of this book. That said, from time to time, I will allude to situations in countries other than the United States to illustrate a point.[11]

When I mentioned this book to various colleagues and friends, a common question was whether I would be discussing critical race theory. As readers can tell by this point, the answer is "no," at least insofar as critical race theory represents a distinct topic.

One reason for this is that critical race theory, as defined by its proponents, has several different tenets. One of them is that race is a socially constructed concept, not corresponding to any underlying biological reality.[12] To a large extent, I agree with that tenet. Genetic populations have an objective, scientific basis, of course, but these populations do not match up with racial categories. Instead, prevailing norms at any given time have greatly influenced how the categories of race have been applied, as confirmed by the infamous "one drop" rule—a rule patently ridiculous when considered from the perspective of genetic endowment.[13] That said, one of the curious and paradoxical aspects of identity politics is that, on the one hand, identity politics ideologues claim race is a social construct, while on the other, they argue that we need to consider explicitly the racial impact of a policy in determining whether it is justifiable. Using a dubious concept as the definitive measuring stick for public policy seems more likely to ensconce the concept deeper in public consciousness than to render it meaningless.

Apart from the position that race is a social construct, there are tenets of critical race theory with which I disagree, such as the claim that racism is endemic and embedded in our public policies, which is used as support for the dogma of systemic racism, and the tenet that people of color have special, privileged insight into certain issues based on their life experience. Both of these tenets are discussed and criticized in the following chapters.

Finally, let me say a few words about the disputes surrounding the alleged teaching of critical race theory in schools. Many on the Left have argued that the worries about the teaching of critical race theory in schools are absolutely unfounded. Indeed, when this controversy was at its height, the claim that critical race theory was being taught in some schools was openly ridiculed in the mainstream media, including on publicly funded radio.[14] However, the contention that critical race theory is not being taught is disingenuous. No, there probably has not been any high school elective expressly entitled "Critical Race Theory." But the tenets of critical race theory have influenced teacher training and, in turn, they have influenced the content of courses.[15] If one is teaching that racism is systemic, one is teaching one of the implications of critical race theory. Under these circumstances, to assert that critical race theory is not being taught would be like maintaining that Marxism is not being taught because there is no elective with that express name even though teachers are required to receive training on the tenets of Marxism and they then teach history as the history of class struggle.

Another tactic used in the disputes over critical race theory in schools has been to argue that those protesting critical race theory want only sanitized versions of history and civics to be taught in schools, versions that would omit the gruesome facts of how blacks were enslaved and then mistreated following emancipation. I cannot read minds, but it seems to me most protests have not been objecting to teaching the facts of history, but rather they have been objecting to the way in which those facts are characterized. For example, *The 1619 Project*,[16] used as part of the curriculum in many schools, appropriately provides factual information about slavery in colonial America not always encountered previously in high school history courses. There is nothing objectionable about that. To the contrary, providing factual information previously overlooked or omitted is a good thing. But *The 1619 Project* also contains highly disputable characterizations of facts, such as the claim that preservation of slavery was the primary motivation for the American colonists' break with Great Britain.[17] Teaching American history, warts and all, is not the issue; teaching a tendentious, ideologically driven interpretation of history is.

Much more could be said about critical race theory and its role in schools and in our broader culture, but I will leave that to those who want to address the theory directly. Here it will be discussed only insofar as it relates to the criticized dogmas.

Finally, one note about wording and one note about notes: I have avoided use of the term "woke" to describe positions I criticize, using instead terms such as identity group politics or ideology, which I believe capture the essence of the left-wing dogmas I address. "Woke" has the virtues of brevity and familiarity, but it has lost some of its utility as it has become a term used by many to reference any position on the Left or even, in the mouths of some, just any position one opposes. Former president Trump has called those who doubt his baseless claims of election fraud "woke."[18] Unfortunately, "woke" is fast becoming the counterpart to the term "racist": a term of insult as opposed to a term conveying accurate, descriptive information.

The reader will notice by now that I use endnotes. I read a lot of nonfiction, and more than a few authors omit footnotes or endnotes on the ground that non-academic readers find them distracting and not useful. I believe that is a disservice to the reader, besides being condescending. In any event, because I am confident many will challenge my arguments, I decided it was imperative to point the reader to my supporting references, many of which can be found online.

CHAPTER 1

Standpoint Theory: Objectivity as a White Male Delusion

In the summer of 2020, the National Museum of African American History and Culture, a museum administered by the federally funded Smithsonian Institution, prominently displayed on its website a "whiteness" chart. The chart purported to describe the aspects and assumptions of whiteness and white culture in the United States. Among the various attitudes listed as "normalized" by whiteness was emphasis on the scientific method, which includes "objective, rational linear thinking" and "cause and effect relationships."[1]

Perhaps to someone totally unaware of the social currents sweeping through the country in the last decade or so, the notion that the scientific method or objective thinking or use of the concepts of cause and effect were mere aspects of white culture as opposed to universally valid standards of inquiry might seem bizarre. After all, wasn't one of the fruits of the scientific method the very technology that allowed the museum to have a website on which to display this chart? But the chart and its display are the foreseeable outcomes of a flawed theory about knowledge and its acquisition that has gained currency both inside and outside academia, namely standpoint theory.

The Claims of Standpoint Theory and Its Appeal

The term "standpoint theory" may not be that familiar to those who have not had the benefit of taking university-level humanities courses, but most people are surely aware of the ways in which this theory has been interpreted and applied in the wider society. Who has not heard the claim that if you're not a woman, or a black, or a lesbian, you cannot speak to issues that might affect women, blacks, or lesbians? Instead, one must defer to those who have the experience of living as women, blacks, lesbians, and so on. One cannot question an oppressed person's lived experience. Moreover, persons in these so-called marginalized groups are not only in a position to speak authoritatively about issues that might affect them but also have enhanced knowledge-producing abilities in general given their oppressed status. Those in "dominant" positions, on the other hand, are disabled from seeing things clearly by their white privilege, male privilege, straight privilege, etc. The only appropriate stance to take for such privileged persons is to "shut up and listen."

These commonly held attitudes and beliefs are the offshoots of standpoint theory, as it has been filtered down into everyday life outside the academy. In a nutshell, standpoint theory holds that knowledge is rooted in and derives from a person's social circumstances and that those who are oppressed (by some criteria) are in a better position to acquire knowledge than those who are not. To use the standard jargon, all knowledge is "situated" and the oppressed are "epistemically privileged." They know better. The "they" who know better are, depending on the context, women, or blacks, or black women (or Latinos or . . . it gets complicated). The epistemically challenged, i.e., ignorant, are whites, but especially white men.

Standpoint theory is Marxist in origin. I say this not to cast any aspersions, but because it is a fact. One of the leading early essays advocating standpoint theory, by the noted feminist Nancy Hartsock, explicitly credits Marx for coming up with the argument that social relations can shape one's knowledge and that oppressed segments of society (in Marx's case, the proletariat) can have a better understanding of the nature of things than the dominant group.[2] Those who hold power don't have the proper perspective to recognize their oppression of others and just accept the current structure of social relations as normal. By contrast, as the oppressed struggle against the dominant class, they can achieve a critical collective consciousness and they can see through the rationalizations offered by those who hold power.

Updating and revising Marxist theory for the 20th and 21st centuries, advocates of standpoint theory maintain that women or blacks or other oppressed groups of individuals are in a better position to understand the true nature of social relations. For example, with respect to women, Hartsock argued that because material life is structured in fundamentally different ways for men and women, with a sexual division of labor analogous to Marx's class division, and women, through their struggles, can see beneath the surface of these relations, the "female experience . . . forms a basis on which to expose abstract masculinity as both partial and fundamentally perverse."[3] But it is not just social relations which are better understood by the oppressed; the oppressed are also in a privileged position to acquire knowledge about a range of other phenomena, including scientific findings. Sandra Harding, a leading and frequently cited proponent of a modified version of standpoint theory, has argued at length that the findings of natural sciences (physics, chemistry, biology) are affected by bias, which cannot be recognized by the (male) scientists themselves, but only by the oppressed, and in this view she is definitely not alone: "Scientific knowledge, like other forms of knowledge is gendered. Science cannot produce cultural or gender-neutral knowledge."[4] As with sex, so too with race. There is no race-neutral knowledge. Even some aspects of physics are adversely affected by "white empiricism," which is defined as the "specific practice of epistemic oppression paired with a willingness to ignore empirical data."[5] Moreover, "the presence of white empiricism involves a refusal to acknowledge that white supremacy has limited the scientific community's capacity for knowledge production."[6]

If knowledge is always relative to and determined by one's social circumstances, then the notion of a truly objective knowledge which can be attained by all and which applies to all is a fantasy. Worse, it is a fantasy that has been used to exclude the voices of the oppressed. "The conception of value-free, impartial, dispassionate research . . . has been operationalized to identify and eliminate only those social values and interests that differ [from those held by] the researchers and critics who are regarded by the scientific community as competent to make such judgments."[7] Here one can see the genesis of the assertion in the whiteness chart that objectivity is a white "assumption"—and it is an assumption that according to standpoint theory is wholly unwarranted.[8]

One might think the radical nature of standpoint theory might make it a hard sell, but that is not the case. As with any theory that had its origins in academia, it has been repeatedly critiqued, revised, and modified, but its core precepts, including the claim that the oppressed have important insights not available to those in the dominant group, continue to be widely held. Many scholars use it as the basis for research. To quote Sandra Harding:

> [Standpoint theory] as a methodology ... has been disseminated across many research disciplines and is today often used to frame research projects.... Moreover, as a more general 'logic of inquiry'—a trans-disciplinary regulative ideal—standpoint theory is widely used in research projects focused on race, class, sexuality, and studies in postcolonial research, though in these contexts the logic is only occasionally labeled as being in the standpoint tradition.[9]

Moreover, it's not just professional academics who are enchanted by this theory. Standpoint theory has been disseminated among, and embraced by, legions of undergraduates and graduate students over the last couple of decades. Pick up some random term paper or master's thesis these days and you're likely to find such assertions as this:

> FST [Feminist Standpoint Theory] asserts that people have a perspective that incorporates race, class, gender, birthplace, and so on. *Journalists have lived under the misperception that they can be objective and unbiased.* This viewpoint has perpetuated systemic racism, misogyny, and classism.[10] (Emphasis added.)

And from the university to the workplace and all the other settings of everyday life, the notion that members of marginalized groups have special insights and that their lived experience trumps any contrary view is now widely accepted, even by the many who have never heard of standpoint theory.

Is this diffusion of standpoint theory due to the strength of arguments set forth in support of the theory? I think not. I believe it has more to do with non-intellectual features of the theory, including, in part, its echoing of elements of folk wisdom.

But as a key contention of my book is that one should carefully consider opposing views and evaluate them on their merits, I will provide a summary of the arguments in favor of standpoint theory, drawing principally, but not exclusively, on a summary provided by Harding herself. Harding's summary is useful for a couple of reasons. First, her arguments are less burdened by rhetoric than many others. Also, she presents a modified version of standpoint theory which attempts, although not successfully, to overcome the relativist implications of earlier formulations of the theory. (I will evaluate the arguments in a later section.)

As indicated above, standpoint theory's intellectual heritage is found in Marxism, and in Marxism's view that society is divided into social classes, with that division eventually evolving into the two opposed classes of the bourgeoisie and proletariat. The position of individuals within these classes is inversely related to their potential for understanding the true structure of social relations. Simplifying Marxist theory somewhat, those in the upper class have an interest in maintaining the status quo, so they are blind to their exploitation of the workers. Their social position shapes and stunts their knowledge. By contrast, workers are motivated to understand the true state of social relations; they can understand both the distorted viewpoint of the upper classes—they must in order to survive—and the reality of their exploitation. So, they are in position to understand the structure of society better.

There are divisions within Marxist theory as to what conditions actually result in the proletariat achieving revolutionary class consciousness, as opposed to simply being in a position to understand social relations better, but that need not detain us. That said, it is worth noting that standpoint theory suffers from an analogous problem, as will become clear.[11]

Essentially, some feminists took the Marxist construct of class division and refashioned it to fit what they perceived as the stark sex-based divisions of labor and power. As with Marxism, standpoint theory holds that knowledge claims are invariably socially situated, and because of their different social situations, there is a systematic difference between the knowledge acquisition capabilities of men and women. The hegemony of men gives them little interest in examining the social order, whereas the oppression of women puts them in a position to question and understand social relations better:

> Women and men are assigned different kinds of activities in [sex-strat-
> ified societies]; consequently, they lead lives that have significantly dif-
> ferent contours and patterns. Using women's lives as grounds to criti-
> cize the dominant knowledge claims, which have been based primarily
> in the lives of men in the dominant races, classes, and cultures, can
> decrease the partialities and distortions in the picture of nature and
> social life provided by the natural and social sciences.[12]

Moreover, as outsiders to the dominant culture, women "can see patterns
of belief or behavior that are hard for those immersed in the culture
to detect."[13] In addition, women "have less to lose by distancing themselves from the social order; thus, the perspective from their lives can
more easily generate fresh and critical analyses."[14] Finally, insofar as they
struggle to change the existing social order, women can arrive at a deeper
understanding of society's sex-based power relations and the institutions
that support these relations. "Only through such struggles can we begin
to see beneath the appearances created by an unjust social order to the
reality of how this social order is in fact constructed and maintained."[15]
Importantly, this deeper understanding extends not only to legal and
political institutions and their constraints, but also to the enterprise of
science. Scientific results that are based on the contributions of marginalized persons provide a better representation of nature than do scientific
results based on male outlooks. "[A] maximally critical study of scientists
and their communities can be done only from the perspective of those
whose lives have been marginalized by such communities."[16]

There have been some refinements to these contentions; in particular,
some feminists have questioned whether epistemic privilege of the oppressed applies beyond certain limited, specified contexts. Limiting the
scope of the claim of epistemic privilege may seem to make it more de-
fensible. I will consider these refinements in due course, but I believe the
above summary is a fair one which the reader can confirm by consulting
the references provided. The really significant development in standpoint
theory since its initial expositions has been its extension beyond wom-
en to other oppressed groups. Oppressed blacks, Hispanics, gays, lesbians, trans individuals, and so forth can also possess epistemic privilege.
The arguments offered for the epistemic privilege of these different oppressed groups do not differ in substance from the ur-feminist argument,

although the interjection of "intersectionality" into the analysis does add significant complications (see below). The core thesis remains the same: the oppressed can recognize the realities of their situation, whereas, with respect to a racial context, "Whites are imprisoned ... in a cognitive state which both protects them from dealing with the realities of social oppression and, of course, disables them, epistemically."[17]

Are many persuaded by these arguments? Sure, probably a fair number, although they should not be because, as I will point out, the arguments are not sound. In any event, there are other factors, including psychological ones, which help account for the acceptance of the theory.

Among the immediate consequences of accepting standpoint theory are that one can dismiss the positions and arguments of persons in the alleged dominant group (again, typically white men) as being based on an inadequate and distorted perspective. Moreover, one can dismiss their positions and arguments without engaging at any length with them. In other words, such individuals can be dismissed out of hand because they literally do not know what they are talking about. For adherents of standpoint theory, were a white man to address a conference focused on discussing best policies for securing women's rights, the first reaction from attendees should be, "Why is a white man talking to us?" One doesn't need to ponder at length the dynamics of this relationship to see how attractive it is—to the self-appointed advocates for the allegedly oppressed. Just as Marxists dismissed arguments questioning their economics or politics by labeling their opponents "bourgeois," so the views of anyone who might demur from some claim put forth by one of today's spokespersons for the oppressed can be dismissed as "patriarchal," "white supremacist," or "heteronormative," depending on the situation. Of course, when deployed in this fashion, standpoint theory is inimical to rational inquiry and the liberal notion that all parties should listen to each other sympathetically and with open minds. In a liberal society, it is not who puts forth the claim that matters but what facts and reasoning are offered in support of the claim. The standpoint theorist rejects this evidentiary standard. For the standpoint theorist, the identity of the person making the claim *is* of paramount importance.

For this reason, standpoint theory is a fit companion to the all too familiar concept of "privilege," as in "white privilege," "male privilege," "cisgender privilege," and so on. Indeed, although they have slightly different pedigrees, standpoint theory and privilege postulation are mutually reinforcing, and one can often find them combined in denunciations of opposing views. Presumably, except for those who had Rip Van Winkle as a roommate, most everyone has at least a passing acquaintance with the concept of privilege and how it has been wielded as a rhetorical weapon. In essence, privilege is an unearned advantage in some social setting that is said to attach to someone because of their status as a white person, a man, and so forth. For example, according to the original list of white privileges, being white supposedly makes it easier to secure a publisher and find flesh-colored bandages.[18] Moreover, because of a person's privileged status, they may be oblivious to circumstances that affect how others are treated or must conduct themselves. Were a white person to opine in a particular instance that a black driver was pulled over because he was driving erratically, she is likely to be rebuked with the admonition to "check her privilege." What standpoint theory and the concept of privilege have in common is the underlying premise that it is one's status that is the best indicator of whether one's claim is likely to be true, not the evidence that one marshals in support of the claim. So, on the one hand, according to standpoint theory, being a member of oppressed groups gives one more authority to speak to a certain issue, while at the same time, being socially privileged takes away one's ability to speak perceptively and intelligently about that issue. Status makes members of oppressed groups better knowers, and those who are privileged worse knowers. Conclusion: on many issues, no need to listen to whites or males.

Its convenience for dismissing pesky objections is not the only basis for the attractiveness of standpoint theory. There is undoubtedly a certain intuitive appeal to the idea. In common, everyday interactions, the point is often made that if you haven't had a certain experience, you can't really talk about it. You don't get it. You don't know what it's like. This is reflected in the folk wisdom that "you need to walk a mile in my shoes" to have a real grasp of a particular situation. Accordingly, if the issue at hand is racial discrimination, many might think the standpoint theorists have a point: how can a white person, especially a white male person, really know anything about discrimination, given that he is unlikely to have encountered it, especially as a victim? Shouldn't he defer to those with first-hand experience? Similar points could be made about sexual harassment, violence against gay men and lesbians, and so on.

Furthermore, a superficial acquaintance with the history of scientific research seems to lend support to standpoint theory's thesis that all knowledge is socially situated. Various scientific claims which are now universally regarded as erroneous were once widely accepted, for example, the geocentric view of the solar system and phlogiston theory (substances combust because of the presence in them of phlogiston). One explanation for the tenacity with which they continued to be held, even when contrary evidence emerged, is the social context of the relevant scientific community. In the one case, many scholars favored geocentrism because they were still influenced by religious beliefs, and in the other, the consensus of the community of chemists in favor of phlogiston made dissent difficult.[19] I am doubtful that there is anything we could correctly call a biologically based science of race, as opposed to various pseudo-scientific views which were little more than expressions of prejudice, but admittedly some well-regarded scientists held racist views. In any event, the soft sciences, such as psychiatry, anthropology, and sociology, provide us with multiple examples of how social context influences scientific claims. Physicians in the nineteenth century considered masturbation a disease that could prove fatal,[20] and notoriously, the official manual of the American Psychiatric Association categorized homosexuality as a disease until 1973.[21] There is little doubt that prevailing attitudes regarding sexual expression influenced these views.

Standpoint theory also provides an additional rationale for efforts to ensure diversity in corporations, government, faculty positions, and so forth. If members of oppressed groups really do have insights inaccessible to white men, then they should be employed and engaged at the very least in numbers proportional to their representation in the population— arguably, even at even greater rates to compensate for the stunted knowledge acquisition capabilities of white men. Indeed, if marginalized people have experiences that provide them with an epistemic advantage, this requires that their views be an integral part of any research program, including scientific research.

Standpoint theory also dovetails nicely with a favored technique of those who question "linear" reasoning or simply don't want to engage with a long line of analysis, namely storytelling, now very much in vogue by its popularization through critical race theory. Through storytelling, one relates an anecdote, or perhaps a fable, derived from one's own lived experience. These stories serve to undercut and expose dominant racist forms of discourse. Focusing on generally accepted facts may just replicate racist biases; the counter-storytelling of a person of color, by contrast, derives epistemic authority from that person's lived experience and is, therefore, presumptively unimpeachable. "Critical race theory recognizes that the experiential knowledge of people of color is legitimate, appropriate, and critical to understanding, analyzing, and teaching about racial subordination [through] such methods as storytelling, family histories, biographies, parables, *cuentos*, *testimonios*, chronicles and narratives."[22] This methodology "challenges White privilege, rejects notions of 'neutral' research or 'objective' researchers and exposes deficit-informed research that silences and distorts epistemologies of peoples of color."[23]

All these factors, and perhaps others, have contributed to the widespread acceptance of standpoint theory. Before we can begin to assess the merits of the theory, however, we need to look at how "intersectionality" has modified the theory.

Intersectionality

As indicated, standpoint theory was initially developed by feminists borrowing from their understanding of Marxist theory. Just as Marx and his disciples maintained that advanced capitalist society was divided into two classes, the bourgeoisie and the proletariat, and argued that the proletariat could achieve an epistemic advantage because of their oppressed status, similarly, feminists divided society into men and women, with oppressed women now positioned to achieve epistemic advantage.

But matters aren't so simple, are they? What about all the other groups who can assert they are oppressed?

Enter intersectionality.

The concept of "intersectionality" first gained significant traction after the legal scholar Kimberlé Crenshaw wrote an article in which she argued that various court decisions improperly failed to recognize that black women could "experience discrimination in ways that are both similar to and different from those experienced by white women and black men."[24] In other words, the courts did not understand how the intersection of race and sex, as multiple axes of discrimination, could affect black women. "Because the intersectional experience is greater than the sum of racism and sexism, any analysis that does not take intersectionality into account cannot sufficiently address the particular manner in which Black women are subordinated."[25] To put it in plain language, black women might be discriminated against even in a setting where there was no apparent discrimination against black men or white women. For example, in the context of employment discrimination, an employer that had a large number of black male employees and a large number of white female employees might still be guilty of discrimination against black women. As far as it goes, a reasonable point perhaps.

Crenshaw then followed up this critique of legal decisions with a broader argument about societal structures of power and how through complex layers of discrimination they adversely affect in varying ways people of different identities. In doing so, she criticized both feminists who failed to take account of race and antiracists who neglected the impact of sex:

> Feminist efforts to politicize experiences of women and antiracist efforts to politicize experiences of people of color have frequently proceeded as though the issues and experiences they each detail occur in mutually exclusive terrains. Although racism and sexism readily interact in the lives of real people, they seldom do in feminist and antiracist practices.[26]

In contrast to this compartmentalizing approach, Crenshaw argued for "the need to account for multiple grounds of identity when considering how the social world is constructed."[27]

Crenshaw's advice was taken to heart. Most, if not all, advocates for standpoint theory acknowledged that identity categories other than male/female had to be taken into account in analyzing the conditions of knowledge production. One can easily see why standpoint theorists would readily embrace intersectionality. If all knowledge claims are socially situated, then the (presumed) different social situation of a black woman as opposed to a white woman must be considered. Consequently, "[s]tandpoint work must always be 'intersectional.'"[28]

But, of course, race and sex are not the only categories of identity that might apply to a person. If one is to take intersectionality properly into account, one must consider everything and anything that could (allegedly) create stark social divisions and marginalize people. "The term *intersectionality* references the critical insight that race, class, gender, sexuality, ethnicity, nation, ability and age operate not as unitary, mutually exclusive entities, but rather as reciprocally constructing phenomena that in turn shape complex social inequalities."[29] That's a fairly long list of identity categories, but one can add to it. For example, there is also immigration status, mental health, physical health, body shape, religion (or lack thereof), and so on. There are subcategories as well. One should never commit the unforgivable mistake of assuming gay men and lesbians would have the same standpoint, and naturally, their standpoint differs from that of transgender individuals. Similarly, with respect to immigration status, one must differentiate between legal and illegal and among cultures of origin. And once one opens the disability category, there's a virtually endless inventory. A visually impaired person is different from a hearing-impaired person and from a mobility-impaired person, and they all differ from persons with chronic diseases, of which there are dozens, along with dozens of combinations and variations.

This lengthy, and ever-expanding, list of identity categories naturally prompts the thought that the end result of any intersectional analysis must be that we are all simply individuals with our own unique histories and social positions—in which case, what exactly does standpoint theory, as modified by intersectionality, contribute to our understanding of knowledge production? Doesn't it all reduce to an individual's unique viewpoint? "That's your opinion; I have mine."

It is tempting to use a *reductio ad absurdum* argument along these lines, but to begin, one must remember that individuality as commonly conceived isn't recognized under intersectionality analysis. A person is a bearer of group identities; a person is more a collection of Platonic forms than an individual. Those who adhere faithfully to intersectionality analysis expressly reject any "shift from collective identity to multiple subjectivities."[30]

Furthermore, intersectionality analysis uses group identity only as a starting point. Recall that central to standpoint theory is the social division between the oppressed and the dominant. Without this sharp social division, the entire rationale for asserting that the oppressed possess epistemic advantage collapses. So even though a person may belong to multiple identity categories, this does not imply that the person has only his or her individual perspective. To the contrary, to the extent persons are oppressed because of their identities, they can achieve a critical group consciousness.

But although standpoint theory cum intersectionality may narrowly escape the *reductio* argument, it still faces the daunting task of determining exactly who has epistemic privilege, to what extent, and in what context. Here it has failed.

When there is a binary division between the capitalist class and workers or between men and women, it is obvious (in theory) who is dominant and who is oppressed. That task of differentiating oppressed from dominant becomes orders of magnitude more difficult if, when carrying out an analysis, one must consider a set of numerous complex identities. But the problem is deeper than that. One must not only place persons within various group identities, but one must also consider the relationship of persons with group identities WXYZ to persons with group identities ABCD and EFGH within a given social context, because "an intersectional position may be disadvantaged relative to one group, but advantaged relative to another."[31] For example, a "White lesbian may be disadvantaged because of divergence from the heterosexual norm and standard, but relative to other lesbians she enjoys racial privilege."[32]

Advocates for intersectionality recognize that in determining extent of marginalization or oppression, a straightforward additive formula using generalizations and ignoring context will not work.[33] One cannot simply claim that a black woman is doubly disadvantaged compared to a black man. And that is a relatively easy comparison. How does one draw any sort of conclusion from a comparison of an indigenous thirty-year-old gay man who is deaf with a heterosexual Hispanic middle-aged woman with Crohn's disease when the context is their competition for a position in a university's chemistry department? Who is more disadvantaged, and in what sense, and through what mechanism, might their relatively greater disadvantage provide them with more powers of knowledge acquisition in connection with the work of this particular department? (Let us assume both have achieved the requisite state of grievance so their consciousness has been raised.) What method of intersectional analysis will enable us to resolve these questions? Despite the hundreds of articles, dozens of books, and numerous symposia and conferences devoted to the topic of intersectionality, one will search in vain for an adequate explanation. The only firm answer one can find is that a quantitative approach, that is, one that looks to develop an oppression ranking showing, for example, how group WXYZ has an epistemic advantage over other groups in a particular context, is unlikely to work. Yeah, I think we can see that. If we just limit the number of oppressed categories to ten—a very conservative estimate—and bearing in mind that we need to consider the relationship of each of these categories to the other categories in a given social context and then rank them, we would have at a minimum 10! (10 factorial) possible configurations of oppression. That's 3,628,800 possible rankings.

Instead of any comprehensive, definitive analysis of how to determine who is best situated to make a superior knowledge claim in each context, we get a lot of hand-waving, with feminists, for example, anxiously acknowledging the importance of considering the insights of other identity groups, but declining to specify the level of deference to be accorded these insights. Here, again, is Harding:

> Moreover, [women's] speech competes for attention and status as most plausible not only with that of misogynists but also with the speech of other Others: African Americans, other peoples of color, gay rights activists, pacifists, ecologists, members of new formations of the left, and so on. Isn't feminism forced to embrace relativism by its condition of being just one among many counter-cultural voices?
>
> This description of the terrain in which feminists struggle to advance their claims, however, assumes that people must choose only one among these countercultures as providing an absolute standard for sorting knowledge claims, or else regard all of them as competing and assign them equal cognitive status. Actually, it is a different scenario that the countercultures can envision and even occasionally already enact: the fundamental tendencies of each must *permeate* each of the others in order for each movement to succeed. Feminists should *center* the concerns of each of these movements, and each of them must move feminist concerns to its *center*.[34] (Emphasis added.)

"Permeate." "Center." Murky metaphors in place of analysis—the type of analysis one would expect and require from those advocating a wholesale revision of how science is to be done. And as to "centering," if each identity group centers the concerns of the others—well, that's a pretty crowded center.

In short, the very complexity of intersectionality, which in one sense is supposed to be its virtue, is also the source of its weakness as a theoretical tool of analysis on the issue of the supposed epistemic advantage of the oppressed. Given the many different possible bases of identity and the myriad ways in which they can relate to one another, a precise, persuasive defense of group WXYZ's epistemic advantage with respect to other groups seems unfeasible—at least it has yet to materialize.

That applying intersectionality can create a conceptual tangle is conceded by some advocates. How to extricate oneself from the tangle? The remedy, according to some, is to think "intersectionally about how intersectionality is and should be deployed" and thinking "intersectionally includes the possibility that *stepping back from intersectionality* may in some cases work as a strategy."[35] In other words, the theory may work best when it is not applied.

Not unexpectedly, the shakiness of the underlying premises of intersectional analysis has not diminished the intensity or frequency of the claims of oppression. To begin, recognition that there are many distinct identity groups, which can be in competition in the victim sweepstakes with each other, opens up additional avenues for criticism and denunciation. For example, some black scholars complain bitterly that certain feminists have undertaken the "whitening of intersectionality" by "decentering the constitutive role of race in intersectional thought and praxis."[36] A film celebrating the human rights work of gay activist Peter Tatchell is lambasted because too much emphasis is placed on the white subject of the film, Tatchell, while neglecting the struggles of black civil rights activists and black trans women.[37] Self-criticism being a gesture expected of those in identity politics, there are also many examples of persons asserting that yes, while their group X is oppressed, group Y is even more so. Thus, a gay white man chides his fellows for ignoring their own "racism, sexism, xenophobia and transphobia,"[38] and a straight black man advises other straight black men to recognize their (relative) privilege and informs them that he and they are the "white people of black people."[39]

In addition, of course, although the various marginalized groups may experience oppression differently, in ways exceedingly difficult to specify, they are confident they are all oppressed by some domineering central locus of power—whose contours, however, can be delineated only by opposing its identity to the identities of the oppressed groups. One gets the impression from reading many of the papers advocating standpoint theory cum intersectionality that government, the business sector, and academia are all thoroughly dominated by wealthy, height-weight proportionate, straight, cisgendered white males with perfect health who belong to a majoritarian religion and whose ancestors were on the *Mayflower* and who are both incapable of understanding social realities and resistant to new ideas.

Finally, although advocates of intersectional standpoint theory may not be able to specify with precision how different groups are epistemically advantaged in particular contexts, that they themselves suffer oppression and possess epistemic advantage is beyond dispute. As these advocates are often found in universities, that is the setting where their oppression may be manifested, and that oppression can take the form of other scholars questioning their oppression and the authority they derive therefrom. As one advocate complains, "elite academics" argue that "standpoint epistemology [is] a limited and potentially biased form of knowing" which enables these elites to commit "epistemic injustice" by "discrediting the epistemic agency of oppressed subjects."[40] Here, again, we see one of the appeals of standpoint theory. Those who take issue with your claims are not simply disagreeing with you; they are committing an injustice.

In sum, even though it is a rare advocate of standpoint theory nowadays who doesn't subscribe to intersectionality, intersectionality has not provided any support for the key tenets of standpoint theory. To the contrary, its unwieldiness, internal tensions, lack of specificity, and rejection of the binary model of oppression tend to undercut standpoint theory. But we cannot leave it there. To be fair, we need to consider whether standpoint theory can stand on its own, without the encumbrance of intersectionality.

An Assessment of Standpoint Theory

Arguably, enough has been said already to indicate the infirmity of standpoint theory, but to do standpoint theory justice, I need to evaluate carefully the arguments offered to support it. All of this must take place before examination of its progeny, the "lived experience" doctrine, can be properly critiqued. So, bear with me. You'll find the journey worth it.

In assessing standpoint theory, I will make the following arguments: to the extent the situated knowledge tenet has any credibility, it does little more than reflect common sense, and its challenge to objectivity rests on an equivocation between an individual's claims to knowledge and our common body of knowledge; standpoint theorists have failed to establish criteria that would enable us to determine what constitutes oppression, when the oppressed have raised their consciousness sufficiently to achieve their epistemic advantage, or, crucially, how to judge that one standpoint is better than another; there has been an utter failure to provide any probative evidence that women or blacks or any other allegedly oppressed group has been able to produce more accurate results in the sciences than men or whites, and evidence that has been offered sometimes confuses questions about accuracy in research with disputes about what type of research is worth pursuing. A leitmotif throughout these separate arguments is that, in various ways, standpoint theory is internally inconsistent and self-defeating.

Situated Knowledge and Objectivity

That knowledge claims reflect a person's background, including that person's social setting, is true—trivially true if one accepts both the notion of causality and the view that humans are physical beings, within the chain of causation. Part of that chain of causation includes underlying beliefs. How we interpret what we observe is influenced by our beliefs. How could it be otherwise? And, yes, claims made within the realm of science can be and have been influenced by background beliefs, sometimes with what most would regard now as infelicitous consequences. Notoriously, our understanding of the earth's relationship to the sun was for centuries influenced by prevailing religious beliefs.

If this were all that the thesis of "situated knowledge" amounted to, then it would generate no dissent, but also little interest, as it would merely restate the obvious. But it aspires to more than that. In the hands of standpoint theorists, the situated knowledge thesis holds that the inescapability of the influence of background beliefs renders scientific objectivity, as traditionally understood, impossible. Value-neutral knowledge is a myth—a myth perpetuated and sustained only because of "its usefulness and its widespread appeal to dominant groups."[41] What we naively think of as objective scientific knowledge is actually an expression of power of the dominant class and reflects their "political desires, interests and values."[42] Standpoint theory enables us to make "transparent the values and interests, such as androcentrism, heteronormativity, and Eurocentrism, that underlie allegedly neutral methods in science and epistemology, and clarify their impact."[43]

As a corrective to this skewed approach to knowledge acquisition—which Harding characterizes as "weak objectivity"—standpoint theorists argue that we must have "causal analyses not just of the micro processes in the laboratory but also of the macro tendencies in the social order, which shape scientific practices."[44] Naturally, this endeavor requires that we begin our analyses using the perspective "of the systematically oppressed, exploited, and dominated."[45] If we succeed in doing so, we should achieve a more accurate and rational production of knowledge. This production of knowledge using the perspective of the oppressed, exploited, and dominated is what Harding refers to as "strong objectivity." It is "strong" because it works as a corrective to the partial, distorted view of reality we get when we do not defer to the insights of the marginalized. Harding clings to the term "objectivity" because she realizes that standpoint theory is vulnerable to the charge of relativism, and also, as she puts it, "objectivity" has "a valuable political history."[46] Other standpoint theorists reject completely the use of the term "objectivity" because they think it is too tainted with the regressive fantasy of value-neutral knowledge. This intramural dispute need not detain us. The point is that objectivity, as traditionally understood, is firmly rejected by all standpoint theorists.

Before arguing for the possibility of reliable, inter-subjectively valid scientific knowledge, which is not dependent on the identity of the persons responsible for producing the knowledge, let me briefly address some related issues in the philosophy of science. I believe I must do this because at various points in the literature, standpoint theorists have availed themselves of the arguments by Thomas Kuhn and others who have emphasized how observations that provide the underlying data for scientific theories are themselves "theory-laden."[47] In other words, the observations that scientists make are dependent on a body of theoretical tenets through which they are conceptualized. Kuhn famously argued that scientists approach research problems through a prevailing paradigm, which includes a set of methodological presuppositions.[48] The prevailing paradigm remains in place until there is a "paradigm shift," which is not caused by the simple accumulation of more data, but rather by persistent anomalies that eventually precipitate the birth of a rival paradigm, which can eliminate or explain away these anomalies. The shift to the new paradigm is not, or at least not entirely, driven by reason and observation alone. Kuhn gave several historical examples to buttress his arguments, including the well-known conflict between the Ptolemaic (geocentric) and Copernican (heliocentric) systems. To put the implication of observations being theory-laden bluntly, when Ptolemaic and Copernican astronomers saw the "same" phenomenon, Ptolemaic astronomers observed a sun setting below the horizon, whereas Copernican astronomers observed the horizon moving up to a sun stationary relative to the earth.

A similar argument against objectivity builds on Willard Van Orman Quine's contention that all theories are underdetermined by the factual evidence.[49] Any body of evidence can be made consistent with conflicting theories. To claim that some observations count in favor of a certain hypothesis, one must make certain background assumptions; no hypothesis can be tested in isolation. Moreover, no conclusive empirical test can be made of the set of background assumptions themselves. To refer once again to our conflict over heliocentrism, Galileo's telescopic observations, in particular his observations of the phases of Venus, certainly put major strains on the Ptolemaic model of the universe, but ad hoc modifications to Ptolemy's model could accommodate these observations. Furthermore, stellar parallax was not detectable in Galileo's time (parallax being the shift in apparent position of an object when observed from different locations). Ptolemaic astronomers insisted this showed the earth was not moving, whereas those who favored heliocentrism argued that this indicated the universe was much larger than had been supposed.

To thoroughly summarize, analyze, and critique the many discussions of objectivity within the philosophy of science would take a thick book,[50] but fortunately, we do not need to pursue that level of detail.

Kuhn's and Quine's arguments apply at the margins of our concerns here and, anyway, do not provide any help to standpoint theorists. To begin, regarding Kuhn's argument, one can concede that at the level of grand theory, science does not progress through a straightforward accumulation of data producing incremental modifications to our body of knowledge. Instead, problems within a prevailing framework of assumptions produce a rupture resulting in a reframing of key issues and a reinterpretation of observations. But this happens rarely. Kuhn himself provided only a few examples (the rejection of Ptolemaic astronomy, the rejection of phlogiston and development of chemical theory, the modification of Newtonian mechanics by relativity). Moreover, the persistence of theoretical views now considered erroneous was not solely the result of stubborn, value-laden background assumptions, but also the inability to test some of the implications of the rival theory. As mentioned, the inability to detect stellar parallax enabled diehard adherents to the Ptolemaic model to endure until the nineteenth century, when stellar parallax was finally measured. The theory of relativity would have remained speculation had we not the instrumentation sufficient for testing some of its implications (which, arguably, did not happen until the mid-twentieth century).

This last point is important. Science, as we now understand this enterprise, did not get started, even in rudimentary form, until the sixteenth or seventeenth centuries. Essential to the scientific enterprise are the ability to conduct experimental testing and the existence of a community of scientists who can freely subject any claim to critical scrutiny and retesting. It is no accident that the scientific revolutions Kuhn references align with the then state of science. The telescope provided astronomers in the 1600s with at least a basic tool to assess some of the claims of the Ptolemaic model. The chemical revolution at the end of the eighteenth century would not have been possible without the ability to isolate substances and to accurately weigh the reactants and products of chemical reactions. And, as indicated, the modifications general relativity made to Newtonian mechanics could not have been confirmed prior to the twentieth century. As the resources for science increase, the social setting that influences scientific theories is less the dominant social, political, or religious values and more the ability of scientists to test hypotheses—provided scientists remain free to subject claims to scrutiny. (Yes, dictatorships can impede science.) Moreover, as the resources for science increase, the match between scientific claims and reality also tends to increase. General relativity did not wholesale replace classical mechanics as much as it supplemented it in special settings, such as strong gravity fields and extremely high velocities. Study of phenomena at the atomic level resulted in the development of quantum mechanics, a system of physical laws distinct from classical mechanics, but classical mechanics still matches our everyday macroscopic reality, as witnessed by the fact that it is still taught in university physics courses. The bottom line is that Kuhn's infrequent scientific revolutions do not entail the conclusion that there is no such thing as objective knowledge or that all knowledge is merely a reflection of dominant social or political values.

But what of the claim that theories are underdetermined by the evidence, with the implication that many incompatible rival theories could be made to fit with the available evidence? Except for theories that are at the frontiers of science (for example, string theory or the claim that quantum theory implies the existence of many worlds), the "underdetermination thesis, in its usual guise, is a product of the underrepresentation of scientific practice."[51] As a matter of logical possibility, sure, one could construct numerous incompatible theories based on the same body of evidence. One could claim that Homeric gods are responsible for the movement of the planets, and they just happen to move them consistent with our accepted laws of physics. If one posits that the gods are undetectable by our scientific instruments, then we could not conclusively disprove that claim. But the constraints of scientific practice rule out most such theories or render them otiose. Among other things, they lack explanatory power and cannot be fruitfully applied. Logical possibility is not the same as practical possibility. Significantly, when arguing for the underdetermination thesis, Quine resorted to the possibility of "pleading hallucination" when confronted with observations that stubbornly resist one's speculative theory.[52] We know already from the failure of the Cartesian project of securing absolutely certain knowledge that once one seriously entertains the possibility that it's all a hallucination, there's no way out of that rabbit hole—other than by recognizing that claiming it's all a dream or a hallucination makes no practical difference to our lives. The currently fashionable version of the Cartesian hallucination hypothesis is the speculation that we are all living in a computer simulation. Difficult, if not impossible, to disprove, but what difference does this make?

Admittedly, there may be at any point in time rival theories that are consistent with scientific practice but which reach radically different conclusions based on the available body of evidence. One current example is string theory which, effectively, is a rival to standard model particle physics.[53] String theory holds that infinitesimal vibrating strings are the fundamental units of reality, instead of atomic particles. Advocates of string theory argue that it allows for the merger of general relativity and quantum mechanics, something that has eluded rival theories. Opponents argue, among other things, that most versions of string theory require supersymmetry, that is, all particles of the standard model have partner particles. These particles have not yet been found. String theory also requires an enormous number of vacuum states, or possible universes. Critics argue this large number of possible universes makes the theory vacuous and lacking in testable predictive power. Currently, there is no set of experiments that can refute or confirm string theory (and some question whether there can be any such experiments).[54]

But the existence of rival theories at the edge of science—where comprehensive testing of theories remains out of reach—does not undermine in the slightest the position that we do have objective knowledge about a wide range of scientific matters, and this knowledge will not change whatever the outcome of the debate between strings and particles. (Some descriptions at the fundamental level may change, but not our knowledge of the behavior of objects at the macro level. Strings, not atoms, may be the ultimate building blocks of a gas, but the volume of a gas will remain inversely proportional to its pressure when temperature is held constant.) In fact, if one just pauses to reflect on all the facets of modern life that depend on the objective knowledge science has provided us over the last couple of centuries, it is astonishing that anyone could claim objectivity is an illusion. Perhaps it is a question of not seeing the forest for all the trees. Consider: We design curves in roads to take account of our knowledge about force, acceleration, and friction. The car driving around those curves is engineered (if it has an internal combustion engine) using knowledge about the effect of compressing gases and the relationship among pressure, volume, and temperature. Without our knowledge of physical strengths and stress, including thermal stress, safe bridges could not be built. The hydraulic lift that your mechanic uses to work on your car is an application of Pascal's Law on fluid pressure. Our effective indoor plumbing makes use of knowledge of water pressure, gravity, and the incompressibility of water. We can drink water in an urban setting because our waste-water treatment systems make use of our knowledge of chemical processes such as coagulation and the chemical properties of disinfectants such as chlorine. Objective knowledge of chemistry and biology has not only provided safe drinking water but also given us thousands of medications that cure disease or alleviate symptoms and vaccines that prevent or ameliorate disease. It is an objective fact, not a value judgment, that smallpox has been eradicated. Our effective harnessing of electricity, in all its myriad applications, requires knowledge of electric fields, electric currents, potential energy, conductors, capacitors and so on. The relationship between electricity and magnetism is fundamental to the creation and use of many devices, including MRI (magnetic resonance imaging) machines. Lasers, of course, are based on the stimulated emission of electromagnetic radiation, and we now rely on lasers routinely for everything from surgery to laser printers; no doubt many a paper advocating standpoint theory was produced via a laser printer.

This list could go on indefinitely, but let me close this summary with two recent, extraordinary examples of the application of objective scientific knowledge. In roughly a year after the first appearance of Covid-19 infections in China in late 2019, Pfizer-BioNTech and Moderna had produced effective vaccines—a stunning result given that vaccines typically take over a decade to develop. But these companies were making use of mRNA (messenger RNA) technology and research, and decades of work on various aspects of mRNA by hundreds of scientists from many different organizations and institutions was necessary to lay the groundwork for these vaccines. Scientists first uncovered the functions of mRNA over sixty years ago and knew, in principle, that mRNA could be used to code cells to make a wide range of proteins. One problem was the stability of mRNA and the need for a delivery mechanism for transferring mRNA into cells. Eventually, various scientists developed the necessary transfer methods using liposomes. Other problems that needed to be researched and overcome included the immune reaction which occurred when the synthetic mRNA entered human cells. Modifications to mRNA code allowed the mRNA to evade the cells' immune defenses. Alongside these developments, there were efforts to use mRNA-engineered proteins to combat cancers and diseases and to produce vaccines, including a vaccine against AIDS, with decidedly mixed results. One problem in particular with respect to the AIDS vaccine was how to target the spikes that enable HIV to penetrate and invade cells. The shape-shifting proteins on HIV spikes stymied researchers. Eventually, some researchers began working with the spikes on coronaviruses; these spikes proved, with some tinkering, to be more amenable to research and testing. As a result, when Covid-19 appeared, the tools were in place for rapid production of a vaccine.[55]

Another recent noteworthy achievement was the construction, launch, and successful deployment of the James Webb Space Telescope. The wide range of knowledge of applied physics and chemistry that went into this achievement is astonishing. Construction of the telescope began in 2004, and given the scope of the telescope's mission, designers were faced with the challenge of applying their knowledge to build cutting-edge instruments and test cutting-edge technologies. The huge, three-story high telescope had to be folded into the rocket transporting it into space, with its components unfurling in delicate maneuvers once it reached its destination. These components include a multilayer, 21 by 14 meter sunshield with an ultrathin layer of gold foil and eighteen individual mirrors that comprise the telescope's 705 kilogram primary mirror. Its location is a million miles from earth, at the second sun-earth Lagrange point, which it needed to reach on a precise trajectory. Its instruments include a state-of-the-art infrared camera and spectrograph, with the latter boasting of 250,000 microshutters, with the size of each shutter a mere 100 by 200 microns. Given the device's complexity, there were over 300 ways in which the mission could have failed. It has not.[56]

No objective knowledge? No match between our understanding and reality? The fact that all the tens of thousands of things that applied science has provided us *work* reveals the absurdity of such claims.

These examples also highlight a key flaw in the argument of standpoint theorists, namely their insistence that value-neutral science is impossible because scientists necessarily select background assumptions based on their values, and this can distort their findings. On an individual scientist basis, it is difficult to refute this claim. No matter how conscientious an individual scientist might be, there is certainly the possibility that values, perhaps held unconsciously, could affect his/her research and observations. But science, as practiced, is both a collaborative and a competitive enterprise, with hundreds, if not thousands, of scientists likely working on the same or related projects as any individual scientist. Any significant skewing of reality due to the ideology of any one scientist will probably be caught by other scientists as they test and retest the scientist's claims. One does not have to imagine that all scientists are purely rational robots, wholly dedicated to the ideals of science—although, to be fair, many are dedicated to the ideals of science—to understand why scientists might challenge a skewed claim. It is not in their self-interest to adopt an erroneous view—which will likely result in an embarrassing failure when put to practical use—while it is in their self-interest to point out errors in another scientist's claim.

The fact that science is practiced by a community of researchers is one reason I have used the terminology "value-neutral" as opposed to "value-free." As indicated, it is impossible to prove that an individual scientist's claims have not been affected, and possibly distorted, because of that scientist's values. But any factual distortion will be eventually canceled out by the critical scrutiny to which that scientist's claims are subjected. It may not happen instantly, but over time it is exceedingly unlikely that a claim that does not match reality will be incorporated into our common body of knowledge (again, assuming we retain the freedom of scientists to evaluate and criticize).

I stated earlier that any credibility that standpoint theory's tenet of situated knowledge possesses is based on an equivocation between a knowledge claim and knowledge. Yes, how we interpret what we observe is influenced by our beliefs, and there is always the possibility that a claim by an individual scientist reflects a distorted view of reality. But before that claim is considered part of our body of knowledge, it must be tested and retested by many other scientists. Unless the community of scientists is working under the constraint of a religion or ideology which demands adherence to certain doctrines and excludes contrary claims as *a priori* unacceptable, the chances of an erroneous claim being incorporated into our body of knowledge are small, as indicated, again by, among other things, the fact that our cars don't routinely explode, bridges don't routinely collapse, antibiotics doesn't routinely poison us, and laser printers can usually be relied upon to produce our texts, no matter their content. Our scientific knowledge is "situated" within a community who have as an integral part of their work the critical scrutiny of knowledge claims.

Before I pass on to the next section, a few brief points. I claim that science can be value-neutral, but aren't values involved in the selection of phenomena to be investigated, and don't values determine when an appropriate level of confidence can be reached that we can apply a scientific finding? Yes, undoubtedly that is true. Scientists are motivated to study certain phenomena because they see value in that study, and to the extent their research is supported by governments, those who control the government's purse strings must also see value in the study. The judgment that smallpox is a scourge that should be prevented and the judgment that side effects from the smallpox vaccine were tolerable in light of the results to be achieved were value judgments. These types of values do not undercut the objectivity of empirically supported findings about the cause of smallpox or the means to prevent it. The value-neutrality that objectivity requires relates to the processing of observations and data and the use of background principles. Are scientists so biased or trapped in an ideology that they cannot impartially assess the empirical adequacy of their claims? For the foregoing reasons, that seems unlikely if we take the scientific community as a whole.

Finally, the argument that science cannot be objective because all knowledge is "situated" is self-defeating. If knowledge claims can never be truly impartial, then the standpoint theorist's claim that the marginalized have an epistemic privilege that enables them to acquire knowledge better than the dominant group is itself "partial," that is, infected by an ineradicable bias. To argue otherwise, one must assume there is some standard of objectivity that could permit the conclusion that the marginalized know things better—that their socially grounded viewpoint does not distort reality. But standpoint theorists claim there is no such standard of objectivity. True, Harding argues that if we bring the perspective of women's lives to bear on our research, we can obtain "strong objectivity." But she fails to explain why bringing another perspective that is socially situated to bear on an existing socially situated perspective can produce anything other than a mélange of subjective perspectives. Once one discards objectivity, one can't reel it back in to fill gaps in arguments. Objectivity is not a yo-yo.

Furthermore, as we have seen, some standpoint theorists also argue that all theories are underdetermined by the evidence. But that claim also applies to standpoint theory. Feminists may be free to approach data using standpoint theory, but everyone else is free to reject standpoint theory and use different background principles, and there is no way to decide between these competing approaches.

This self-referential character of the claim that all knowledge is so-cially situated is what is known in the literature as the "bias paradox" of standpoint theory. It is sufficient by itself to prove standpoint theory is fatally flawed. Standpoint theory is exposed as the equivalent of the philosophy undergraduate's contention that "There is no such thing as knowledge," to which the appropriate reply is: "How do you know that?" However, to be fair, some standpoint theorists have recognized this problem with their theory, and they have made heroic efforts to work around it. These efforts have failed, as the next sections of my argument will establish.

The Murky Conditions for Epistemic Advantage

In the prior section, I listed some of the many ways we have utilized the objective knowledge science has provided us. Many of the underlying discoveries of physical and chemical laws that permitted these appli-cations were the result of work by white men: Boyle, Lavoisier, Carnot, Joule, Maxwell, Planck, Einstein, and so on. This, of course, in no way shows that white men are especially gifted when it comes to scientific investigation. The relative lack of women and people of color in scien-tific work prior to the twentieth century was the result of lamentable prejudice that prevented many individuals from developing their talents and the historically contingent uneven global distribution of scientific resources. Nonetheless, that white men were able to contribute to our increasing body of objective scientific knowledge does suggest that being a white man is no handicap to doing science.

But this is what standpoint theory denies. Those who are oppressed (women, blacks, dealer's choice) can achieve an epistemic advantage over the dominant white men precisely because they are oppressed. But how is this? And what counts as sufficient "oppression"?

Certainly, given the legal and customary exclusion of women and blacks from higher education, many professions, and political engage-

ment which sadly prevailed in the United States, and many other countries, until the mid-twentieth century, one can state with assurance that in
the generally accepted understanding of "oppressed" women and blacks
were oppressed. But are they oppressed now? Leaving aside the dogma
of systemic racism (see next chapter), current claims for oppression rest
principally on the statistical underrepresentation of women and blacks in
some professions, the allegedly high incidence of sexual or racial harassment, the alleged denial of equal pay, the still prevailing division of labor
based on sex, through which women are expected to do more housework
and child-rearing in addition to working regular jobs, and micro-aggressions. However, whether these conditions, to the extent they exist,
constitute oppression is debatable. To begin, the legal system provides
remedies for the exclusion of women and blacks from any job and for
the denial of equal pay, whether in the sciences or elsewhere, and similarly, it provides remedies for harassment. Many individuals have taken
advantage of these legal remedies and prevailed, some receiving substantial damages, so the contention that the remedies are toothless is simply
false. As to the division of labor, that division is nowhere as stark as it
used to be, with men assuming more responsibility for housework and
childrearing. Moreover, the "double-day" of work that feminists often
cite conveniently ignores the "double-day" that many men experience.
"Honey-do" lists do not execute themselves, and just as it is probably
still predominantly women who do the dishes and change the diapers,
it is predominantly men who fix the toilets and sinks, install the shelves,
etc. The reality is that most couples sort out household responsibilities
according to what they perceive as their talents and limitations and time
constraints, and most seem content with the division of labor. Finally, as
to micro-aggressions, their very name indicates the weight they should
be given. Do sex- or race-based insensitive remarks or behavior occur?
Undoubtedly, but how often is disputed—in part because it is unclear
what constitutes a "micro-aggression"—and it is similarly disputed the
extent to which these micro-aggressions have an adverse effect on a recipient's mental or physical health.[57]

The changing legal and social landscape and the shrinking territory
on which a plausible claim of oppression can stand have pushed some
advocates of standpoint theory to come up with other mechanisms of
oppression. For example, if one does not cite scholarly papers written by

women or people of color as often as one cites papers written by white men, this is now considered by some as a form of oppression known as citational injustice. Apparently, the relevance of the paper or the merit it has is not sufficient to warrant citation. The identity of the person who wrote it is what counts.[58] Arguably, though, the state-of-the-art form of oppression is epistemic oppression, which is "persistent epistemic exclusion that hinders one's contribution to knowledge production," with "exclusion" being an "unwarranted infringement on the epistemic agency of knowers."[59] Such an epistemic injustice can be a matter of "dominantly situated knowers [discounting] the knowledge claims of marginalized knowers."[60]

Here we see hints of the ultimate bootstrap. Oppression supposedly gives the oppressed better insight, and the oppression that can give them this better insight is the failure to recognize their better insight. Standpoint theory requires an oppressed group, but given the current state of affairs in Western democracies, with all citizens enjoying the same legal rights and laws prohibiting discrimination in employment, housing, public accommodations, and other areas on multiple bases (sex, race, sexual orientation, color, religion, disability, age, etc.), the claim of oppression rests on a very thin reed.

However, there is no need to argue this point extensively because for standpoint theory to have any merit, it must not only convincingly claim that some group suffers oppression, but it must be able to show how, because of this oppression, its members can achieve better powers of knowledge acquisition, that is, they can obtain an epistemic advantage. But to date, standpoint theorists have been unable to specify the exact criteria by which one could determine whether members of a group have achieved epistemic advantage.

When reading some of the literature, one can have the impression that all women, or all blacks, and so on, are alleged to have an epistemic advantage. But that would be a mistake. Just as in Marxist theory not all workers achieve an appropriate level of class consciousness, similarly, the predominant view in standpoint theory is that not all women (or blacks, etc.) have an epistemic advantage. Most standpoint theorists maintain they are against "essentialism," in other words, that women have an epistemic advantage qua women (or blacks qua blacks). Instead, the epistemic advantage is something that must be achieved. As Sandra Harding emphasizes, "a standpoint is an achievement, not an ascription," and it requires both "scientific work in order to see beneath the ideological surface of social relations" and "political organization to do that work."[61] Put another way, being a member of an oppressed group is a necessary condition for having epistemic advantage, but it is not a sufficient condition.

This qualification is important; it certainly preserves standpoint theory from being dismissed immediately as laughable because it is obvious that Harding's values are not the same as Laura Ingraham's, and Clarence Thomas and Al Sharpton have sharply divergent viewpoints. But passing the laugh test through this qualification comes at the cost of presenting other troublesome issues: namely, how does one know who has achieved the appropriate standpoint, and if there is no sex-specific set of experiences that unites all women—or race-specific set of experiences that unites all blacks—then how could one claim there is *a* feminist standpoint, or *a* black viewpoint (and if there is more than one, how to decide between them)?

There is no answer to these questions in the literature. There are no objective standards that can distinguish the women who have achieved a feminist standpoint from those who have not. By implication, the suggestion seems to be that one's consciousness becomes sufficiently raised if and only if one sees things the same way that the advocates of standpoint theory see things. This is self-validation with a vengeance, and here again one sees echoes of Marxism, as it was practiced. Whether workers have achieved the proper level of class consciousness depends on whether they accept what the Politburo tells them to think.

One problem in providing an objective test for whether someone has achieved the appropriate state of consciousness is that standpoint theorists have failed to specify the exact set of circumstances that make it possible for the allegedly oppressed to acquire epistemic advantage. What mechanism is at work here? Many explanations have been offered, but they either are question-begging or remain at the level of metaphor. As indicated, Harding states that "scientific work" and "political work" are needed. But which type of scientific and political work? No specificity is provided, other than the requirement that the scientific work must "see beneath the ideological surface of social relations." In other words, research that starts out accepting the standpoint theorist's views has the promise of producing epistemic advantage. Again, self-validation.

Harding also argues that women researchers are both "strangers" to the social order and "outsiders within" and this status enables them to acquire epistemic privilege because "when one works on both sides ... there emerges the possibility of seeing the relation between dominant activities and beliefs and those that arise on the 'outside.'"[62] However, it remains unclear how this social status is reliably going to generate more accurate perspectives on reality than other social statuses.

Giving this argument the most generous interpretation, one might acknowledge that there are two types of situations where women might have insights that could escape men. With respect to scientific research, claims by male researchers regarding sex differences and sexual behavior may reflect biases that women would be able to spot and correct. Certainly, the history of "scientific findings" about the ways in which women are supposedly different from men has been littered with erroneous assertions. But this was largely a problem of the nineteenth and early twentieth centuries, that is, before more female researchers started to work in significant numbers in these fields. In any event, in no way does this very specific situation show that women have an epistemic advantage when it comes to scientific work in general.

With respect to legal or social reform, the indignation or resentment that some women feel about the way they are being treated may motivate them to criticize certain laws or social arrangements. This has happened, and, in some instances, these criticisms eventually have been found by most to be well-taken. This has resulted in changes being made. One instance where women were at the forefront of efforts to make legal changes was the effort to end the exemption for marital rape. That said, there is nothing to differentiate this type of criticism from criticism made by other interested groups—including from time-to-time predominantly male groups (e.g., criticism that has led to the end of the presumption in favor of mothers in custody disputes). Acknowledging that on occasion groups of women have been leaders for needed legal reform is a far cry from saying they necessarily have some general knowledge advantage when it comes to legal or social reform.

Sometimes groups of women have a valid point—just like groups of men, groups of blacks, groups of business leaders, groups of environmentalists, and so forth. The validity of any group's position depends on the strength of their arguments, including the evidence they marshal in support of their arguments, not their identity.

Furthermore, the problems of identifying who has achieved epistemic advantage and delineating the contours of that advantage are exacerbated by the recognition that even the feminists who have achieved enlightened consciousness have differing views. How can one arbitrate among them, given that any attempt to argue for one view over another is merely an expression of one's own "situated knowledge"? Standpoint theorists do not try. In a classic understatement, two advocates of standpoint theory candidly admit that "standpoint theory cannot provide a cut-and-dried formula for identifying particular standpoints that can be counted on to produce more objective knowledge."[63] Bizarrely, some try to make a virtue out of a defect by embracing contradiction. It is worth quoting Harding at length on this point:

> [T]he subjects/agents of knowledge for feminist standpoint theory are multiple, heterogeneous, and contradictory or incoherent, not unitary, homogenous, and coherent as they are for empiricist epistemology. Feminist knowledge has started off from women's lives, but it has started off from many different women's lives: there is no typical or essential woman's life from which feminisms start their thought. Moreover, these different women's lives are in important respect opposed to each other [and produce] multiple, heterogeneous, and contradictory feminist accounts. Nevertheless, thought that starts off from each of these different kinds of lives can generate less partial and distorted accounts of nature and social life.[64]

In other words, we must acknowledge there is not one feminist standpoint, but many contradictory ones. Nonetheless, out of this cluster of contradictory views, we can hope to obtain a less distorted account of reality—but don't ask how. So, instead of a sharply defined claim of epistemic advantage, we get a coin tossed into a wishing well. As one critic of standpoint theory has observed, "A philosophy of science qua social science whose only goal is to tell inconsistent and incoherent stories is not very appealing or sufficiently ambitious."[65]

In light of these problems, some defenders of standpoint theory have abandoned any attempt to assert an epistemic advantage for women in advance of work on any particular research project. There is no such thing as an automatic epistemic advantage for women, including enlightened women, in doing science. Instead, there is a weak presumption "that un-privileged social positions are likely to generate better perspectives on social reality than other social positions."[66] Whether any women actually have an epistemic advantage depends on the context of a particular inquiry, including the results of that inquiry. One "presumes the epistemic relevance of systemic conditions of inequality without specifying in advance what their relevance will be in a given context."[67] The claim of epistemic advantage can be justified only contextually.

This significant modification of standpoint theory supposedly saves it from the "bias paradox" previously mentioned. There is no claim that standpoint theory, which itself is a socially situated thesis, is objectively true. The perspective of women is not necessarily better in terms of knowledge acquisition than other socially situated perspectives. Whether it turns out to provide more insight cannot be determined without assessing, with respect to a particular research issue, the relative merits of the competing perspectives.

It is not entirely clear, however, whether this modification of standpoint theory does enable it to evade the bias paradox, because of uncertainty over the status of the presumption "that unprivileged social positions are likely to generate better perspectives on social reality than other social positions." If standpoint theory is to retain a sliver of consistency, the assertion of this presumption must be a socially situated claim, so how can one impartially judge whether this presumption has merit? One assumes defenders of this claim must be appealing to an argument from induction—that is, feminists can show there is overwhelming evidence from a number of instances demonstrating that women can produce knowledge better. Indeed, advocates who take this contextualist approach put forth what they claim is evidence of better insight by women. But even such an argument runs into trouble unless there is some objective standard that allows us to decide the relative merits of different perspectives. What is that standard? Not clear.

But let us leave the problem of internal inconsistency aside and turn to the evidence offered to show that the allegedly oppressed, whether it be women, blacks, or some other group, have, at least in some contexts, greater powers of knowledge acquisition than the dominant group (meaning white males).

The Evidence for Epistemic Advantage

Carl Sagan famously observed that "extraordinary claims require extraordinary evidence."[68] The claim that a group of persons, in virtue of their allegedly oppressed status and their struggle to achieve an enlightened consciousness regarding their status, can reliably produce knowledge, including scientific knowledge, better than their oppressors is an extraordinary claim. It flies in the face of common sense; it erects a cognitive caste structure, whereas common sense tells us that almost all humans have roughly the same range of cognitive powers. Any difference in knowledge acquisition capability results primarily from training and access to appropriate resources. In fact, this makes the standpoint theory claim even more extraordinary because the oppressed, if anything, are less likely to have advanced training and access to appropriate research tools.

But instead of the extraordinary evidence necessary to establish the credibility of standpoint theory, we have a dearth of any probative evidence. Significantly, in light of proponents' claim that the epistemic advantage of the oppressed extends even to the natural sciences, there has been zero evidence that in physics, chemistry, or biology, women or blacks or any other allegedly oppressed group has reliably demonstrated greater insight than white men. The "idea of a gendered standpoint on science is bankrupt, [not only] beset with formal contradictions [but also] wholly lacking an empirical track record to provide even weak inductive support."[69]

What about the distortions caused by "white empiricism," the subject of a paper by the physicist Prescod-Weinstein? She boldly states at the outset of her paper that "race and ethnicity impact epistemic outcomes in physics, despite the universality of the laws that undergird physics."[70] However, instead of providing examples of some significant scientific advances in physics that can be explained only by the special insight of minorities, the paper principally complains about the fact that blacks' claims of racism are not always accepted simply on their say-so. Prescod-Weinstein contrasts this demand for evidence to support claims of racism with what she regards as the pass given to advocates of string theory, who continue to receive funding for their research despite the hitherto lack of confirming empirical evidence:

In effect, white physicists are considered competent to self-evaluate for bias against other epistemic agents *and* theories of physics where there is no empirical grounding to assist in decision making, while Black epistemic agents are considered incompetent to bring a lifetime of knowledge gathering about race and racism to bear on their everyday experiences. This empirical adjudication is the phenomenon of white empiricism. It is reflected in string theorists' ability to actively argue for continued investment in their ideas via funding and faculty hiring while at the same time Black people—particle physicists or not—are often considered to be making controversial or 'evidently wrong' statements about racism.[71]

To begin, as previously observed (see note 54), string theory has many white physicist critics, so the suggestion that string theory is somehow an outgrowth of a white approach to physics lacks support.

But leave that point aside. The major problem with Prescod-Weinstein's argument is that it compares two completely different things. It's not even apples and oranges; it's more like apples and asphalt. The type of evidence that is needed to support a scientific theory is in a different category entirely than the evidence needed to support a claim of discrimination. In addition, there is no scientific basis for maintaining that we must accept as dispositive a person's claim of discrimination based on their lived experience.

Furthermore, not to conclude immediately that discrimination has occurred anytime a black person complains of discrimination is not treating black people as "incompetent" to make a claim of discrimination. To the contrary, once a complaint has been made, that typically initiates an intensive, and sometimes expensive, fact-gathering process. Universities and other organizations where physicists might work are required by law to take any complaint of race discrimination seriously. Does that happen 100% of the time? Probably not, but there's no indication that race discrimination claims are "often" not treated seriously, and Prescod-Weinstein offers no data or even examples to support this accusation.

The only specific example Prescod-Weinstein offers of the advantages an oppressed person has in doing physics is the case of Vera Rubin, a white woman.[72] Rubin is given credit for developing the theory of dark matter, that is, that the universe contains a large amount of matter that is not visible like ordinary matter, but rather is detected by the force of its gravitational attraction. The observations Rubin made that resulted in the development of this theory were in part due to her inability to get time on telescopes that would allow her to work on more popular lines of inquiry, which Prescod-Weinstein says was the result of sexism. (That's not entirely clear, but no need to dispute this.) But this in no way shows that Rubin—a very talented astrophysicist to be sure—was more gifted than men to do physics. To the contrary, it's a case of serendipity, not unknown in the annals of physics even for male scholars.

At the conclusion of her paper, Prescod-Weinstein offers one final example of white empiricism that only demonstrates how misdirected her arguments are. She asserts that "White empiricism can help explain why the Thirty Meter Telescope was evaluated so differentially by Mauna Kea protectors and telescope-using scientists."[73] This is a reference to the dispute between those in the scientific community who believe this telescope on Mauna Kea would greatly assist in astronomical observations and some native Hawaiians who object to this use of Mauna Kea on environmental, cultural, or religious grounds. Once again, Prescod-Weinstein is making a category mistake. This is not a dispute about how one does physics, but rather a value dispute about what scientific research is worth pursuing, given other interests. In this matter, no one has any special insight, and the matter will eventually be resolved as these things are normally done in a democratic society: the government will decide based on input from those concerned, and whoever is unhappy with that decision can then work to change the composition of the relevant governmental body.

I have spent some time reviewing Prescod-Weinstein's paper because it is one of the few papers put forth by standpoint theorists that offers examples of how the oppressed would do hard science better, as flawed as her examples may be. But there are a few others. Alison Wylie and Sergio Sismondo argue that standpoint critiques of dominant science methodology "are by no means limited to the social sciences."[74] In support of this claim, they offer the example of women being excluded from drug trials and other studies of health conditions, formally from 1977 to 1988 and informally for some time prior. Given how the different biology of women can influence drug responses, this exclusion appears to have been scientifically unjustified, and Wylie and Sismondo contend that it was pressure from feminists which led to the change.

(Let me note here that in an era where the biology of women is often ignored or dismissed as immaterial—e.g., when discussing the participation of trans athletes in women's sports—it is refreshing to note that biology is still considered relevant, at least in some contexts.)

But the situation is more complicated than it might first appear, and upon further examination, it turns out to be, again, a question of values as opposed to an issue of scientific methodology. In 1977 the Food and Drug Administration (FDA) issued guidance banning women with childbearing potential from early phases of most drug trials, and trial sponsors typically excluded women from all phases.[75] But this was not the result of some unscientific, sexist mindset. Instead, based on disastrous outcomes that some drugs had on fetuses (think thalidomide), the guidance was adopted to prevent birth defects, an outcome presumably welcomed by most mothers. The FDA adopted this policy knowing that this might lead to skewed results from drug trials, but weighing the different risks, the agency thought this the better policy. In 1986, for its own sponsored trials, the National Institutes of Health (NIH) issued a partial reversal of this policy, encouraging the participation of women in drug trials. In 1988, the FDA completely reversed its stance and issued guidance specifically calling for drug trials to be inclusive of gender, race, and age groups. These reversals had less to do with pressure from women's groups and more to do with a change in national bioethics policy, with the 1979 Belmont Report calling for greater respect for individual autonomy in medical settings.[76] The consensus view became that women should be allowed to assess the risks themselves, after being informed of the dangers. Women's groups became more directly involved only when they felt the NIH wasn't moving fast enough to implement changes.

In any event, whatever the precise role of women's groups in advocating for change, this was not a scientific dispute over the significance of data; it was a dispute over competing priorities.

Let us move on to the soft sciences, such as psychology, sociology, or anthropology. Here, the case for women having an epistemic advantage has, superficially, a bit more plausibility. Pause to consider why. One reason we have more firmly grounded results in the hard sciences is the ability to test and retest results with reliable equipment. Also, the results of hard science research often have direct, real-world applications, and if you have a wrong theory about, for example, the relationship between the temperature and pressure of a gas, the consequences of that error will not long remain hidden. In the soft sciences, data often comes from qualitative surveys that cannot always be duplicated. Moreover, how does one apply, for example, a theory of moral development to the real world in a way that can show the validity or invalidity of the theory? Can't really be done. Finally, as the subject of the soft sciences is, in some way, human behavior, the scientist has a heightened stake in the results, and the risk of unconscious or conscious bias is greater. There have been a number of psychological surveys that purport to show that conservatives tend to be more intolerant, closed-minded, and inclined to authoritarianism, with the most cited one being, perhaps, the meta-study by John Jost and his colleagues.[77] Query: how many of those studies were authored by political conservatives? (Also, I wonder what Lenin, Stalin, Mao, and Pol Pot would have said about these studies' conclusions.)

Point is, bias is almost surely more prevalent in the soft sciences, and consequently, it would not be entirely surprising if standpoint theorists could point to studies, especially older studies, that may reflect bias against women.

And, sure enough, there is a famous case that shows just that. As Wylie and Sismondo observe, Lawrence Kohlberg notoriously studied only boys and young men in gathering data for his theory of moral development.[78] I have been unable to find a definitive explanation why Kohlberg so limited his data source (access to study subjects?), but it really does not matter what the explanation was. Limiting one's study of moral development to one sex is, at a minimum, going to cast doubt on one's ability to generalize the study's findings, as Kohlberg should have recognized.

In her 1982 book, *In a Different Voice*, Carol Gilligan, who had been one of Kohlberg's students, criticized Kohlberg's failure to include girls and young women in his research, noting that "in the research from which Kohlberg derives his theory, females simply do not exist."[79] Gilligan proceeded to elaborate her own theory of moral development, the data for which she derived from her own surveys. Two of these included both male and female subjects, while one was limited to females.[80] Significantly, the latter study was further circumscribed to women considering abortions. In Gilligan's view, Kohlberg's theory of moral development was too skewed toward a rights-oriented approach to morality, whereas her surveys showed that many women conceptualized morality differently:

> When one begins with the study of women and derives developmental constructs from their lives, the outline of a moral conception different from that of Freud, Piaget, or Kohlberg begins to emerge and informs a different description of development. In this conception, the moral problem arises from conflicting responsibilities rather than from competing rights and requires for its resolution a mode of thinking that is contextual and narrative rather than formal and abstract.[81]

Gilligan's conception of morality became known as the ethics of care.

So, what is the takeaway from this episode in the history of moral psychology? Does it show that women have greater insight in moral psychology than men? No, that conclusion is not warranted. We must distinguish between recognizing a research error and possessing greater powers of knowledge acquisition. There's really no dispute that Kohlberg's sample was skewed if he was aspiring to a theory of moral development applicable to all children. In fact, nowadays the error is obvious, and the fact that it wasn't obvious in the 1950s (when Kohlberg started his research) probably says more about the cultural differences between that time and ours than it does about the different cognitive capabilities of men and women. Still, give credit to Gilligan for highlighting this error, and, at least arguably, her status as a woman made this error more obvious to her than others.

But Gilligan went on to formulate her own theory of moral development that has been the subject of as much criticism as Kohlberg's. Many see the care ethic as just as partial as the rights ethic; they both capture only aspects of moral development.[82] Moreover, although Gilligan was careful at the outset of her book to caution that her association of an ethics of care with women was not "absolute,"[83] the book lends itself to an essentialist interpretation, with men and women having significantly different approaches to moral issues. Not only does this seem to group all women together in terms of their moral development—a conclusion difficult to justify—but it threatens to give credence to discredited notions about women's favoring of emotion over reason. Finally, Gilligan committed her own research error by relying, in part, on a survey of women considering abortion. It seems apparent that survey results may have been different if the sample also included women who had rejected the option of abortion.

In the end, all the Kohlberg-Gilligan episode shows is that women might be quicker to cry foul if some social science researcher were so benighted as to exclude women from a survey whose data was being used to draw conclusions about humans in general. Not likely to happen today, but, in any event, conceding this narrow point does not support the ambitious claims of standpoint theory.

Let's consider two final examples of evidence that could be used to support standpoint theory—or at least a significantly scaled-back version of standpoint theory. They may be the strongest examples for standpoint theory precisely because, in one case, its proponent has so pruned the theory that its most dubious claims have been discarded, and in the other, standpoint theory isn't even mentioned—the author merely argues that feminist science can produce, in some cases, more epistemically fruitful results.

In focusing on the issue of sex discrimination in the academic scientific community, Kristina Rolin, a philosopher of science, concedes that a feminist standpoint cannot "determine whether there is any evidence of subtle forms of gender discrimination" nor can this standpoint "determine how much such evidence can be found."[84] Epistemic advantage is limited to bringing feminist values to bear, that is, "feminist values function as a reason to consider certain kind of evidence as relevant for a study on gender discrimination."[85] The implication is that male researchers on sex discrimination will be more likely to overlook or ignore relevant evidence.

To prove her point, Rolin contrasts a book first published in 1979 by a male researcher, Jonathan Cole, with a 1999 paper by two female Finnish social scientists, Saija Katila and Susan Merilainen.[86] Cole, by examining hiring and promotion patterns and correlating these with indica of academic merit such as productivity, concluded that, in significant part, the unequal numbers of men and women in the sciences is a result of self-selection rather than discrimination. The paper by Katila and Merilainen, Rolin maintains, offered evidence of subtle forms of discrimination that could affect female academics' productivity, which Cole failed to take into account.

The extent to which there is discrimination against female scientists is much debated, being the subject of scores of articles and books, and is beyond the scope of our argument.[87] The issue here is not whether there is such discrimination but rather whether male researchers, because they are male, are much more likely to overlook relevant evidence of discrimination. The sole example Rolin provides cannot carry the weight she ascribes to it.

To begin, Rolin's assessment of Cole is not entirely accurate or fair. His 1979 study was a large-scale statistical study, and its primary focus on the correlation between productivity (in this context, principally research culminating in publication) and hiring and promotion was clearly justified. Statistics are often used to determine whether there is a prima facie case of discrimination, and for any large-group analysis (as opposed to individual claims of discrimination), one typically begins with a statistical analysis. The "subtle discrimination" referenced by Katila and Merilainen was simply outside the scope of Cole's research. Granted, some wording by Cole in summarizing the results of his research was incautious. Instead of claiming there was a high degree of fairness in the distribution of rewards in the scientific community, he should have simply stated that his research did not detect any marked unfairness. But if inflated claims were an indicator of defective social science, then 99 percent of the papers published by standpoint theorists would qualify.

Second, the study of sex-specific working conditions that might affect women's productivity, in particular sexual harassment, was just getting underway in the late 1970s. Cole's book came out in 1979; Katila and Merilainen wrote in 1999. In twenty years, the landscape of research can change in any science, including social science. One cannot fault a researcher for failing to consider a possibly relevant causal factor that was not widely considered relevant at the time.[88]

Furthermore, examination of the Katila/Merilainen paper indicates that it may not support the claim Rolin makes for it, namely that it "shift[s] the debate on gender discrimination" by suggesting we should consider not only evidence on sex discrimination in hiring and promotion "but also evidence on those social processes that generate gender differences in scientific education and productivity."[89] The evidence offered in their paper consists in large part of anecdotes about what is commonly referred to as "micro-aggressions." For example, the authors mention: 1) a male scholar who is giving a talk on an article entitled "Voicing Seduction To Silence Leadership" stating, as a female colleague enters the classroom late, "Here comes our expert on seduction"; 2) this same male scholar referring on this occasion to female scholars by their first names; and 3) a professor referring to the "female Mafia" at an academic journal.[90] The paper also mentions some incidents that are difficult to categorize but, at least arguably do not constitute instances of sex discrimination: female scholars do not speak up as much at weekly seminars—although they are perfectly free to speak up if they want—and at one seminar a male professor harshly criticizes a presentation by a male student but then subsequently encourages the student to continue his work.[91] How is a professor tempering prior criticism anything other than the professional conduct one would expect? Some of the "subtle discrimination" allegedly set forth in the Katila/Merilainen paper is more elusive than subtle. Upon inspection, it fades into non-existence.

Moreover, Katila/Merilainen fail to establish any causal link between incidents such as these and any shortfall in academic productivity. Remember, the claim Rolin makes for them is they have identified social processes "that generate gender differences in scientific education and productivity." Such a link would require, at a minimum, a longitudinal study, preferably one with a comparison between those scholars who suffered from micro-aggressions and those who did not. Instead of a scientifically rigorous study, Katila/Merilainen offer stories gathered during the course of one year at the very university department where they worked. Normally, when a researcher has a personal interest in the outcome of her research, it raises red flags regarding the possibility of bias. However, Katila/Merilainen, consistent with feminist ideology, see this personal stake as a positive, since through their paper they aimed "to place [their] organization in a state of flux and to tweak the power relationships."[92] So, their paper is less a scientific study than a denunciation.

One observation by Katila and Merilainen merits special attention. They assert "several men in our department including professors, research fellows and PhD students share a collective view that men, in general, are best suited to study women's issues."[93] Such a viewpoint *is* discriminatory, and although the authors offer no evidence of a causal link between this viewpoint and the productivity of female researchers, one could reasonably presume there would be some negative impact on those female researchers in their department working on women's issues. But the thing is, this is not some subtle discrimination visible to the feminist standpoint only. Anyone can see this attitude reflects blatant bias. No doubt Jonathan Cole, an experienced sociologist, would have identified this viewpoint as a factor that could affect productivity had he been conducting a micro-study of prejudices in one university department.

In sum, Rolin does not prove her point. The feminist epistemic privilege that she thinks she finds by contrasting Cole with Katila/Merilainen is an illusion fostered by an improper comparison between two distinct types of studies taken two decades apart and sustained by accepting anecdotes of micro-aggressions as evidence of career-impacting discrimination in the absence of any established causal link between such conduct and lesser productivity on the part of female researchers. What presumably injurious bias Katila/Merilainen do mention could have been recognized as such by any impartial man or woman.

Before leaving our discussion of Rolin's paper, we need to consider from another angle her assertion that "feminist values function as a reason to consider certain kind of evidence as relevant for a study on gender discrimination." As we have seen, this claim is not persuasive insofar as it pertains to evidence for sex discrimination, as commonly understood. But, admittedly, values, feminist or otherwise, could be the basis for arguing for a reconsideration of what counts as sex discrimination. But to acknowledge this is simply to acknowledge the quotidian give-and-take of democratic societies. Different groups often have different interests and values, and they argue for recognition of these interests by others. Whether they prevail in their arguments depends, at least ideally, on the merits of their arguments, objectively considered, not on their identity. It's certainly possible that women (or a segment of women—remember, not all women think alike) could highlight certain patterns of events and cite these patterns in successfully arguing for changes in laws or customs that otherwise would not have come about. However, it's also possible that their arguments could fail because they lack merit. Recall (if one is old enough, if not look it up) the efforts in the 1980s and 1990s to require employers to pay women their "comparable worth."[94] Just as we do not have cognitive castes regarding facts, so too do we not have axiological hierarchies regarding values.

Feminist values are also the focus of the final scholarly work we will review, namely an essay by Elizabeth Anderson. Anderson is widely acknowledged to be one of the leading philosophers in the United States (she was the recipient of a grant from the MacArthur Fellows Program),[95] so her argument merits attention if only for that reason. Furthermore, she doesn't couch her argument in terms of standpoint theory, thereby avoiding many of the pitfalls of the theory. Instead, she simply maintains that feminist values can be more "epistemically fruitful" than competing values that may guide research.[96] (Because she is not an advocate for standpoint theory, strictly speaking, I could omit discussion of her essay, but I do not want to be accused of ignoring any evidence that might be interpreted as supporting even a weak version of standpoint theory.)

To support her claim, she cites a study of the effects of divorce conducted by a team led by psychologist Abigail Stewart, who, apparently, undertook research on divorce using a consciously feminist approach, which included, among other things, no presumption in favor of traditional family structure.[97] Without going into all the details, Anderson's take on Stewart's study is that it provided a less skewed, less partial analysis of the effects of divorce because it produced a wider range of evidence than comparable studies, and it had this result precisely because the research was guided by feminist values:

> Thus, a noncognitive value judgement is more epistemically fruitful than another, relative to a controversy, if it guides a research program toward discovering a wider range of evidence that could potentially support any (or more) sides of a controversy. For example, the conception of divorce as loss, presupposing a negative evaluation of divorce, will be able to guide research toward discovering the negative but not the positive features of divorce. By comparison, the Stewart team's value-laden conception of divorce as involving both loss and opportunities for growth is more epistemically fruitful, relative to controversies about the *overall* value of divorce, in that it allows us to uncover evidence bearing on both the pros and cons of divorce.[98]

One does not need to dispute Anderson's claims about the value of Stewart's analysis to see that it doesn't lend any support to standpoint theory, even in its most modest form, nor does it lend any support to the notion that, in general, feminist values produce more accurate results. As I have already remarked, researchers may be motivated by their values to approach research differently than other researchers in the same field, and, on occasion, their different approach may yield results that many find illuminating. Even assuming that Stewart's analysis is more illuminating than other studies on divorce, this does not show that either women, in general, or feminists, in particular, are reliably better social science researchers. (Significantly, one of the studies Anderson criticizes was carried out by a woman.) Consider: A study on the unemployment effects of minimum wage legislation by two white male economists that used a different methodology (actual payroll records as opposed to telephone interviews) than a comparable study may arguably be more illuminating, and perhaps their different approach was motivated by skepticism regarding the value of minimum wage laws.[99] If true, this does not establish that, in general, white males are better researchers if they are motivated by free market values.

Diversity in background and values among social science researchers is probably a good thing, especially given the role that values may have in shaping social science (as opposed to hard science) research and the limitations on the testing of conclusions of such research. But no sex, race, ethnicity, or other grouping of individuals has any greater powers of knowledge acquisition than any other, whatever their values—provided their values do not affect the objective processing of data.

This last point is key, of course—as Anderson recognizes. She states that although value judgments may appropriately guide inquiry, "facts—evidence—tell us which answers are more likely to be true" and these "two roles must be kept distinct so that inquiry does not end up being rigged simply to reinforce our evaluative preconceptions."[100]

Rigorous, impartial evaluation of the data by scientists is necessary. Objectivity is important and attainable. In this enterprise, no individual or group has any advantage over others.

Conclusion Regarding the Evidence for Standpoint Theory

Our survey of the evidence either directly offered in support of standpoint theory or arguably supportive of standpoint theory reveals a nearly complete lack of probative evidence. Some women on occasion may adopt a research approach that, in some ways, is better than other competing approaches—but the same could be said for some men or members of any other identity group. The extraordinary evidence that would be required to establish that women with raised consciousness constitute a privileged cognitive class just isn't there.

Standpoint theory represents an ideologically motivated challenge to the possibility of objective scientific knowledge—but for all the foregoing reasons, it is a failed challenge, despite the fact that its proponents resolutely continue to promote its self-defeating claims. The theory is internally inconsistent, fails to provide clear, verifiable criteria for some of its key claims, and, as we have seen, has no supporting evidence.

Were this theory confined to the university setting, one might think it erroneous, but relatively harmless. However, its influence has extended way beyond academia. The form it has taken outside the university does not always mirror the dense philosophical arguments found in academic papers, but its connection to the underlying tenets of standpoint theory is clear. And because this cruder form is now embedded in everyday discourse and is wielded as a weapon in public policy discussions, it is arguably more pernicious. It is time to turn our attention to the doctrine of "lived experience."

Lived Experience as a Trump Card

"Lived experience," as now commonly understood, is the first-hand account of living as a member of an oppressed group. Described this way, without elaboration, the concept seems innocuous enough. After all, first-hand accounts of anything can be informative. It is possible such accounts can improve our understanding of a situation. They can also foster empathy with a person who has undergone unpleasant or injurious experiences and help us better appreciate this person's stance on some issues. But acknowledging the possible value of first-hand accounts does not capture the significance that those immersed in identity politics attach to lived experience. "Lived experience" of oppression is not comparable to any other type of experience one may have had. Experience of oppression is categorically different than other experiences and endows the oppressed person with knowledge not obtainable by those in dominant positions. Here we see the connection with standpoint theory, where being oppressed—some way, somehow—enables one to acquire better insight. Consequently, persons with experience of oppression are the authorities on any topic relating to their oppression; all others (white males) must defer to them.

All the different groups of the oppressed have their own unique lived experiences, but the use of lived experience as a criterion for truth has become especially prominent in the context of race relations. The importance of lived experience as a source of knowledge is a central tenet of critical race theory:

> A final element [of critical race theory] concerns the notion of a unique voice of color. Coexisting in somewhat uneasy tension with anti-essentialism, the voice-of-color thesis holds that because of their different histories and experiences with oppression, black, American Indian, Asian, and Latino writers and thinkers may be able to communicate to their white counterparts matters that the whites are unlikely to know. Minority status, in other words, brings with it a presumed competence to speak about race and racism.[101]

This viewpoint is echoed throughout the literature on critical race theory and race discrimination. "CRT believes that People of Color are creators of knowledge and have a deeply rooted sensibility to name racist injuries and identify their origins."[102] Similarly, Patricia Hill Collins argues there is a "Black feminist epistemology [that] calls into question the content of what currently passes as truth and simultaneously challenges the process of arriving at that truth," and "[f]or most African-American women those individuals who have lived through the experience about which they claim to be experts are more believable and credible than those who have merely read or thought about such experiences."[103] As previously noted, physicist Prescod-Weinstein maintains that when black women are "speaking up about their experiences with discrimination" they should be offered "axiomatic acceptance of their agency in discourses about race and gender/sex," and the failure to do so forms part of her indictment of white empiricism.[104] The Urban Institute maintains that the lived experience of those in marginalized communities gives them "expertise" so they know their needs better than any "scientist, government official, funder, or policymaker."[105] And the weight given to lived experience is not solely an American phenomenon. Anywhere there are race issues in Western countries, advocates of identity politics "tend to stress the 'lived experience' of the groups they seek to protect with less emphasis on objective data."[106]

The extent of deference one should give to claims based on lived experience varies from author to author, but it definitely would be far more than giving the benefit of the doubt to a claim of discrimination when the evidence is in equipoise. At the extreme, it can mean accepting a black person's assertions despite overwhelming factual evidence to the contrary, as indicated by the Black Lives Matter statement on the Jussie Smollett trial. After observing that in "an abolitionist society [that is, where police are abolished] this trial would not be taking place," the statement makes clear that "we can never believe police . . . over Jussie Smollett, a Black man who has been courageously present, visible, and vocal in the struggle for Black freedom."[107] In other words, don't believe your lying, racist eyes, ears, and brain; you must believe the black man instead.

To dispute the conclusions that an oppressed person of color draws from their experiences is, at best, a display of white privilege, and more likely an example of white supremacist thinking and an instance of epistemic injustice. It is just not to be done. As one journalist has observed, "'Lived experience' is the great incontestable. No doubt may be expressed about a person's lived experience. It is the truth and nothing but the truth."[108] Lived experience is so sacred that questioning or "minimizing" an oppressed person's lived experience will get you expelled from some museums.[109] Of course, it is even worse if one were to question claims of discrimination on more than one occasion. In that case, you are probably engaged in "gaslighting," which the University of Cincinnati's racial resources web pages helpfully define as "doubting or outright denying . . . negative experiences" of people of color.[110] It is called gaslighting because by asking for additional evidence, one must be effectively implying the person of color is crazy—why else would one not simply accept as absolute truth whatever that person claims based on their lived experience?

What is the appropriate response to an oppressed person discussing discrimination? Silent acceptance—certainly if one wants to be an "ally." Syracuse University provides guidance: "If your friends who are part of marginalized communities decide to engage with you on the subject of discrimination, listen to them and offer support where appropriate. As an ally, your job is to listen and learn."[111] This advice to remain silent and not to question is the nearly uniform counsel of American universities, all of which established racial resources pages after the death of George Floyd, if they did not have them already. For example, George Mason University offers as one of its recommended antiracism resources an article in *Teen Vogue* that unambiguously declares, "It isn't up to white people to decide what is and isn't racist. It's our job to listen to black people and people of color when they say something is inherently racist."[112] That universities, supposedly centers of critical thinking and inquiry, would unqualifiedly endorse the approach of "shut up and listen" with respect to any factual claim is especially poignant.

But at least most universities still cling to the possibility that whites and blacks and other people of color can be in conversation, although the role of whites is largely confined to that of mute agreement. Some people of color are so confident of the infallibility of their lived experience—and so emotionally exhausted by having to talk to whites who do not immediately acknowledge the reality of systemic racism—that they have decided the best alternative is to stop talking to whites. British journalist Reni Eddo-Lodge wrote a bestseller with the forthright title *Why I'm No Longer Talking to White People About Race*, in which she bemoaned white reactions of skepticism when she articulated her lived experience.[113] In 2021, Yale University sponsored a talk by psychiatrist Aruna Khilanani, daughter of parents from the Indian subcontinent, with the blunt title, "The Psychopathic Problem of the White Mind." In her talk, Dr. Khilanani advised against talking to whites at all, saying doing so was "useless" because on issues of race whites are "demented."[114]

Well, at the risk of being considered demented, I am going to challenge the view that we should always defer to the lived experience of people of color.

Fortunately, in assessing the merits of the lived experience doctrine, we have already laid the groundwork through the prior discussion of standpoint theory. There is nothing special about oppression that gives people special insight, and no one has provided any evidence to the contrary, apart from question-begging assertions. Moreover, the lived experience doctrine suffers from the same incoherence that undercut its standpoint theory parent. Each of the oppressed groups will have its own unique experiences, so when they clash, how are we supposed to resolve any conflict? No answer. In addition, the specter of essentialism hangs over the doctrine, as is even conceded by some of its proponents. (See prior quotation from *Critical Race Theory: An Introduction*, which admits the doctrine coexists "in uneasy tension with anti-essentialism"). If all the oppressed in a particular group, such as blacks, have special insight into their oppression, then they should all have similar answers at least with respect to the issues dealing with racism. But if anyone has had an oppressed, poverty-stricken upbringing—one with its share of discrimination and racist remarks—it is Supreme Court Justice Clarence Thomas. Yet he adheres to a libertarian approach to most social issues and firmly rejects affirmative action. Whose lived experience should we defer to, Clarence Thomas's or Ibram Kendi's?

Pointing out the logical inconsistencies in the doctrine is probably not going to persuade any of its adherents, however. In part, this is due to the intuitive appeal of the doctrine, in addition to its reflecting the temper of the times. It is part of our received wisdom that we can learn things from those who have had experiences that we have not had. This is true. It is also true that we cannot really dispute how someone felt about their experience. "You need to walk a mile in my shoes to understand how I felt" is an observation with which it is difficult to disagree. Furthermore, with respect to some feelings, the option of donning another's shoes is not available. For example, men will never know exactly what it feels like to be pregnant, so there is no alternative to taking a woman's word for it.

But notice that this truism is about one's feelings, one's sensations, one's impressions. It is not about factual assertions relating to how one came to have a particular experience, much less is it about the public policy ramifications of one's experiences. It is possible to understand, describe, and even provide advice about a wide range of human experiences without ever having lived through a particular experience oneself. This capacity is what makes much of our communication possible. If one's own limited life experiences placed a hard ceiling on what one could understand and discuss, then we would have an extremely difficult time communicating with each other and establishing and maintaining a community.

A few examples will suffice to confirm this point. Many of us will never experience prison or the effects of heroin or meth, but that does not prevent us from discussing intelligently the public policy issues relating to incarceration or drug use, nor would it prevent us from disputing the factual claims of a former inmate or drug addict relating to the circumstances of their imprisonment or drug use. If a former inmate claims he felt bored and frustrated in prison and was never provided opportunities for rehabilitation, we cannot dispute his feelings, but if, in fact, the prison offered multiple classes in a variety of subjects and the inmate never took advantage of these, we might dispute his factual claims regarding lack of rehabilitation opportunities. Certainly, we can agree or disagree with him about broader policy issues, such as the severity of prison sentences. Likewise, if a former addict states that the feelings of euphoria the drugs provided her made it difficult to break her habit, we are not really in a position to challenge that claim. But if she asserts that the ready availability of oxycodone was entirely to blame for her decision to start to use drugs, we might question this attribution of responsibility, especially if she were not prescribed this drug. And, of course, on policy matters, we are free to agree or disagree with her on best policies for curbing drug use and assisting those with drug dependencies. Point is, having a certain experience does not imply that one has indisputable knowledge about the facts relating to that experience, and it definitely does not entail that one has better insight regarding policy matters relating to that experience.

Indeed, as a competing partner to the common wisdom about the need "to walk a mile in my shoes," we also have the common wisdom that someone "may be too close to an issue" to discuss it objectively; that is, they are too emotionally involved with a matter to deliver an informed, impartial judgment. We apply this adage routinely, for example, by carefully screening potential jurors in an effort to ensure they have no connection to the parties and have not had any experiences similar to the ones at issue in the case. Consider also the role of a marriage counselor. Not only is it not a requirement to be a marriage counselor that one have been married to a spouse who was physically or emotionally abusive, or adulterous, or financially imprudent, and so forth, but someone with such experiences probably would not be trusted to provide impartial advice. Were this received wisdom about the dangers of emotional involvement to be applied mechanically, it would actually instruct us to give *less* weight to claims of discrimination from those in groups that have historically been the victims of prejudice, as they may be more inclined to find racism or sexism in the absence of supporting facts. Given the contemporary wave of cries of "racism!" and "sexism!" over every imaginable human interaction, it is tempting to adopt that presumption.

But it would be a mistake to go that far. Those in allegedly oppressed groups have no special insight into discrimination or other acts of oppression, but neither should there be any presumption of skepticism regarding their claims. Personal experience should not be ignored, and it can provide a starting point for any discussion either of a particular alleged incident of discrimination or of appropriate public policy. It is just that it should not provide both a starting point and an endpoint. With respect to the "Shut up and listen" meme, it is the "shut up" part that is troubling, not the "listen" part. Listening is good. People do have different life experiences, and many blacks, women, and members of other groups have had experiences and perspectives from which white men can and should learn. But having had certain experiences does not automatically turn one into an authority to whom others must defer. One should listen carefully, but where appropriate, one should question and engage. In commenting on the use of lived experience to squash debate, philosopher Kwame Anthony Appiah had this to say: "We go wrong when we treat personal history as a revelation, to be elevated above facts and reflection. Talk of lived experience should be used not to end conversations but to begin them."[115]

Conclusion on Standpoint Theory

The suppression of women and their treatment as inferior, subordinate beings has a long history, encompassing virtually all human cultures. The silencing of women was an integral part of that suppression, as 1 Timothy reminds us. ("Let a woman learn in silence with all submissiveness. I permit no woman to teach or to have authority over men; she is to keep silent.")[116] Fortunately for all of us, that situation began to change in modern times and now, at least in Western countries, only the most pig-headed bigot thinks women are not as capable as men with respect to scientific or academic endeavors. But the attainment of full civil and social equality was fairly recent, being a matter of decades, not centuries.

Racism followed a different historical track, but for the last several centuries, its evolution has been substantially similar to sexism: brutal suppression, including attribution of intellectual inferiority, followed by a slow, gradual change in beliefs and attitudes, so that today, just as with women, only a scorned minority believes blacks are not as capable as whites. Again, though, in the United States, widespread acknowledgment of the equality of blacks did not occur before the mid-twentieth century.

Given this history, it is not surprising that women and blacks raise their voices and demand to be heard. They should be heard. Quite apart from their moral right to equal treatment, we will all benefit from their contributions in every aspect of our shared life, including the sciences. The more capable minds we have doing science, the more progress we will obtain. But to acknowledge that we need and should have their contributions does not imply that women or blacks—or any group of human beings—have powers of knowledge acquisition greater than any other group of human beings. There is no evidence to justify the erection of such a cognitive class system. To maintain otherwise is, in the final analysis, to substitute for the white male bigotry of the past a new prejudice that is just as intellectually infirm and, if the eventual result is the discarding of the belief in objective knowledge, just as pernicious.

CHAPTER 2

The Unproven Claim of Systemic Racism

On any given day, read a major newspaper, log onto a university website, listen to a network news show, and one will likely read or hear phrases like these: "blacks are disproportionately affected . . ."; "studies show an adverse impact on blacks from . . ."; "racial minorities will bear a disproportionate burden . . ."; and so on. Why is this? Because the concept of disparate or disproportionate impact is central to the doctrine of systemic racism, and if one were to select one notion that has rapidly come to dominate American culture within the last several years—and especially since the death of George Floyd—it would be the widespread belief that the United States is systemically racist, that is, racism is deeply embedded in the laws, policies, practices, and institutions of the United States. Indeed, saying that the concept of disparate impact is central to the doctrine of systemic racism may be an understatement. It may turn out that the claim of systemic racism amounts to little more than the observation that certain statistical disparities exist combined with the assumption that these disparities are caused by a vaguely sketched "system."

This chapter argues that the claim of systemic racism has not been proven. Unlike standpoint theory, which lacks probative supporting evidence altogether, the claim of systemic racism has, in limited respects, some supporting evidence. Nonetheless, the evidence is insufficient. Moreover, because the evidence of systemic racism is so tenuous, while the belief in it is so tenaciously held, and the disincentives to questioning it are so powerful, it is appropriate to classify the notion of systemic racism as a dogma.

Let me elaborate on this last point. Disputing the claim of systemic racism places one squarely at odds with virtually every institution of higher education, the federal government and many state and local governments, dozens of major nonprofits, almost all major media outlets, and legions of academics. Even one's own computer may counsel adherence to the prevailing doctrine, as Microsoft software automatically links the user to a host of antiracism resources on Bing, including instruction on systemic racism. Challenging the doctrine of systemic racism gives one the sense of being like a dissident in sixteenth-century Spain, asserting that the consecrated host really is just a wafer. Fortunately, the penalty for questioning systemic racism nowadays is merely thundering accusations of racism and social ostracism, although social media dogpiles do share certain aspects of *autos-da-fé*.

Or perhaps the better analogy would be to the Soviet Union, where dissent from the party line was treated as a psychiatric problem. In a recent essay in the most prestigious science journal in the United States, two academic psychologists argued that those who question the existence of systemic racism suffer from a high level of social dominance orientation (SDO), and their efforts to deny systemic racism "likely reflect a motivation . . . to maintain their place atop the status hierarchy."[1] Oh, yes, that's it. Dissent has nothing to do with legitimate questioning of the evidence for systemic racism; it's just a psychological disorder. No better way to avoid having to engage with an argument than to focus on its alleged motivations and dismiss it as the product of a disturbed mind.

Before proceeding further, and perhaps to defer my involuntary commitment, let me emphasize that denying systemic racism is not to deny the existence of racist attitudes or acts of racial discrimination. Among some in the general public, "systemic racism" may be taken to mean "a whole lot of discrimination." But that is not what those who claim there is systemic racism mean by the term. Quite to the contrary, they maintain that focusing on intentional acts of discrimination is to divert our attention from the real problem, which is the set of laws, policies, practices, and institutions of the United States. The metaphor used in the literature is that intentional discrimination is just the tip of the racist iceberg. The iceberg's base, the really destructive part, is systemic racism. Individuals may or may not be racist, but the *system* is definitely racist, and blame for the various disparities between blacks and whites must be assigned primarily to this system. As the Center for American Progress proclaims, "the disparities between white and black Americans can nearly always be traced back to policies that either implicitly or explicitly discriminate against black Americans."[2]

As indicated, the claim that the United States is systemically racist is based on statistical disparities between whites and blacks in a number of areas. The information summarizing these disparities is widely available. Four readily accessible, perspicuous sources are the aforementioned Center for American Progress, the Brookings Institution, *Vox*, and, interestingly, *Insider*.[3] All four have websites with many charts showing statistical differences between blacks and whites in such areas as wealth accumulation, income, educational attainment, debt burden, home ownership, incarceration rates, and health outcomes. No reason to think these charts are materially inaccurate—although, as we will see, different ways of organizing the underlying information can result in charts with different implications. (For example, the wealth gap disappears when comparing a black family with two parents with a white single-parent family.) But for now, the point to bear in mind is this: statistical differences by themselves do not prove anything. Consider: the percentages of players in the National Basketball Association (NBA) and the National Football League (NFL) who are black are wildly out of proportion to the percentage of blacks in the general population. Although blacks account for 12.4 percent of the American population (per the 2020 census), around 74 percent of the NBA's players are black, as are 58 percent of the NFL's players.[4] Mind you, these are well-paid positions, with the median annual salary of NBA players being over $4 million—much more than most Americans will earn in a lifetime.[5] Is this disparate outcome the result of systemic racism against whites? No one has made that suggestion, despite these glaring statistical disparities. No, everyone seems content to assume these players earned their positions through merit in their fields.

In relying on statistical disparities as proof of systemic racism, advocates of that doctrine are effectively implying that when blacks fare worse, statistics can be an appropriate substitute for direct evidence of invidious intent. For the time being, let's accept that argument. Nonetheless, at a minimum, for statistics to constitute evidence of systemic racism, one must first identify the "system," then establish that this system consists of policies or practices that cannot be justified on grounds independent of race, and then, finally, establish a firm causal link between the statistical disparity and the specifically identified policy or practice. I will argue that proponents of the doctrine of systemic racism fall short with respect to all three conditions: no nationwide racist policies are clearly identified, apart from policies that existed prior to the mid-twentieth century, and even with those policies, their long-term causal effect is not always established; key policies that have been characterized as racist have had independent, nondiscriminatory justification; and factors other than the identified policies have contributed significantly to the statistical disparities, in particular with respect to the key categories of wealth and income. All three conditions are necessary, but the establishment of a causal link is the most obvious prerequisite; without it, a statistical disparity proves nothing, as illustrated by our NBA/NFL example. And, as we will see, despite the oft-repeated claim that disparities trace back to racist policies, causes other than the identified policies provide a better explanation.[6]

Before proceeding to discuss the shortcomings of the dogma of systemic racism with respect to these elements, however, it is worthwhile to first take a look at the history of disparate impact analysis in the context of illegal race discrimination to illustrate the type of showing that courts have required.

An Abbreviated History of Disparate Impact Analysis

Disparate impact analysis in the context of race discrimination became common as a result of Supreme Court decisions in the early 1970s that interpreted the prohibition on employment discrimination set forth in Title VII of the Civil Rights Act of 1964.[7] The crucial issue before the Court was whether a showing of intentional discrimination was necessary to a finding of liability under Title VII. The Court concluded it was not necessary. Specifically, the Court ruled that the disproportionate exclusion of blacks from certain jobs pursuant to facially neutral selection criteria could, under certain circumstances, result in a violation of the law.[8]

One reason that prompted the Court to make this interpretation was undoubtedly the suspicion that some employers confronted with Title VII's ban on race discrimination were implementing new selection criteria as a tactic to continue discriminatory practices. In fact, the employer in the first case presented to the Court on this issue not only had a history of intentional discrimination but also had adopted the requirement of a passing grade on an aptitude test on the effective date of Title VII. Upholding the use of facially neutral selection criteria, without qualification, would have gutted the protections of Title VII. Nonetheless, the Court did not limit its ruling to the need to eliminate such subterfuges. Instead, the Court reasoned that because Title VII aims to enlarge employment opportunities for blacks and other minorities, it should be expansively interpreted to be consistent with that goal. Therefore, the Court held that Title VII is not limited to prohibiting intentional discrimination, but also prohibits "practices that are fair in form, but discriminatory in operation."[9]

Significantly, however, the Court ruled that statistical disparities are not by themselves sufficient to establish discrimination. There must be a causal nexus between the challenged practice and the disparate impact, and furthermore, the employer can still avoid liability if it can establish that the challenged practice is consistent with business necessity.[10] That is, a practice may still be lawful despite any side effect it has of adversely affecting blacks if it serves the needs of the business. When, in 2015, the Supreme Court extended the theory of disparate impact liability to actions under the Fair Housing Act, it emphasized again that liability for discrimination cannot be imposed solely "on a showing of a statistical disparity."[11] There is a "robust" causality condition requiring plaintiffs to point to a specific policy or policies causing the disparity. Further, analogous to Title VII's business necessity defense, a housing discrimination defendant can prevail if it can show that the challenged policy is necessary to protect a valid interest.[12]

Following the Court's Title VII decisions, scholars analyzing policies and practices have increasingly adopted disparate impact analysis, in both legal and non-legal contexts, in the course of making their arguments. That trend has only accelerated after the Floyd-inspired racial reckoning. Indeed, it's the rare paper on public policy today that does not consider the possible disparate impact on blacks, or women, or other allegedly marginalized groups. Now, even ads from the 1950s for vaginal douches have been analyzed for their disparate impact.[13] Perhaps more typical are arguments against capital punishment and legal assisted suicide that have been predicated, in part, on their perceived disparate impact on blacks or other "vulnerable" groups.[14]

Considering disparate impact in the context of public policy analysis is not, in itself, necessarily a bad thing. Having benefits and burdens roughly evenly distributed among all racial/ethnic groups may promote social harmony and reduce racial and ethnic discord. The U.S. Constitution designates "domestic tranquility" as an important value. That said, an equal distribution of benefits and burdens as measured by group identity cannot be said to be an intrinsic good, any more than a similar distribution among all individuals, irrespective of group identity, could be said to be an intrinsic good. It is certainly not a compelling, final goal that overrides what are typically regarded as key elements of a desirable society, such as individual autonomy and responsibility for giving shape and direction to one's life and the opportunity to engage in activities commensurate with one's personal interests and abilities. (The Constitution also states that the government should secure for us the "blessings of liberty.")

Moreover, the emphasis on disparate impact and on balancing burdens and benefits can sometimes lead arguments astray. Consider the aforementioned arguments against the death penalty and legal assisted suicide predicated on disparate impact. These two contexts bear emphasis because they involve two topics where the disparate impact argument is singularly inapt. Familiar to many will be the claim that the death penalty is legally or morally infirm because the number of persons executed, as well as the number of persons sentenced to death (most of whom will probably never be executed), is disproportionately black. Now, there are several solid arguments against the death penalty, arguably the most important one being the troubling rate of error in convictions, including capital convictions, but the argument based on the racial composition of those executed does not seem especially forceful or even relevant. Consider: if we could impose death penalty quotas so that the number of capital convictions of blacks and whites mirrored their percentages in the population, would that really make capital punishment significantly more acceptable? I think not. The disparate impact argument adds nothing of substance to the policy debate over capital punishment.

Similarly, around the time Oregon enacted its statute legalizing assisted suicide (also known as assisted dying), there was much hand-wringing over the projected disparate impact legalization would have on women and minorities, with fears that members of these groups would be disproportionately the victims of abuses, including pressure, overt or subtle, to "choose" assisted dying. To begin, anyone familiar with prevailing black attitudes toward assisted suicide would know such fears were overstated (whites constitute the overwhelming percentage of those who have requested assisted dying in Oregon and other states).[15] More important, the underlying premise of the argument is questionable: one must believe that it makes a significant moral difference whether more blacks than whites are pressured into choosing assisted suicide. But it's the concern that *anyone*—regardless of their race or ethnicity—would be pressured into assisted suicide that is morally relevant, isn't it? Would the concern about legalization disappear if it turns out that it's almost always whites who choose assisted dying? Again, as with the debate over the death penalty, the disparate impact argument in this context seems nothing more than a makeweight.

The foregoing examples underscore the point that statistical disparities do not themselves demonstrate an injustice. The disparity must, in some sense, be morally significant, and it must be traced back to some specific policy or practice (or perhaps interlocking policies or practices) that cannot be justified despite any disparate impact it may have. In setting forth these conditions, I am obviously being guided by the standards used by the Supreme Court in its disparate impact cases. One modification is that in the context of public policy, one cannot meaningfully speak of "business necessity." The test should be whether the policy or practice at issue serves an important policy goal that cannot be met by a different policy or practice that avoids a disparate impact.

Of course, it is open to a proponent of systemic racism to slough off this burden. Kendi appears to do this. Regarding various disparities, his suggestion is that it is a matter of either/or: "Either racist policies or Back inferiority explains why White people are wealthier, healthier, and more powerful than Black people today."[16] But this is just reductionist rhetoric, essentially claiming one must either accept systemic racism or be a racist. The claim of systemic racism is a powerful, searing indictment with consequential implications for public policy. It demands more support than posturing via the posing of a false dilemma.

Identifying the "System"

It is customary nowadays to hear or see statements such as this one that appeared in a *Washington Post* article: there is a "well-established link between structural racism and health disparities."[17] But to have a "well-established link" between cause and effect, one must, at a minimum, identify with precision the cause. Despite the fact that structural or systemic racism is often cited in the abstract, rare is the effort made to describe this "system," and most such efforts either amount to little more than handwaving or confuse effect with cause: there are disparities along racial lines so that shows there's systemic racism. That's equivalent to saying a fire was caused by combustible material or a person's death was caused by a fatal condition. Whenever one hears the claim of systemic racism, one should always ask for the system to be clearly identified.

Of course, if one were discussing the topic of systemic racism in 1923, as opposed to 2023, the task of identifying the system and its various elements would be, unfortunately, easy. Segregation in education was legally mandated in much of the United States, depriving blacks of educational opportunities available to whites. (The separate "but equal" requirement was a farce.) Although the Supreme Court in 1917 held that governments could not mandate housing segregation,[18] private parties could and did enforce segregated housing through restrictive covenants. The Supreme Court would not render such covenants unenforceable until 1948.[19] Shamefully, Woodrow Wilson's administration segregated the federal workforce, and segregation of government employees was also the rule in various states. This segregation had the effect of diminishing the income of black employees.[20] With respect to private employment, there was no protection against discrimination, and there is no doubt that discrimination was widespread—especially in the South, but it existed throughout the country. This discrimination adversely affected the immediate income of blacks as well as their longer-term financial prospects. Although the Fifteenth Amendment prohibited denial of the right to vote based on race, blacks still were prevented from exercising their franchise, particularly in southern states, through various mechanisms, such as literacy tests, poll taxes, or outright intimidation.[21]

So, in the first decades of the twentieth century, there was systemic racism in the sense that laws, regulations, and practices across a wide range of areas significantly disadvantaged blacks. No question. But the situation began to change by mid-century. In 1948, President Truman issued executive orders integrating the Armed Forces and the federal workforce.[22] As indicated, that same year, the Supreme Court rendered racist restrictive covenants in residential housing unenforceable. In 1945, New York became the first state to outlaw race discrimination in employment, and Connecticut followed shortly thereafter.[23] In 1954, the Supreme Court outlawed segregated public schools.[24] Granted, there ensued "massive resistance" to the Court's order, with some school systems dragging their feet for nearly a decade, but the path toward integrated public schools was laid. In 1957, Congress enacted the first civil rights bill since Reconstruction; the law created the Commission on Civil Rights, with the power to investigate allegations of voter intimidation and other actions depriving blacks of equal protection of the laws.[25] In 1961, within weeks of his inauguration, President Kennedy issued an executive order creating the Committee on Equal Opportunity with a mandate to combat discrimination in private employment arising out of government contracts.[26] A year later, he issued another executive order banning race discrimination in federally funded housing.[27]

The year 1964 witnessed the passage of the historic, monumental Civil Rights Act, prohibiting discrimination on the basis of race (as well as other bases) in employment and public accommodations.[28] The act created an agency, the Equal Employment Opportunity Commission (EEOC), to administer and enforce the employment discrimination provisions and also provided charging parties with the ability to sue. The act also authorized the attorney general to bring desegregation lawsuits against school systems still failing to adhere to the Supreme Court's ruling. Adoption of this law was quickly followed by the Voting Rights Act of 1965,[29] which effectively eliminated state and local regulations and tactics designed to prevent blacks from voting, and the Fair Housing Act of 1968,[30] which prohibited discrimination in the sale, rental, or financing of housing. Given the discrimination blacks experienced when applying for loans, an especially important piece of legislation was the 1974 Equal Credit Opportunity Act (Title VII of the Consumer Credit Protection Act), which prohibited discrimination in the extension of credit and required creditors to provide applicants with the reasons for any denial of credit.[31]

Expanded protections against discrimination came not just from new legislation but also from judicial interpretations of old legislation. In 1968, the Supreme Court revitalized the dormant 1866 Civil Rights Act, interpreting it to provide a private cause of action against entities engaging in housing discrimination based on race.[32] This ruling was followed a few years later by another case interpreting a separate section of the 1866 Civil Rights Act, which found that the act provided a remedy against employment discrimination based on race.[33] This last decision was especially significant because, under Title VII of the 1964 Civil Rights Act, there was no right to a jury trial or compensatory or punitive damages (until 1991). Plaintiffs alleging race discrimination, therefore, were in better litigation posture than plaintiffs alleging other types of prohibited discrimination.

Furthermore, apart from overt changes in the law, many employers and educational institutions began voluntary efforts to increase employment and educational opportunities for blacks by, to some extent, taking their race into consideration as a positive selection factor: what became known as affirmative action. The term "affirmative action" made its first appearance in Kennedy's 1961 executive order applying to federal contractors.[34] The order required contractors to "take affirmative action" to ensure that applicants and employees are treated without discrimination. Plainly, this verbiage required more than just refraining from discrimination; some positive—affirmative—action was required. However, the nature of the required affirmative action was not at the time detailed. Within the specific arena of federal contracts, that term took on a specialized meaning, but for many other employers and educational institutions, the concept of affirmative action, as applied, came to be understood as providing some sort of loosely defined edge to black applicants—preferential treatment within the contours of a "holistic" approach. The vagueness of the edge offers legal protection because undisguised use of quotas is a step too far. This is what drew the Supreme Court's attention in the famous *Bakke* case, decided in 1978.[35] In *Bakke*, the medical school at the University of California at Davis set aside for minorities sixteen of the one hundred slots in its entering classes. The Court found the set aside unlawful but also concluded that the university had a substantial interest in promoting a diverse student body and, to that end, could use an applicant's minority status as a "plus" factor in evaluating the applicant's candidacy. Quotas bad; plus factors okay.

Affirmative action remains a controversial subject, and the extent to which employers or educational institutions can legally provide and have provided preferences to black applicants has been subject not only to the evolution of federal law but also to changes in state laws, as well as voluntary changes in admission criteria by some employers or universities. Supreme Court litigation involving Harvard University, pending at the time of this writing, may curtail the extent to which educational institutions may give preference to applicants based on their race. Nonetheless, broadly speaking, since the 1970s, some level of preferential treatment has been afforded to black applicants across a wide range of employment sectors and with respect to admission to many educational institutions. In other words, for over fifty years, not only have governments and institutions strictly prohibited race discrimination in employment and education, but blacks, as a group, have been granted a not inconsiderable edge. This is not a picture of systemic racism against blacks.

In addition, the mid-twentieth century not only witnessed a transformation in employment, educational, and housing opportunities for blacks but also the launch of an array of spending and social programs designed to bolster the incomes and well-being of poor people: the so-called "War on Poverty." President Lyndon Johnson successfully pushed for a policy agenda that he envisioned as bringing an end to both poverty and racial injustice.[36] Roughly two dozen programs were implemented or strengthened, including most notably, Medicaid,[37] food stamps,[38] the programs of the Child Nutrition Act of 1966 (principally, free school meals for the needy)[39] and the initiatives of the Economic Opportunity Act of 1964, which, through several different programs, provided jobs and job training, supplemental education, and financial assistance.[40] (Head Start is perhaps the most well-known program that was launched by this legislation.) These programs benefited all persons below certain income levels, but because blacks were disproportionately represented among the nation's poor in the 1960s (just as they are today), blacks received a disproportionate share of the benefits from these social welfare programs.

Social welfare programs have expanded, contracted, been replaced, or otherwise changed over the decades since the 1960s, with the largest changes coming with the emphasis on greater assistance for the working poor, for example, via the Earned Income Tax Credit (EITC) and the replacement of Aid to Families with Dependent Children (AFDC) with the Temporary Assistance for Needy Families (TANF) program. Whatever the changes, the fact remains that, proportionately, blacks have continued to receive the greatest value in benefits. For example, in 2019, almost 33 percent of the recipients of Medicaid were black[41] and 25 percent of food stamp (SNAP) recipients were black.[42] EITC has also favored blacks disproportionately, especially black women; as of 2019, 21 percent of black women received payments via EITC versus 9 percent of white women, and their average benefit was hundreds of dollars larger as well.[43]

At this point, some exasperated readers may be thinking, "Well, of course, percentage-wise blacks have received more benefits from the social safety net *because they needed it*." Sure. But if the "system" had racism deeply embedded within it, presumably no set of policies in the system would have the task of meeting that need. That's emphatically not the case, and it has not been the case for decades. Far from ignoring the needs of economically disadvantaged blacks, the federal government's poverty programs have provided them with assistance at levels disproportionate to their share of the general population. (Disproportionality has to cut both ways: if a disproportionate share of burdens has significance, then so too must a disproportionate share of benefits have significance.)

It is important to note that the amount of public funds poured into these programs has been far from trivial. On the fiftieth anniversary of the War on Poverty, a careful calculation of the amounts spent, both federal and state, showed that more than $19 trillion had been expended.[44] That is as of 2014—nearly a decade ago.

Finally, the foregoing combination of civil rights protections and benefit programs resulted in a significant improvement in blacks' economic conditions in the period between 1964 and 1975. There was a marked decline in the gap between black and white earnings during this period. The ratio of aggregate black-to-white earnings rose sixteen percent during this period, from 0.62 to 0.72.[45] Academic research has confirmed this was not a mere coincidence, but rather that "Federal civil rights policy was the major contributor to the sustained improvement in black economic status that began in 1965."[46]

To summarize our argument to this point: A dispassionate review of the civil legal and social systems that have been in place largely since the 1960s indicates that blacks have been legally protected from discrimination in employment, education, housing, and public accommodations, that they have received preferential treatment (to some extent) in employment and education, and that they have received huge amounts of public resources to help them meet their needs, including nutritional and health needs, in a share disproportionate to their percentage of the population. There is no racism embedded in these systems. The laws and policies of the United States have not been systematically racist for at least the last fifty to sixty years.[47]

Proponents of systemic racism would beg to differ, but when one reviews their arguments, one notices something immediately: they rarely discuss the legal protections and social welfare systems that have been in place since the 1960s. This omission is glaring. The failure to acknowledge the disproportionate benefits blacks have received from social welfare programs is especially conspicuous, given that some of the more prominent claims regarding systemic racism do not focus on policies that impose disproportionate burdens on blacks but rather on policies that allegedly disproportionately benefit whites. In evaluating whether a "system" as a whole is racist, should one not weigh the benefits disproportionately received by one group against the benefits disproportionately received by the other group?

Let us look at some of the current civil policies often mentioned as being part of a racist system: the tax policy that allows favorable treatment (income deferral) for certain retirement plans; the tax policy of granting a deduction for mortgage interest; and lending policies that either result in many blacks being denied needed loans or being charged higher interest rates.[48] The arguments for systemic racism here follow the same pattern, running as follows: percentage-wise, fewer blacks have retirement plans or accounts or can take full advantage of them due to their relative difficulty in saving money; similarly, regarding the mortgage deduction, far fewer blacks are homeowners and, therefore, far fewer blacks can take advantage of this deduction; regarding loans, under prevailing policies, fewer blacks qualify for loans at manageable rates.

To show that these policies are racist, one must first establish that these policies do not have any independent justification. Recall from our prior discussion of disparate impact analysis that before a policy that has a disparate impact can properly be considered racist, one must show it does not serve an important, nondiscriminatory purpose, or that this purpose can be served equally well by a different policy which would have no disparate impact. Without getting into a deep discussion of tax policy, which is beyond our scope, one can make a compelling argument that incentivizing retirement accounts obviously helps seniors avoid poverty and reduces the burden on social welfare programs. It is not clear why we should abandon these appropriate, race-neutral goals merely because members of one ethnic or racial group are not presently in a position to take full advantage of this policy. Nor has anyone put forward a different policy that would achieve the same goals without the disparate impact.

The mortgage deduction is more problematic only because scholars disagree over whether it is really achieving its objectives. This policy is supposed to increase homeownership and sustain the housing industry, a source of jobs for many, including blacks. However, some argue that the policy has done little to increase homeownership and that most of the benefit of the deduction goes to the wealthy, as middle- and lower-income homeowners do not typically itemize deductions and would not get much benefit if they did.[49] But the reform that many policy experts have suggested, that is, converting the deduction into a tax credit to enable more homeowners to partake of the advantage, would still probably proportionally benefit whites more than blacks. Does that make the policy racist if it achieves important goals that are ultimately beneficial in some way to American society?

Moreover, as a general matter, once we delve into the areas of tax and economic policy, it can be difficult to determine whether a policy has a beneficial or detrimental effect on blacks, in particular black income and wealth. For example, many who accept the doctrine of systemic racism contend that one thing the government should do to help boost black income is increase the minimum wage substantially, as this would have "a disproportionate positive impact on African Americans."[50] But many economists reach the precisely opposite conclusion, arguing that a high minimum wage would have a disproportionate adverse effect on blacks because it would reduce black employment opportunities substantially, affecting not only current income but also the ability to acquire much-needed training. "They are not only made less employable by minimum wages; opportunities to upgrade their skills through on-the-job training are also severely limited."[51] So, if the effects of a policy, and not its intent, determine whether it is racist, we can have a situation where opposing sides on a policy issue can each hurl denunciations of racism. All this accomplishes is to make policy disputes even murkier, turning economic issues into moral ones. The takeaway point is that the argument that the "system" is racist is even more untenable when the argument relies on tax and economic policies whose effects are disputed by qualified experts.

Similar points apply to the argument that lending policies adversely affect blacks. Those who posit systemic racism argue that blacks are too often denied credit or can obtain credit only by paying higher interest rates. However, the net worth of a loan applicant is a legitimate factor in determining credit risk, and, as all agree, the median wealth of black families is far less than the median wealth of white families (see discussion in next section). Differences in how loans are distributed to blacks and whites are largely a reflection of this underlying economic reality. Financial institutions will lend money to those who are considered more of a credit risk only if they can structure the loan to minimize the risk. To require them to do otherwise is to require them to make irrational economic decisions. As an illustration of this point, consider how lending restrictions on mortgages were loosened in the late 1990s and early 2000s as, in part, a reaction to a push by the government on banks to lend to less creditworthy customers.[52] The result was a significant increase in loans given to individuals with low credit scores, including many blacks, but the lending institutions sought to protect themselves by issuing subprime mortgages, i.e., a mortgage loan with a higher interest rate and/or adjustable rate. Then, when the financial crisis of 2008 hit, with its associated increase in mortgage defaults, the charge was that banks had "steered" blacks into subprime mortgages. So, to the advocates of systemic racism, banks were racist when they did not provide the loans and then racist when they did. As one commentator noted as the subprime crisis was winding down:

Prior to the emergence of the subprime market for home mortgages, lending institutions rationed credit by denying risky loans and those involving some property locations, a practice that became known as redlining and was attacked as race discrimination. Interestingly, now that legal ceilings on home mortgage interests have been relaxed, enabling less creditworthy people to secure loans, the racial discrimination charges focus on higher loan-default rates experienced by people who would have otherwise not been able to secure a loan.[53]

The reality is that people with poor credit have a more difficult time securing loans at standard rates or securing loans altogether. Within a market economy, that fact reflects sound business practice by lending institutions, not race discrimination.

Before leaving this topic of discriminatory lending, we should discuss the case of *Pigford v. Glickmore*, a lawsuit that some have cited as illustrating contemporary systemic racism.[54] In this case, a class of black farmers sued the U.S. Department of Agriculture (USDA), alleging they had been discriminatorily denied loans or had their loans delayed in violation of various statutes and USDA regulations. The USDA's credit and benefits program for farmers was administered locally, at the county level, by committees elected by local farmers, and this is where the discrimination took place. Unfortunately, during the relevant period (roughly 1981 until 1996), the USDA exercised very little oversight over the county committees and, therefore, did nothing to forestall the committees' discriminatory actions, despite receiving some complaints about them. A federal district court approved a settlement of the lawsuit in 1999, and over $1 billion was paid out to aggrieved black farmers. Furthermore, because there were complaints that some black farmers, through no fault of their own, missed the deadline for filing claims under the settlement, Congress in 2008 passed legislation to provide these farmers with additional time to pursue their claims, and in 2011 a $1.25 billion settlement was reached on these additional claims.[55]

But as despicable and as widespread as the actions of these local committees were, the *Pigford* case does not exemplify how systemic racism harms blacks. The system itself—the laws and policies governing the allocation of USDA funds—was perfectly colorblind. It was the actions of bigoted individuals that caused the harm. Moreover, the relevant laws and policies provided for redress of the legitimate grievances of these black farmers.

No one in their right mind would claim that discrimination does not take place. Although overt prejudice is waning, bigotry can still cause harm. The issue is whether today, unlike the situation in 1923, there are laws and policies in place that prohibit such discrimination and provide for appropriate relief when it occurs. We have such laws and policies. There continue to be bigots, but the system itself is not racist.

Wealth Disparity and Past Systemic Racism

While public policies have protected and benefitted blacks since at least the 1960s, as previously stated, systemic racism prevailed for much of American history. For how long racism could be said to have been systemic would be a matter of debate (the period from the late 1940s until the 1960s could be said to be a time of transition), but no fine-tuning is necessary to consider this argument: Current policies and practices in and of themselves may not be racist, but the effects of prior racist policies and practices continue to this day, and it is these persisting effects that account for the disparities among blacks and whites in various areas, in particular wealth. Leave aside the concession about current practices and policies not being inherently racist, and this is the preferred argument of some of those who contend there is systemic racism. The system is racist because it perpetuates past racism.[56]

There is some plausibility to this argument because systemic racism did exist, and, obviously, changes in laws and policies, however beneficial, cannot be expected to eliminate instantly all the ill effects of a racist system. Moreover, the focus on wealth accumulation is justified, because if there is one disparity that can be singled out as the most crucial disparity, it is the disparity in wealth, given its significance for one's general condition, including health and educational achievement. As the Center for American Progress notes, wealth "is the most complete measure of a family's future economic well-being."[57] And there is no doubt a disparity between the median wealth of black families and the median wealth of white families. In 2016, the median wealth for white families was $181,900, whereas for black families it was $18,200.[58] In 2019, the median wealth for white families was $188,200, whereas for black families, it was $24,100.[59] Although the size of the gap has waxed and waned over the decades, in the last thirty years, black wealth has never been more than 18.8 percent of white wealth, and has been as low as 8.1 percent.[60] The gap could be made smaller by age-adjusting the median wealth—wealth tends to increase with age and the median age for a black person is over a decade younger than the median age for a white person—but however one slices the numbers, the gap is substantial.

Given the civil rights protections, affirmative action initiatives, and assistance programs that have been in place for over fifty years, it does not seem likely that this gap is due to "systems" that have been put in place in recent times. Necessarily, if one seeks a systemic cause, one must look to the more distant past. But the further back in time one goes, the more difficult it is to trace a chain of causation between past racist policies and current disparities in wealth. There are too many possible intervening causes, along with background changes in conditions unrelated to specific policies. Consider, for example, how wealth can be acquired in a predominantly agricultural society versus how it can be acquired in a post-industrial, urban, service-oriented economy. However, most proponents of systemic racism do not think we have to go back beyond the 1930s and 1940s. According to them, policies of the New Deal era created advantages for whites and disadvantages for blacks that continue to affect wealth accumulation to this day. They point to two sets of policies in particular: Social Security and the various programs that provided for government-backed home mortgages.

With Social Security, the contention is that the decision to exclude agricultural and domestic workers from coverage under the act was motivated by racism. Many workers in these occupations were black. The political power of southern Democrats supposedly forced their exclusion from this important social safety net. Ta-Nehisi Coates has flatly stated that the "omnibus programs passed under the Social Security Act in 1935 were crafted in such a way as to protect the southern way of life."[61] Political scientist Robert C. Lieberman was even more unqualified in attributing the exclusion of agricultural and domestic workers to acquiescence in the racism of southern politicians, stating that the "Old-Age Insurance provisions of the Social Security Act were founded on racial exclusion. In order to make a national program of old age benefits palatable to southern congressional barons, the Roosevelt administration acceded to a southern amendment excluding agricultural and domestic employees from OAI coverage."[62] (Citation omitted.) This claim has now been repeated so often that it forms an indispensable component in the standard recitation of the ills of systemic racism, whether that recitation occurs in a denunciation of wealth, education, housing, or health inequities. According to an essay in *Lancet*, the exclusion of domestic and agricultural workers undoubtedly was "racially motivated" and has had critical "ongoing intergenerational effects."[63]

However, this claim does not withstand scrutiny. A thorough analysis of the legislative background of the Social Security Act reveals that the exclusion was the result of recommendations from staff, technical advisors, the Social Security Advisory Council, and, ultimately, from Treasury Secretary Henry Morgenthau—hardly a southern congressional baron.[64] This recommendation was based on the need for administrative simplicity: there was a concern that the frequent absence of adequate accounting records for agricultural and domestic workers would make appropriate tax collection for these workers nearly impossible. As Morgenthau stated in his testimony before Congress, inclusion of these workers in the legislation would "impose[] a burden on the Treasury that it cannot guarantee adequately to meet."[65] Southern Democrats did not "create the exclusion or push it through Congress."[66] Moreover, although many black employees were among the workers not included, 74 percent of the excluded workers were white.[67] Thus, the notion that the exclusion specifically targeted blacks is also false. Finally, it is worth noting that the exclusion was short-lived. In 1950 Social Security was extended to farm and domestic workers employed by a single employer; in 1954, it was further extended to farm and domestic workers employed by multiple employers.[68] In sum, the claims that the Social Security Act was racist and that it had a significant lasting impact on wealth accumulation by blacks are unsupported.

The question of discrimination in government-backed home mortgages is more complicated, and here we will see some solid pieces of evidence that suggest the possibility of enduring effects of past racially motivated policies. But we need to be careful in our analysis for at least three reasons. First, indisputably racist policies are often conflated with policies that may have had a disproportionate impact but were nonetheless grounded in legitimate business considerations. Second, the actions of one federal agency do not necessarily reflect the actions of a separate agency, even when their programs are similar. Finally, and more important, the past policies and practices that had an enduring effect on wealth were arguably not so much discrimination in the issuance of mortgages but the failure of the government after the Civil War to place emancipated slaves in a tenable economic position, that is, a position where they and their descendants would be regarded as an acceptable credit risk for a mortgage. In other words, it's not the policies of the New Deal era that may have had an enduring impact but the policies of the post–Civil War era.

The Great Depression resulted in a rash of foreclosures and a steep decline in home prices. As part of the New Deal, the federal government created various agencies and programs to stabilize home ownership and home prices. One of the agencies created was the Home Owners Loan Corporation (HOLC), which had as one of its tasks the purchase and refinancing of troubled home loans. Beginning in 1933 and during the course of its existence, the HOLC purchased over a million loans from lenders—20 percent of all mortgages on owner-occupied homes outside of farm areas. Another task the HOLC eventually undertook was a systematic appraisal of neighborhoods in connection with establishing policies with regard to the servicing of its own loans and the management of acquired real estate. In developing its appraisal, the HOLC relied principally on information from local real estate professionals, including bank loan officers and realtors, and local officials. The HOLC classified neighborhoods based on loan-related, risk-based characteristics, grading them A to D, with A indicating low risk and D high risk; the maps the agency eventually developed were color-coded as well, with the D areas marked in red. Hence the term "redlining."

However, contrary to what is so often implied in the literature, the HOLC's "redlining" had little to no direct impact on HOLC loans, to blacks or others, for the simple reason that the HOLC did not undertake its survey and the development of its maps until it had already made the vast majority of its loans.[69] Nor did the maps reflect the loans the HOLC made; the HOLC made substantial loans in areas that eventually were D-rated; in Philadelphia, 60 percent of HOLC loans went to D-rated areas.[70] Furthermore, with respect to the racial breakdown of HOLC loans, black households accounted for 4.5 percent of its loan portfolio; this percentage "matched the black share of nonfarm homeowners in 1930 and 1940."[71] Thus, the objective evidence indicates that racial bias did not deprive blacks of their fair share of HOLC loans.

But did the HOLC's maps affect how other lenders made mortgage loans, and were the maps themselves a product of racial bias? The answer to both these questions is a qualified "no."

Another federal agency, the Federal Housing Administration (FHA), began insuring home mortgages in 1935, principally with respect to new construction. In connection with its loan guarantee program, the FHA undertook its own study of local markets and created its own set of color-coded maps to indicate relative lending risk. Some scholars have suggested that in creating its maps, the FHA relied on HOLC's maps, but there is no direct evidence of this—most FHA maps were destroyed decades ago. The surviving maps do not match the HOLC maps, although there is some resemblance. Furthermore, the FHA maps were developed with a different methodology, using property inventories with block-level data, and covered many more cities than the HOLC maps.[72]

With respect to whether the HOLC maps were racially biased, many of the area description files that accompanied HOLC's survey maps did contain racial references, sometimes characterizing the presence of a high concentration of blacks as having a negative influence on a neighborhood's risk assessment. Moreover, 95 percent of black-owned homes were placed in red zones. However, the vast majority of homeowners in red zones were white; specifically, whites owned 92 percent of the homes in red zones. In other words, in absolute numbers, the red zone classification affected more whites than blacks.[73] Significantly, the redlined areas with larger white concentrations had better economic conditions overall than redlined areas with larger black concentrations, which is "the opposite of what we would expect if black neighborhoods had been disproportionately targeted for the D rating."[74]

The most reasonable conclusion is that the placement of most black homeowners in red-shaded areas was primarily the result of their pre-existing bleak economic situation, not intentionally biased placement by the HOLC. Although there were both poor whites and poor blacks in the 1930s, just as there are today, blacks, in general, were substantially more impoverished than whites and, therefore, were concentrated in municipal areas with the least desirable housing. This fact can be confirmed by reviewing census data from 1930 and 1940 on the range of values of homes owned by whites and blacks. In 1930, 39.3 percent of the nonfarm homes owned by blacks were valued at less than $1,000; the comparable percentage for "native" whites was 6.6 percent. Meanwhile, 21.8 percent of native whites owned nonfarm homes valued between $5,000 and $7,500; the comparable percentage for blacks was 6.5 percent. In 1940, the percentages for nonfarm homes under $1,000 were 56.4 percent black and 13.5 percent white; and for nonfarm homes between $5,000 and $7,500, the percentages were 2.7 percent black and 15.1 percent white. (The decline in value for all homes reflects the loss of value resulting from the Great Depression.)[75] In other words, black homeownership was already concentrated in the more economically challenged areas before any New Deal housing programs took effect. "The patterns in the [HOLC] maps were also driven by decades of disadvantage and discrimination that had already pushed black households into the core of economically distressed neighborhoods prior to the government's direct involvement in mortgage markets . . . [and] the HOLC maps are best viewed as providing clear evidence of how decades of unequal treatment effectively limited where black households could live by the late 1930s rather than reflecting racial bias in the construction of the maps themselves."[76]

Of course, even if the HOLC did not discriminate in providing loans or in classifying neighborhoods, blacks may have suffered mortgage discrimination via other agencies. In fact, there is persuasive evidence that the FHA, as a result of its backing of segregation, did discriminate in providing loan guarantees, at least during the period from the mid-1930s through 1948. One reason for this difference is the difference in agency missions: the HOLC guaranteed refinancing of existing mortgages, whereas the FHA focused on new construction. In stabilizing the existing supply of owner-occupied homes, the HOLC could not deny mortgages to black homeowners without undercutting its mission. The FHA was not similarly constrained.

The FHA's written policies confirm that racism had some influence on its distribution of loan guarantees. FHA's 1938 Underwriting Manual contained several references to the negative effect that the presence of mixed races presumably would have on a neighborhood's rating. For example, the manual stated that:

Areas surrounding a location are investigated to determine whether incompatible racial and social groups are present, for the purpose of making a prediction regarding the probability of the location being invaded by such groups. If a neighborhood is to retain stability, it is necessary that properties shall continue to be occupied by the same social and racial classes. A change in social or racial occupancy generally contributes to instability and a decline in values.[77]

More significant, because it set forth a condition for a high rating, was the manual's express statement that in evaluating "undeveloped" neighborhoods, a high rating "should be given only where [adequate zoning exists] or where effective restrictive covenants are recorded against the entire tract."[78] One restrictive covenant the FHA recommended was a "prohibition of the occupancy of properties except by the race for which they are intended."[79] Put more plainly, it was a major plus factor for a mortgage loan if the tract on which the house was situated required sales to be limited to whites or blacks. Indeed, although the FHA did not word this section of its manual as a segregation mandate, it effectively operated as one.

The references to the undesirability of mixed neighborhoods and the conditioning of a high rating on racially restrictive covenants are obviously troubling; they evince a morally reprehensible segregationist outlook. And there is no question that the FHA fostered segregated neighborhoods through its distribution of loans.[80] However, we are considering the long-term effects of the government's mortgage programs on black wealth. Here the issue is not so much whether the FHA fostered segregation but whether the agency improperly denied loan guarantees to blacks altogether, despite their creditworthiness. There is evidence that some blacks did not receive loans they should have received; they were denied loans for homes in white neighborhoods even though they were financially qualified.[81] However, blacks certainly were not shut out completely. As of 1950, 2.3 percent of FHA loan guarantees went to black homeowners. This may seem like a very small percentage, but in that year, only 5.6 percent of homeowners were black.[82] Of course, this does indicate that the percentage of FHA loan guarantees to black homeowners represented less than half the total percentage of black homeowners in the population, which is in marked contrast with the HOLC loan program, which, as indicated, provided loans to black homeowners commensurate with their rate of homeownership. In assessing the significance of this gap, though, we should not assume that this gap was entirely the result of racial discrimination. Bear in mind that the racially discriminatory sections of the FHA's manual were just a fragment of literally dozens of rating criteria that took up over a hundred pages in the underwriting manual. In other words, their importance should not be exaggerated; it's not as though the manual was exclusively focused on the racial composition of neighborhoods. Most of the manual set forth criteria that one would expect an agency to use in determining the advisability of making or insuring a loan, such as the soundness of a house's structure and the financial ability of the borrower to meet the obligations of the loan.[83] Indeed, in its first decades, the FHA was notorious for its conservative underwriting.[84] Given the less favorable financial condition of blacks compared to whites, objective loan risk considerations indicate that prospective black homeowners, regardless of any racial discrimination, would likely have received proportionally fewer loan guarantees than whites.

All that being said, even assuming that the relatively worse economic situation of blacks played a role in their being considered poor risks for loans, it's a fair inference that racial discrimination, as reflected in the FHA's manual, deprived *some* blacks of loans to which they would otherwise have been entitled. This practice had an adverse effect on their wealth which, in time, likely had some adverse effect on the wealth of their heirs.

However, in assessing the extent of the adverse effect on black wealth, it is important to note that federal policy changed after the 1948 Supreme Court ruling invalidating racially restrictive covenants. Following the Supreme Court decision, the FHA revised its manual to delete racial references, including the reference to the conditioning of high ratings on racially restrictive covenants, and advised its field offices not to reject mortgage applications that violated such restrictive covenants. Counsel for FHA's parent agency, the Housing and Home Finance Agency, expressly stated that "underwriters are no longer free to write-down an evaluation because non-white races are involved in the transaction."[85] Furthermore, in December 1949, FHA ruled that it would not provide mortgage insurance for properties in which racially restrictive covenants were recorded after February 15, 1950.[86] Then, in 1952, the agency directed its field offices to give preference to open-occupancy (that is, nonsegregated) developments.[87] In 1954, the FHA announced it would take active steps to encourage the development of open-occupancy projects in key areas. Thus, according to the 1961 report of the Civil Rights Commission, "in the 7 years from 1947 to 1954, FHA moved from a policy requiring segregation to one expressly encouraging open occupancy."[88]

What was the overall effect of FHA's mortgage policy from the mid-1930s until 1950? Some commentators argue it increased white homeownership dramatically while doing next to nothing for black homeownership. In a leading article on FHA policy, John Kimble stated that by "equating African Americans with risk, the FHA . . . directed the rain of capital to fall exclusively over homogeneous, white suburbs."[89] But census data does not support this conclusion. In 1940, in urban areas, black homeownership was at 19.9 percent, with white ownership at 39.1 percent, for a gap of 19.2 percent. In nonfarm rural areas, black ownership was at 35.2 percent, with white homeownership at 53 percent, for a gap of 17.8 percent.[90] By 1950, nonwhite homeownership in urban areas had jumped to 32.5 percent, with white homeownership also increasing to 52.2 percent, for a gap of 19.7 percent. In nonfarm rural areas, nonwhite homeownership was at 45.9 percent, with white homeownership at 64.3 percent, for a gap of 18.4 percent.[91] In other words, between 1940 and 1950, the heart of the period when the FHA's discriminatory policies were in effect, homeownership increased for both blacks and whites, and the gap between their rates of ownership increased only slightly, from 19.2 percent to 19.7 percent in urban areas, and from 17.8 percent to 18.4 percent in rural areas. Housing capital was sprinkled more liberally among whites, but it was hardly the deluge for whites and drought for blacks that some commentators assert.

It is true that even though the FHA changed its stance in the early 1950s from one of opposition to integrated housing to one of encouragement, the agency still continued to fund some segregated housing, depending on the state and locality. With respect to housing law, the 1950s was a time of transition, with a handful of states, including New York and New Jersey, prohibiting segregated housing built with public assistance, including FHA-guaranteed loans.[92] Where these laws were in effect, the agency "adopted a policy of refusing to insure loans for discriminatory builders."[93] Unfortunately, that policy did not apply in the majority of states where builders and brokers were still free to discriminate. It was only in 1962 that the FHA refused completely to fund segregated housing, as a result of President Kennedy's executive order prohibiting discrimination in federally funded housing.[94]

Did this interim period of disfavoring segregated housing but still funding it in many localities result in a major setback for black homeownership? Not according to the 1960 census. According to the Bureau of the Census, the rate of increase for homeownership among nonwhites was greater in the 1950s than the rate of increase for whites. "Between 1950 and 1960, the number of units occupied by nonwhite owners increased from 1.4 million to 2.0 million, or 46 percent; whereas the number occupied by white owners increased from 22.3 million to 30.5 million, or 38 percent."[95] Federal policy was not as generous as it should have been to black homeowners, and especially in the 1940s, it had the deplorable effect of reinforcing racist stereotypes, but it cannot be said to have substantially diminished black homeownership.

In addition to the argument that many blacks in this time period were improperly denied loans, there is also the contention that the federal policy disfavoring mixed neighborhoods—however limited it may have been in time—and the relative lack of mortgage funding for redlined neighborhoods kept blacks concentrated in impoverished neighborhoods with substandard housing, with this effect continuing to this day. A perpetual ghetto. This argument, however, is not supported by studies of formerly redlined neighborhoods. The Brookings Institution, an organization, it should be noted, that favors remedial measures for what it regards as historical racial inequities, conducted a study which found that most formerly redlined areas are not today majority black.[96] That is to say, federal policy did not have the effect of confining blacks to these areas. Moreover, although the Brookings study states that the redlined areas still suffer from disinvestment, the economic conditions of the formerly redlined areas do not starkly differ from other areas in the same cities. In cities with the ten most populous formerly redlined areas, the median annual household income in these areas was $48,663 (± $2,395), whereas in the other areas of these cities the median annual income was $56,945 (± $2,952). Similarly, the difference in the median value of owner-occupied homes was $368,492 (±$100,664) versus

$408,494 (± $42,142).[97] Some difference to be sure, but about what one would expect given that in the 1930s and 1940s these areas had been labeled as very risky for investment principally because, at that time, they were relatively impoverished and had lower valued, substandard housing. Is the current roughly 11 percent difference in home value between a home in a formerly redlined area and a home in other areas of the city the result of New Deal federal housing policy or merely a reflection of the worse starting position of the homes in the redlined areas? No definitive conclusion can be given one way or the other, but as the Brookings study points out, this 11 percent difference is not even statistically significant.[98]

We have covered a lot of ground in the last few pages, so it's appropriate to take stock. The claim under consideration is that New Deal housing policies created a significant gap in homeownership rates between whites and blacks, and this is a major cause of today's racial wealth gap. Furthermore, the way in which agencies characterized neighborhoods when determining loan risk served to perpetuate discrimination and confine blacks to blighted urban areas. Neither claim is adequately supported. The HOLC insured black homes in numbers commensurate with the percentage of black homeownership. For a period of time, the FHA did disfavor mixed neighborhoods, and it did fail to insure mortgages for blacks in numbers commensurate with black homeownership, but part of that shortfall can be attributed to objective financial considerations, and in any event, the racial gap in homeownership did not balloon between 1940 and 1950. An increase in the gap from 19.2 to 19.7 percent cannot be a major cause of today's racial wealth disparity. Regarding redlining, the areas that were redlined by the HOLC did not turn into perpetual black ghettos.

That said, there is a large gap in homeownership currently between blacks and whites. In fact, it's much larger now, at least with respect to nonfarm homes, than at any other point since 1900. As of the first quarter of 2022, 74 percent of non-Hispanic whites owned their homes, whereas 44.7 percent of blacks owned their homes, for a gap of 29.3 percent.[99] And, of course, we have already noted that there is also large gap in wealth between white and black households. What accounts for these large gaps? As we have seen, only a small fraction of these yawning gaps can be attributed to New Deal policies. The homeownership gap is especially perplexing if we focus only on federal housing policy because beginning in the late 1960s and continuing from time to time thereafter, the FHA actually reversed course completely and went out of its way to favor minorities in its loan guarantee programs, such as by its Section 235 program, which helped finance homes for about 400,000 low and moderate-income families.[100] Unfortunately, the Section 235 program and subsequent initiatives ran into foreclosure problems in principal part because, to accommodate low-income borrowers, the agency had to loosen its credit requirements. As one commentator has observed, "FHA underwriting went from being prejudicially restrictive for households of color in its early years to being irrationally loose in its later years."[101] Part of the problem with trying to boost black homeownership is precisely the fact that as a group blacks are more likely to be financially challenged, which makes it more difficult to balance increased access to credit with sustainable homeownership.

So where to look for explanations of the gaps? We might begin by looking at data from the late nineteenth and early twentieth century. Census data for 1890 reveal that the overall percentage of black homeownership was 18.7 percent, compared to 54.7 percent for "native" whites, for a gap of 36 percent; with respect to nonfarm homes, the percentages were 16.7 for blacks and 42.1 for native whites, for a gap of 25.4 percent.[102] What this shows is that as the twentieth century approached, blacks started substantially behind whites in homeownership—not surprisingly given that in 1890 most blacks were former slaves or children of former slaves and the financial assistance given to former slaves varied from inadequate to negligible to nothing. Moreover, as we have seen, the value of the homes owned by blacks was generally substantially less than the value of homes owned by whites. This circumstance negatively affected not only the wealth of black homeowners but also their ability to obtain financing for their current or future homes and reduced the wealth, if any, they could pass on to descendants.

In addition, a recent draft study that has taken a close look at wealth data from the late 1800s and early 1900s has concluded that although the gap between white and black wealth narrowed precipitously in the immediate aftermath of Emancipation (when people go from nothing to something, that's to be expected), it began to level off by the turn of the century and has changed little since 1920. As the study's authors observe,

"Remarkably, the racial wealth gap in 1920 was only moderately higher than it is today."[103]

A fair inference from these sets of data is that after the Civil War, black families—almost entirely without assistance—were able to put together a modicum of wealth, but naturally still lagged behind white families because they were mostly starting from scratch. So, some of the gap in homeownership and wealth resulted from the lingering effects of slavery and the failure of the government to provide sufficient assistance to blacks following Emancipation. But this does not explain why the gap failed to narrow further after 1920. Of course, during the period from 1920 to around 1960, blacks had to endure discrimination in employment, education, and housing and were largely shut out of the political process, so that can explain why little progress was made during those decades. But what about the lack of gap narrowing in the decades following 1960?

We have now had over fifty years of civil rights protection, affirmative action, trillions of dollars in federal and state assistance, and multiple attempts by the government, including the FHA, to boost black homeownership. It is true blacks started behind, but why, after the systemic benefits of the past five decades, do they remain behind? The devastating effects of slavery cannot provide the entire explanation—not after one hundred and sixty years, and, as indicated, through their efforts, black families were able to gain economic footing and make up much ground during the decades immediately after the Civil War. There must be other causes—causes that may not be part of a racist system.

Non-Systemic Causes of Wealth Disparity

One of the obvious causes of the continuing racial wealth disparity is the persistence of racial discrimination. It may strike some as peculiar to label discrimination as a non-systemic cause, but, again, recall that systemic discrimination does not refer to bigoted actions by individuals.

Racial discrimination can occur in any area of life, but in terms of its frequency as well as its effect on income and wealth, discrimination with respect to employment may be the most significant. That race discrimination in employment is still a problem is not debatable. How much of a problem is debatable. It is challenging, if not impossible, to quantify the amount of discrimination that continues to occur for a few reasons. First, it's difficult to get an exact count of the number of annual charges and complaints of discrimination because each state has its own civil rights agency, and for some discrimination claims (e.g., an action under 42 U.S.C. §1981), the complainant can go directly to court without first filing an administrative charge. Second, not everyone who suffers discrimination seeks a remedy for it. Third, on the other hand, not everyone who complains about discrimination has a meritorious claim. In fact, according to the EEOC, the federal agency responsible for processing employment discrimination charges under federal civil rights laws, very few do.

Let's look at the EEOC statistics. The number of race discrimination charges that the EEOC receives (which are overwhelmingly charges that allege discrimination against blacks) varies from year to year but has hovered around 25,000 since the late 1990s, with some decline in recent years.[104] In the overwhelming majority of cases (around 70 percent), the EEOC concludes there is "no reasonable cause" to believe the allegations have merit.[105] The EEOC finds reasonable cause in only a very small fraction of the charges—around 2 percent to 3 percent— although it does obtain relief for charging parties (so-called "merit resolutions") in around 15 percent of the cases; neither percentage has changed much over the years.[106]

Thus, a very rough, and generous, calculation of the number of discriminatory actions against black employees and applicants may be about 10,000 a year; this estimate reflects approximately 3750 charges filed with the EEOC where relief was obtained, double that amount to include charges handled by state agencies, and a few thousand incidents where either no charge was filed or where a meritorious charge failed, for whatever reason, to obtain relief. Is this enough to present such a serious hurdle to blacks accumulating wealth that it can account for the failure of the wealth gap to narrow?

Not likely. Bear in mind that, as indicated, those with meritorious charges typically obtain some relief; in many cases, they obtain full relief. So, we are really looking at cases where a meritorious charge failed to obtain relief or no charge was filed. In other words, perhaps at most two to three thousand cases a year of unredressed race discrimination. What the actual damages would be obviously would vary from case to case, but for most jobs actual damages from a failure to hire, an unlawful discharge, or unequal pay, would usually be in the low-to-mid five figures. Therefore, although continuing race discrimination does have a negative effect on income for blacks and, consequently, their ability to accumulate wealth, it cannot account for a substantial portion of the gap in wealth.

A final consideration confirms that discrimination is not sufficient to explain the continuing wealth gap. As we have seen, the wealth gap today is about the same as it was in 1920—when discrimination against blacks was both rampant and legal. Although we cannot precisely calculate the amount of discrimination suffered today, it is surely much less than the discrimination endured one hundred years ago. We need to look elsewhere for an explanation of the continuing wealth gap.

We don't have to look far. One salient factor accounts for much of the continuing gap in wealth. Yet, this factor, well-documented in multiple studies, receives scant notice by proponents of the doctrine of systemic racism. A major contributor to the inability of blacks to overcome the gap in wealth is the disproportionately large percentage of black families with children who have only a single parent, typically an unmarried mother.

It doesn't take a PhD in economics or sociology to grasp the point that the income that one person brings home is, on average, much less than the income that two persons bring home. Similarly, common sense and some basic understanding of the costs involved in raising a child let us know that a single parent with children is likely to face more economic challenges than a single parent without children. The challenges are, in most cases, severe enough that the single parent will have difficulty setting aside any funds for savings, which will, over time, negatively affect the family's accumulation of wealth.

Common sense is supported by academic studies. "The theoretical arguments for the benefits of marriage are supported by a large body of research, including research on parents' economic and social resources as well as research outcomes for children and young adults."[107] Family structure is a strong predictor of wealth outcomes. "Married families have substantially more wealth than any other family type, with never-married mothers having the lowest levels. Couples without children are better off than couples with children. Yet, coupled parents are better off than singles and single parents."[108] Compared with all other family types, single parents who have never married "will have had the least opportunity to accumulate joint wealth and thus may be most vulnerable to economic hardship."[109] The difference in wealth between single-parent families and those headed by couples is sizeable, especially when the single parent is a mother. In 2019, the median net worth for all U.S. households was $121,700; for single mothers with children, it was $7,000.[110] This wealth disparity is no surprise because the median annual income of unmarried households is a fraction of the income of married households, and it has been that way for decades.[111] According to the Bureau of Census, 38.1 percent of families with minor children headed by single mothers live in poverty, compared with 7.5 percent of families with two parents.[112]

The more favorable economic conditions that two-parent families enjoy cut across racial lines. In fact, "marriage is a better predictor of family income than are education, race, and ethnicity."[113] Marriage is economically beneficial to all races as marriage is "a route to greater family wealth insofar as black women . . . and women in general enjoy higher family incomes when they are married."[114] Significantly, the median net worth of black two-parent families exceeds the net worth of white single-parent families, confirming that family composition is a major contributor to any racial wealth disparity.[115]

There is no need to belabor this point: As the nonpartisan Pew Research Center has pointed out, "It is well-established that married parents are typically better off than unmarried parents."[116]

Importantly, and not unexpectedly, family structure has consequences beyond the accumulation of assets. "Children from intact, married families headed by biological or adoptive parents are more likely to enjoy stability, engaged parenting, and economic resources, and to gain the education, life experience, and motivation needed to flourish in the contemporary economy"; furthermore, stable, two-parent families "are associated with a variety of positive social and health outcomes for children and adults alike."[117] In contrast, "non-marital childbearing reduces children's life chances by lowering parental resources and the quality of parenting. Unmarried mothers experience less income growth, more mental health problems, and more mental stress than married mothers."[118] Their children "are more likely to commit delinquent acts, engage in violent criminal behavior, and use drugs and alcohol than those who grew up in intact families."[119]

Moreover, single parenthood not only has a tendency to impoverish the family but can also have long-term, multigenerational consequences. The poverty of the single-parent family is reproduced in the poverty of the children of that family when they become adults. Children of single-parent families are more likely to drop out of school, to have lower earnings in young adulthood, and to be poor. Growing up with only one parent reduces a child's chances of obtaining a high school degree by 40 percent.[120] Girls who grew up in mother-only households are more likely to become single mothers themselves.[121] It is not impossible to break the cycle of poverty, but it is very difficult.

The economic and social ills associated with single parenthood affect whites and blacks alike. However, in terms of percentage, single mothers with children are disproportionately black and have been for decades.[122] The ratio of the percent of black children born to unmarried mothers compared to the percent of white children born to unmarried mothers is about 2.5 to 1.[123] Since 1990, roughly 70 percent of all births to black mothers have been to unmarried mothers.[124] A staggering 64 percent of all black children live in single-parent households, compared to a figure of 24 percent for whites.[125]

The disproportionate impact that this pattern of family composition has had on wealth accumulation is undeniable. A family cannot save if it does not bring in sufficient income, and too many black families have found themselves in this position. As we have seen, black families started behind white families with respect to wealth because of the failure of Reconstruction policies to put them anywhere close to an equal footing with white families. But their inability to make up much ground, especially since the implementation of civil rights and social welfare policies in the 1960s, in large part reflects the high percentage of single-parent families and the consequent severe adverse effect this has had on the ability to save and accrue wealth.

What is stated here is not some new, surprising revelation. Almost sixty years ago, the sociologist Daniel Patrick Moynihan warned about the consequences of the increase of single-parent (effectively single-mother) families among blacks, underscoring the detrimental effects this trend would have on the economic and social well-being of black families.[126] (Interestingly, at the time of Moynihan's 1965 report, about

25 percent of black children lived in families headed by a single mother—a fraction of the number today.) Moynihan's report wasn't ignored; on the contrary, it prompted an avalanche of criticism, with many accusing Moynihan of racism.[127] The tactic of dismissing inconvenient facts through accusations of racism is not new; it is just more prevalent today.

There are a couple of reasons why some are eager to dismiss the relationship between family structure and wealth disparity, despite their undeniable connection. First, this sociological fact doesn't fit the narrative of "systemic" racism. Because there is so much investment in this dogma, there is, consequently, a pronounced disinclination to consider any facts that cast doubt on this doctrine. Second, many mischaracterize the observation of a connection between family structure and poverty as tendentious moral criticism, especially when this observation is made by a white person: privileged whites criticizing blacks for lack of self-restraint. A "blame the victim" approach. Nope. The approach here is a causal analysis, not a moral critique. Unfortunately, on race issues, morality and causality are often confused, perhaps because slavery was not only immoral but also had a significant causal effect on wealth disparity. But these two aspects of analysis are distinct; they are not necessarily conjoined. Federal housing policy in the 1930s and 1940s was immoral, to the extent it reinforced segregation, but, as we have seen, it has had a relatively minor effect on wealth disparity. Conversely, having children while unmarried does not implicate morality (as far as I'm concerned, at least), but this behavior has a manifest effect on the inability to generate wealth.[128] This is just a fact, a fact that plays an important role in the analysis of the causes of the continuing wealth disparity between white and black families. Noting this fact is not a moral judgment. The decision of whether to bear a child is rightfully left up to the mother. Presumably, many mothers decide the value of having a child outweighs any detrimental effects it may have on their financial status. Fine, it's their choice. Because it is their choice to prioritize having children over wealth accumulation, blaming the wealth gap on systemic racism is not only an illicit inference but a demeaning denial of agency to black parents.

It is worth noting that some black scholars are in general agreement with the argument advanced here. Distinguished economist Glenn Loury argues that although historical injustices undoubtedly have played a role in creating disparities in wealth, income, and other areas, we should "consider the possibility that problematic patterns of behavior could be an important factor contributing to [the] persisting disadvantaged status [of blacks]."[129] Loury maintains that we should "chart a middle course," acknowledging the role discrimination has played, and continues to play, in holding blacks back, while also insisting we address "the patterns of behavior that impede black people from seizing newly opened opportunities to prosper."[130] Chief among those patterns is the high number of single-parent families, with Loury contending that it is an "absurdity" to attribute the entirety of black underachievement to "institutional forces" when about "70% of African-American babies are born to a woman without a husband."[131] Similarly, Ian V. Rowe has observed that "while strengthening family stability would not single-handedly close the racial wealth gap, it is a controllable factor that heavily influences economic outcomes," and in support of this observation, he cites data showing black households with two parents have more net worth than white single-parent households.[132] With respect to wealth accumulation, family composition matters.

This concludes our discussion of wealth disparity, although as we will see, this issue bleeds into the discussion of disparities in education, health, and criminal justice. To summarize: although there is a legacy effect from slavery and the shortcomings of Reconstruction, which resulted in blacks starting their financial journey with a significant disadvantage, the principal cause of a continuing large racial wealth gap over the last fifty years is the predominance of single-parent black families, who, understandably, face extreme difficulty in accumulating wealth.[133]

The Disparity in Educational Achievement

Proponents of the doctrine of systemic racism point to various disparities in educational achievement and the treatment received in educational institutions: proportionally fewer blacks take advanced placement courses, complete high school, attend elite colleges, and graduate from college. Their scores on mathematics and reading achievement tests continue to lag behind whites and Asians. Numerically, blacks are ahead of whites and other races in one area, but this is not an indicator of academic success: their rate of school suspensions for misconduct is significantly higher than that of other races/ethnicities, especially Asians.[134]

Do these disparities reflect systemic racism? The evidence indicates they do not. We have already discussed two major causes of these disparities, namely relative lack of financial assets and family composition, with the latter, of course, being a major reason for the lack of assets. In general, students from lower socioeconomic backgrounds do not do as well as students from higher socioeconomic backgrounds; this is true for all racial and ethnic groups. The Annie E. Casey Foundation, a committed advocate of racial equity, has concluded that family "assets strongly correlate with indicators of child well-being—such as academic performance and self-esteem—and can help children avoid negative consequences such as behavioral problems and teenage pregnancy."[135] Other organizations and scholars have reached similar conclusions, as discussed in the prior section. For example, children of single mothers are much more likely to drop out of school. It is not a mystery, then, why black students, statistically more likely to come from economically challenged backgrounds, are also statistically more likely to trail behind other students in academic performance. Family composition influences income and, ultimately, wealth, while wealth in turn influences educational achievement. Family structure is key across the board. It is undeniably more difficult to achieve academic success and break the pattern of poverty when a single-parent family is one's starting point.

Although few dissent from the view that poor academic performance is correlated with lower socioeconomic status, some have argued the real fault is with the failure of state or local governments to properly fund school districts that have higher poverty rates. This contention has sparked an academic debate regarding the exact level of per-pupil funding for black students.[136] That debate need not detain us long because even the data offered by those claiming racially disparate funding show that in forty out of fifty states, the per pupil funding for black students was no less than 95 percent of the per pupil funding for white students; moreover, in twenty states, the funding for black students exceeded the funding for white students.[137] An arguably significant funding gap in ten states cannot explain the nationwide underperformance of black students in an array of academic measures, such as mathematics and reading achievement tests, especially given the overfunding of black students versus white students in twenty states.

So, with the above-referenced data regarding the financial assets and family composition of black families, we already have much of the explanation for the comparative underachievement of black students, and this explanation owes nothing to supposed systemic racism of current laws and policies.

But do some black students suffer from discrimination from teachers or their fellow students? Sure. Prejudice remains, although again, it is nowhere near as prevalent as it was decades ago. Moreover, given all the resources that school systems have invested in diversity training for educators in recent years, one must assume either prejudice is waning or diversity training is wholly ineffective. In any event, the prejudice of individual educators or students is not a "system," especially when there now exist avenues of redress for alleged discrimination.

Poverty and single-parent families, along with some continuing discrimination, can account for most of the gap in academic achievement, but these factors don't explain why black students from middle-class or upper-class backgrounds also often lag behind similarly situated white or Asian students. One noted study focused on this precise issue, namely anthropologist John Ogbu's in-depth study of the Shaker Heights, Ohio school district.[138] Shaker Heights was an integrated, upper-middle-class neighborhood with a relatively well-educated local population. Nonetheless, year after year, there was a noticeable achievement gap between black students and white students, so much so that Ogbu was asked by both the black community and the school district to undertake a study of the problem. After comprehensive research, Ogbu concluded that the primary reason for underachievement was black students' disengagement. "A kind of *norm of minimum effort* appeared to exist among Black students at Shaker Heights schools."[139] Many black students admitted they could work harder but said it wasn't "cool" to do so and being studious was considered acting "white." Peer pressure played a significant role. Fear of being accused of acting white "discouraged some students from engaging in their schoolwork."[140]

Significantly, in the course of his research, Ogbu considered and rejected other explanations sometimes put forward as explanations of the racial achievement gap, such as IQ scores, social status, segregation (Shaker Heights was integrated), language differences, and teacher expectations. The last item merits some comment because it is often advanced as part of the reason for low achievement: white teachers do not expect black students to do well, and so they don't. But as Ogbu explained, the role of students themselves in creating teacher expectations is often overlooked. Through his observations, Ogbu found that "low teacher expectations coexisted with students' unwillingness or refusal to do classwork or homework," and it was "difficult to determine which came first."[141]

Ogbu's study has obvious limitations: it addressed just one school district at a certain point in time, so one cannot assume his findings can be generalized. Still, the Ogbu study provides a plausible explanation for why even black students in affluent school districts may lag behind their white peers. Of course, we still need to understand why some black students feel disengaged. Ogbu speculated that part of the explanation may be a legacy of the discrimination endured by prior generations, which resulted in some black families developing "anti-establishment beliefs and behaviors, which were partly expressed in peer pressures against the school norm of achievement."[142] In a recent book, John McWhorter expands on this explanation, noting that white resistance to school integration, and the accompanying hostility toward blacks, caused a sense among some blacks that school was for white children, creating "a cultural meme casting school as 'white.'"[143] Unfortunately, this cultural attitude has persisted even though the conditions that created it no longer exist. Thus, one might plausibly claim that the discrimination endured by prior generations has played a role in discouraging blacks from pursuing academic achievement, but that is different from maintaining that the differences in academic results between blacks and whites is due to current systemic racism, with the implication that somehow we need to change grading criteria, eliminate standardized tests, or otherwise modify traditional ways of measuring academic success.

School discipline warrants special attention because it has been the focus of many who claim our education system is systemically racist. In particular, some maintain that the use of suspensions and expulsions as a mechanism for controlling student behavior is a racist disciplinary method, given that proportionally more black students than white students are suspended and expelled. Giving credence to this kind of argument, the Obama administration, in 2014, issued guidance on school discipline policies (a guidance subsequently rescinded by the Trump administration, but as of this writing now under renewed review) which expressed concern that suspensions and expulsions resulted in students "losing important instructional time" and warned schools that the Departments of Education and Justice would review school policies that, among other things, sanctioned students of a particular race at higher rates.[144] If there were a disparate impact—and there would be if the comparison were between blacks and whites—the school would be found to have discriminated unless its disciplinary policy served an important educational goal that could not be met by other means. Given the skepticism regarding the need for suspensions and expulsions set forth in the guidance, that burden would likely be nearly impossible to meet. What is especially troubling and revealing about the mindset behind this guidance, though, is the emphasis the guidance placed on the instructional time suspended students would miss. This focus is incongruous and paradoxical as it is precisely the disruptions to class instruction caused by misbehaving students that is the more pressing problem in education today. A report from the Department of Education indicates that although in-school bullying incidents have decreased since 2009–10, verbal and other abuse of teachers has nearly doubled, and "widespread disorder in the classroom" has increased by over 160 percent.[145] This increase in classroom disorder came during a period of time when, due to pressure from government agencies, suspensions were significantly decreased. Sure, suspensions mean the offended student isn't in class, but shouldn't we be more concerned about the students (often black students) who want to learn but cannot because their teachers are precluded from taking appropriate disciplinary measures? As one scholar has noted: "Losing classroom time as a result of suspension has a small negative impact on the performance, whereas exposure to disruptive behavior significantly reduces achievement."[146]

A disparate impact straitjacket imposed on public schools would encourage tacit quotas, which will mean either that black students who should be removed will not be, which will result in further deterioration of the classroom environment, or that white students or Asian students (who currently are suspended even fewer times than whites) will be suspended even when such discipline isn't warranted.

But isn't it true that black students are disciplined with suspension or expulsion more often than whites even though they do not commit more suspendable offenses than whites? This common claim was a key finding of a 2019 report by the U.S. Commission on Civil Rights. That report unqualifiedly asserted that "Students of color as a whole, as well as by individual racial group, do not commit more disciplinable offenses than their white peers, but black students, Latino students, and Native American students in the aggregate receive substantially more school discipline than their white peers and receive harsher and longer punishments than their white peers receive for like offenses."[147] As the dissent of Commissioner Gail Heriot pointed out, however, there was no probative evidence to support this sweeping assertion.[148] The majority heavily relied on a chart of self-reported offenses (not teacher-reported offenses) by a group of 10th graders which actually shows there *are* differences in rates of offense between whites and blacks. Moreover, the chart indicates that Native Americans are suspended more often than blacks and that whites are suspended more often than Asians. In fact, the chart indicates white students are suspended or expelled 41 percent more often than Asian students. As Commissioner Heriot observed, if these school suspensions and expulsions are the consequence of discrimination, then we must infer that "huge numbers of white students would not have been suspended if they had been Asian," which would imply that teachers and school officials are not just racist but irrational and arbitrarily racist.[149] Although most teachers are white, the prejudice attributed to them results in a disproportionate discipline of whites!

Moreover, the claim that black students are disciplined more harshly than white students has been refuted by studies that take into account the student behavior that preceded the offense leading to a suspension:

> The inclusion of a measure of prior problem behavior reduced to statistical insignificance the odds differentials in suspension between black and white youth. Thus, our results indicate that odds differentials in suspensions are likely produced by pre-existing behavioral problems of youth that are imported into the classroom, that cause classroom disruptions, and that trigger disciplinary measures by teachers and school officials.[150]

A "principal's choice of punishment is primarily driven by two factors, the type of offense committed and whether the student has committed any offense in the past."[151] Failure to take into account students' prior offenses when comparing the discipline rates of various groups will necessarily result in incomplete and misleading data.

Accordingly, it is implausible to maintain that discrimination is a major cause of black students proportionally receiving more discipline or stronger discipline, such as suspensions. Indeed, no study has been able to conclude there has been a direct cause-and-effect relationship between educator bias and discipline imposed on black students. Significantly, even those organizations that argue that discrimination must be responsible for some of the gap in discipline concede that studies they cite for support "do not come close to suggesting that discrimination is responsible for the entire gap."[152] But there is no need to scratch our heads regarding possible explanations for the aggregate differences in discipline between black students and white or Asian students. As previously discussed, a higher percentage of black students come from single-parent homes and/or live in poverty. Such circumstances have been reliable predictors of a higher rate of delinquent behavior regardless of a person's race or ethnicity—and students who engage in a higher rate of delinquent behavior are going to be disciplined more often. Putting caps on school suspensions or other forms of discipline would worsen the problem of disruptive behavior, especially in majority-minority schools, thereby leading to an enlargement of the achievement gap, and will only serve to mask the underlying causes of school misconduct.

Systemic racism is not the cause of the gap in educational attainment or the gap in school discipline.

The Disparity in Health and Healthcare

A large number of studies, as well as routine statistical reports from government agencies, show that with respect to many measurements of health blacks tend to fare worse than whites. To jump to the ultimate bottom line, for decades, life expectancy for blacks has been less than life expectancy for whites, although black women have a longer life expectancy than white men.[153] As with other disparities, the claim by many is that health disparities are the result of systemic racism. Indeed, with respect to some disparities at least, the connection between systemic racism and more unfavorable health outcomes for blacks is deemed a "scientific fact," the questioning of which is unconscionable.[154]

But, to begin, even organizations which are vociferous in their claims of systemic racism acknowledge that the "connections between poverty, lack of education, and health are well-established."[155] Poor people have worse health. Not a shocker. Of course, these organizations also argue that poverty and lower educational attainment are themselves a product of systemic racism, but as we have seen that claim does not hold up. Lack of adequate health insurance, which goes hand-in-hand with relative lack of income, also plays a significant role in adverse health outcomes—again, as proponents of systemic racism concede.[156] So, unsurprisingly, those with less income or inadequate health insurance tend to have more health problems, and because, proportionally, blacks are overrepresented in these categories, these circumstances by themselves account for much of the disparities in health outcomes. A 2003 National Academy of Sciences (NAS) study concluded that racial and ethnic disparities in health "are associated with socioeconomic differences and tend to diminish significantly, and in a few cases, disappear altogether when socioeconomic factors are controlled."[157]

What has helped sustain the claim of systemic racism in healthcare—other than the unsupported assertion that socioeconomic conditions themselves invariably reflect systemic racism—is the fact that many studies indicate that socioeconomic factors cannot account for all the disparity. These studies have suggested that even when controlling for socioeconomic conditions, statistical disparities remain. As stated in the NAS report, a "majority of studies . . . find that racial and ethnic disparities remain even after adjustment for socioeconomic differences and other healthcare access-related factors."[158]

But here some words of caution are appropriate. As the NAS report advises:

> Assessing sources of disparities in care in the current literature is also complicated by many methodological considerations. Attempts to control for SES [socioeconomic status] are inconsistent, with some researchers employing patient income or education as sole indicators of SES, and others using proxy variables such as estimates of income on the basis of patients' zip code information. Most studies control for insurance status, but some combine data from patients insured via different types of health systems (e.g., HMO or fee-for-service) or different sources of insurance coverage (e.g., public vs. private).[159]

In other words, even though some studies might assert that disparities still exist after control for socioeconomic factors, this conclusion can be a function of a failure to carry out a comprehensive, fine-grained analysis of the study subjects' socioeconomic situation. Data indicating that one ethnic group of patients had fewer visits with a physician for condition X than another ethnic group are of limited value—even if all study subjects had similar incomes—if most members of the former group typically had to wait months for an appointment with a health maintenance organization (HMO) whereas most members of the latter group had insurance that allowed them to select a responsive provider. And it is not only differences in insurance coverage that affect the quality of care, but differences in the medical facility providing the healthcare service. Not all hospitals or clinics are alike. For example, one study found a six-fold difference in maternal morbidity rates among New York City hospitals.[160]

Nonetheless, despite the caveats in the NAS report, even more recent studies continue to use limited data to categorize people as having similar socioeconomic circumstances, such as using education level as a proxy for status, considering all college graduates as possessing equivalent status.[161] This despite the fact that most people do not consider an Ivy League education equivalent to an education from Southwest Substate College, at least as indicated by the competition for spots in the former. The takeaway from the imprecise categories utilized in most studies is that a complete profile of the socioeconomic circumstances of study subjects would likely show that much less disparity would remain unaccounted for than is usually supposed.

In addition, the role of behavioral and metabolic factors (e.g., obesity) is too often ignored. A 2017 analysis of life expectancy carried out at the county level in the United States found that these factors explained more of the variation in life expectancy than socioeconomic and race/ethnicity factors.[162] In fact, 74 percent of the variation in life expectancy was explained by these factors. Globally, the leading risk factors for cancer, namely alcohol use, smoking, and obesity, are all behavior-related, and many negative behavioral and metabolic factors contributing to lower life expectancy, including obesity, hypertension, and diabetes, are more prevalent among blacks than whites.[163] And, significantly, the second leading cause of death contributing to the difference in life expectancy between black males and white males is "homicide."[164] Although this cause of death does not necessarily fit neatly into the category of behavioral factors, as many innocent bystanders may be murdered, it is not totally divorced from that category either. Anyway, this statistic cannot be chalked up to an inhospitable living environment created by systemic racism, because homicide does not figure into the differences in life expectancy between black women and white women, and we can safely assume that black men and women tend to share the same living environment.

In sum, were an analysis carried out that combined detailed categories of socioeconomic status, including access to care and a breakdown of the exact type of care, with consideration of behavioral and metabolic factors, little unexplained disparity likely would remain.[165] Unfortunately, no study exactly matching these criteria has been carried out.

While there are practical hurdles to carrying out such an analysis, one reason no such analysis has been made is that the proponents of the doctrine of systemic racism see no need for such an analysis to support their claims. They attribute virtually every factor affecting health and healthcare to systemic racism, as they assert that the lower socioeconomic status of blacks relative to whites, the use of substandard medical facilities, and the behavioral and metabolic factors connected to adverse health outcomes are all aspects of systemic racism.[166] Even the supposed "targeted marketing" of heroin is characterized as a "pathway" between racism and health outcomes.[167] Given this outlook, it is pointless to try to separate factors unrelated to systemic racism from factors arising out of systemic racism when accounting for racial disparities. The governing, seemingly irrebuttable presumption is that *everything* arises out of systemic racism.

There is no need to repeat here the previous arguments that disparities in wealth, income, and educational attainment are not products of systemic racism. But let us briefly consider the habit of attributing behavioral factors (e.g., obesity, single-mother pregnancies, illicit drug use) to systemic racism. This argument demeans blacks, denying agency to a group of people based on their ethnicity by assuming they cannot take any responsibility for their actions. I will say this for the proponents of the claim of systemic racism, though: they are candid that the elimination of individual responsibility is part of their program. As the authors of one paper on the connection between systemic racism and poor health outcomes maintain: "It [the framework of systemic racism] shifts accountability from individuals to systems by acknowledging that the context of people's lives determines their health and that blaming individuals for poor health or crediting them for good health is therefore inappropriate."[168] I do not think "blame" is the proper term to use in describing the consequences of an individual's choices, but I do think recognizing the causal connection between an individual's choices and subsequent health consequences is essential if we are to retain the concept of individual responsibility—and if we do away with that, then what is left of human dignity?

If we do not buy into the dogma that all or virtually all health disparities arise out of systemic racism, are there reasonable arguments that at least some health-related laws or policies constitute a racist system? Some have argued that the failure of the United States to provide universal health coverage is racist, as this failure has a disparate adverse impact on blacks.[169] It is probably true that universal health coverage would eliminate some of the disparity in health outcomes between blacks and whites, as it would improve healthcare for those with lower socioeconomic status. But here, as with any disparate impact argument, one has to consider whether the policy at issue serves some legitimate public purpose. As with tax policy (see above), a deep discussion of healthcare financing is beyond our scope, but at least at first glance, the argument that universal health coverage is unaffordable and would have collateral adverse effects cannot be dismissed as pretextual. What is often overlooked by those who point out "every other developed county has universal coverage" is that every other country has nowhere near the defense budget of the United States. Given the situation in the world, with authoritarian countries not only threatening but also actively attacking democracies, a strong defense is not optional. I am not arguing against universal coverage; I am merely arguing that the failure to provide it cannot automatically be characterized as racist. One other thing to bear in mind is that universal coverage is not likely to eliminate more than a portion of the disparity. If one has the goal of eliminating the disparity completely—and why settle for half-measures—the United States would have to adopt a comprehensive system of socialized medicine, with no opportunity for private coverage outside the system. One cannot achieve the same health outcomes for everyone unless everyone receives more or less the same level of care, however good or bad it might be. Interestingly, some studies have indicated that there is not much disparity in outcomes for patients in the Veterans Administration system.[170] But, of course, this is the same system that has been excoriated for providing deficient services to its patients.[171] Making sure everyone receives unsatisfactory healthcare would be one way of achieving equity. Anyway, whatever one may think of socialized medicine, there are familiar arguments against it, and these arguments have nothing to do with race.

So, if there is no current policy or law relating to health that can be properly characterized as racist, and socioeconomic and behavioral and metabolic factors account for most of the disparity in health outcomes, where does that leave us? It leaves us with whatever portion of the disparity cannot be explained by these factors, however much this is, and speculation about what the causes of this disparity might be. Bias by providers, explicit or implicit, has been offered as a possible explanation.[172] As has been previously acknowledged, prejudice is still with us. There is no doubt that some physicians, nurses, and other healthcare professionals may harbor prejudicial attitudes toward black patients. That said, it is difficult to believe that, in 2023, such prejudice can account for more than a small fraction of the disparity in health outcomes. We are not all living in Alabama in 1950. Medical schools are awash in diversity, inclusion, and equity initiatives and training on how to reflect self-critically on one's own possible biases. If widespread bias still remains, then pessimism is the only appropriate response because, apparently, racial prejudice cannot be eradicated. Interestingly, one study probing why black patients may receive less pain medication than white patients found that the explanation was not so much racial bigotry, but ignorance. Some medical students held false beliefs about physiological differences between blacks and whites.[173] In a way, this finding is encouraging because ignorance can be alleviated easier than bigotry. In the final analysis, I am not pessimistic about the extent or persistence of bias, as lamentable as any bias is, because I believe bigotry has diminished significantly in the last several decades and biased providers affect healthcare only marginally—and no study shows otherwise.

It may be frustrating not to have a complete and persuasive explanation of all the disparities in health outcomes between blacks and whites, but we should note that there are unexplained disparities going in the other direction as well. Certain causes of death are far more prevalent among whites than blacks. Suicide is predominantly a white thing (or white and Native American thing, to be more precise). Compared to whites, relatively few blacks commit suicide.[174] Why remains a puzzle. It is especially puzzling because, allegedly, blacks suffer much more stress than whites due to discrimination, but if so, this stress does not result in suicide.[175] Similarly, a leading cause of death for whites is chronic respiratory diseases, but not so much among blacks.[176] Why? There has been no answer, and again, this is a bit of a puzzle considering how much emphasis has been placed on blacks being more exposed via their housing to pollutants. The point is that there are racial disparities in various areas relating to health outcomes, but these statistical disparities do not necessarily imply a racist cause.

Let me close this section of the chapter by discussing maternal mortality and the claim that it is a "scientific fact" that racism is a major cause of the higher maternal mortality rate among black women.[177] The existence of the disparity itself is "scientific" to the extent that statistics can be considered a science, but it is questionable whether the purported link between racism and higher rates of maternal mortality is an established scientific fact, as opposed to being an ideologically driven conclusion. Women belonging to racial minorities have "elevated rates of obesity, hypertension, diabetes, and chronic illness," all of which have a "strong link" with "adverse maternal outcomes."[178] In fact, non-Hispanic black women have an obesity rate approaching 57 percent, almost 20 percent higher than non-Hispanic white women.[179] "Maternal obesity has been consistently reported to increase the risk of pregnancy complications" and is considered a "risk factor" for maternal mortality.[180] In fact, a study has shown that the increase in maternal mortality in recent decades has had more to do with obesity and diabetes (often associated with obesity) than the race of the mother.[181] A study from France—significant because it shows that the connection between obesity and maternal mortality is not just a by-product of American racism—concluded that the risk of death from pregnancy for overweight women was 1.65 times greater than that for women with proportional body mass. For women with class 2–3 obesity, meanwhile, the risk was 3.4 times greater.[182] (The risk of maternal death for black American women is about 3.5 times greater than it is for white American women.)[183] Preeclampsia and eclampsia are the leading causes of maternal death for black women,[184] and both are closely associated with obesity.[185]

None of this is to suggest that obesity and associated health conditions explain all the difference in maternal death rates between blacks and whites, but it does indicate clearly that these conditions are a major factor in explaining the disparity. To ignore this fact in favor of ideologically motivated allusions to a racist system is neither scientific nor of much help in achieving the goal of reducing maternal deaths among black women.

Disparities and the Criminal Justice System

In the area of criminal justice, there is statistical evidence suggesting blacks are treated more harshly than whites in certain respects; moreover, in particular communities, this adverse impact may be directly linked to deficient policies. To that limited extent, at least in some communities, one can speak of a systemic problem. In addition, some laws and policies that adversely affected the treatment of blacks within the criminal justice system were revised or removed significantly later than the civil rights/ social welfare revolution of the 1960s. That said, there is insufficient evidence to sustain the charge that the criminal justice system as a whole is systemically racist.

Furthermore, the one aspect of the criminal justice system that has drawn the most attention, and the most vehement denunciations, namely, police killings of blacks, is, ironically, the one aspect where the charge of systemic racism may be most easily refuted. The attention given to this issue, fueled by massive media coverage of isolated incidents where blacks are killed by police, has resulted in many Americans mistakenly thinking that a black man's risk of being killed by police is higher than the risk of dying in a car accident.[186] Systemic racism dogmatists have even labeled police killings of blacks "genocide."[187] The reality is the thing that is being widely, deliberately, and systematically destroyed is the truth.

First, let us talk about absolute numbers. Based on the database compiled by the *Washington Post* since 2015, roughly 1,000 people a year are killed by police shootings. In 2021, police shot and killed 1,055 persons, of whom 302 were white and 177 were black (the rest were of unknown race or Hispanic). In 2020, police shot and killed 1,020 persons, of whom 459 were white and 243 were black (again, the remainder being unknown or Hispanic).[188] So, on average, a little over 200 blacks per year are shot and killed by police, with almost all of these being black men. The number of black men in the United States is approximately 23 million.[189] This means the percentage of black men shot and killed each year is about 0.00087 percent. Hardly a genocide. Moreover, as indicated, every year the (predominantly white) police kill more whites than blacks. It is a strange genocide where the alleged perpetrators of the racial genocide kill more of their own race.

But, of course, the argument is that even though police kill fewer blacks than whites, blacks are disproportionally targeted by the police. In making this argument, those who posit systemic racism typically compare the percentage of persons killed who are black (20–25 percent) with the percentage of the population that is black (less than 13 percent). However, looking at the raw census numbers does not allow one to make an adequately informed judgment because that approach omits any consideration of context.

Considering context is no easy task, as there are a number of variables that need to be taken into consideration, and doing the research necessary to incorporate the variables into a sound statistical study requires significant time and effort. Fortunately, a few years ago, a team of researchers headed by Harvard economist Roland G. Fryer, Jr. tackled this assignment. The Fryer team carried out a detailed analysis of police shootings (all shootings, not just fatal shootings) which included consideration of factors such as whether the suspect attacked, what charges were eventually filed against the suspect, what the reason was for the police responding to the scene, and, of course, all pertinent demographic characteristics of the suspect and responding police officers.[190] Fryer's team could consider this wide range of factors because they pored over detailed event summaries of police shootings for over a dozen police departments. The conclusion of this rigorous study was that there was "no evidence of racial discrimination in officer-involved shootings."[191] In addition, more detailed information from Houston arrest records permitted the team to analyze situations where police were authorized to use lethal force but refrained from doing so. Based on the data from

Houston, the study concluded "that blacks are 27.4 percent less likely to be shot at by police relative to nonblack, non-Hispanics."[192]

Obviously, the Fryer study has limitations. First, it is based on a small portion of American police departments. Second, the summaries of shootings are prepared by the officers themselves. Although the summaries are subject to review, so blatant lies are unlikely, there is nonetheless an incentive for officers to describe the events in a way favorable to them. That said, police shootings of all suspects of whatever race are closely reviewed, so there is no more incentive to shade the truth for black as opposed to white suspects.

Is the Fryer study ideal? No, but given how relevant data currently are collected and how the data would have to be collected, reviewed, and analyzed to produce the perfect study, it is unlikely such a study is forthcoming anytime soon. As one scholar has observed, "the ideal benchmark does not exist: there is no data set of every police-civilian interaction in the whole country, objectively graded as to the degree of threat that the civilian posed to the officer or others, much less a data set that also includes situations where cops *could* have stopped someone but did not."[193] In addition, it's difficult to envisage how we could obtain a data set of police-civilian interactions that is perfectly, objectively graded from a neutral standpoint. Do we send monitors to accompany police? Who chooses the monitors? Body cameras have been introduced in an attempt to provide an objective factual record, but the footage doesn't always capture all details and can be inconclusive. There is no escaping the reality that all studies will have some limitations. The key point is that despite its limitations, the Fryer study remains the best study to date with respect to taking into account situational factors. Accordingly, its conclusion that there are no racial differences in shootings once these factors are taken into account is entitled to considerable weight.

This judgment is buttressed by a recent meta-analysis that reviewed numerous studies undertaken since 2015.[194] Most studies found that when the black share of fatal police encounters was compared with benchmarks such as number of weapons arrests, murders, and various other crime rates, the racial disparities disappeared or were greatly reduced.[195] Nonetheless, the meta-study cautioned that more research was needed, especially with respect to possible variations among police departments, as some studies suggest that in certain police departments there may be an unexplained and significant disparity in the use of lethal force.[196] This makes intuitive sense. Given the thousands of different police departments in the country, it would be extraordinary if there were no departments where inadequate training, perhaps combined with implicit or explicit bias, resulted in disparities that were race-based. But the major takeaway from the studies so far is that there is no proven systemic racism, at least at the nationwide level, in police shootings.

Of course, police killings of blacks represent just one of the many ways the police and the black community interact, and police-community interactions represent just one of the many different components of our criminal justice system, so finding no systemic racism in this one area does not necessarily imply there is no systemic racism affecting outcomes in other areas. This is a point that Fryer himself has emphasized as he has expressed frustration that those who are skeptics of systemic racism have utilized the portion of his study dealing with police shootings while ignoring that portion dealing with police use of nonlethal force. As Fryer summarized his findings in an opinion piece, data from New York City's Stop and Frisk program showed police "were 53% more likely to use physical force on a black civilian than a white one"[197] (in the published study, after accounting for all variables, the odds ratio for blacks was 1.178).[198] For purposes of the study, nonlethal physical force encompassed everything from putting hands on persons to striking them with a baton. In addition, data from a nationwide Police-Public Contact Survey (PCPS) indicated blacks were 2.8 times more likely to report use of force by police than whites.[199] These data suggest, although they certainly do not prove, that police may be rougher with black citizens than white citizens. One important caveat with respect to the PCPS is that the information is based only on the civilian's account of events. Just as police reports may be shaded to place police actions in a favorable light, similarly, civilian reports may exaggerate the force used by police.

So, Fryer's study implies that the oft-heard complaint that the police harass blacks more than whites may have some truth to it. Fryer's study does not explain why this might be the case or why there may be a disparity in the use of nonlethal force but no disparity with respect to shootings. One possibility is this: police recognize the importance of confining their use of firearms to extremely threatening circumstances, whereas they feel much less constrained in applying nonlethal force, where the potential for inflicting serious harm is much less. Bias, explicit or implicit, may manifest through this relative lack of constraint. Tension between the black community and police—certainly evident in New York City during its Stop and Frisk program—can contribute to an officer's perception that a more assertive posture is required.

Does the disparity in use of nonlethal force indicate that systemic racism is influencing police interaction with black civilians? Again, to begin, if the cause of the disparity is explicit prejudice on the part of some officers, then this is interpersonal racism, not systemic racism. If it is implicit racism or deficient training in appropriate interaction with civilians, an argument could be made that there is a systemic fault: a lack of programs to deal with implicit bias or a lack of other appropriate training. Because Fryer's study does not assign a cause, no inference can be made from that study regarding systemic faults. Other studies, however, have assigned causes. Notably, the Justice Department's analysis of the policies and practices of the Baltimore City Police Department (BPD) squarely attributed police use of disproportionate force in stops, searches, and arrests of blacks to deficiencies in "BPD's policies regarding the use, reporting, and investigation of force" which consequently failed "to provide officers with clear and consistent guidance."[200]

So, to sum up the issue of systemic racism in police interactions with the public: no evidence of nationwide systemic racism in the use of lethal force; some evidence suggesting in some cities that deficient training policies and practices have resulted in inappropriate interaction with civilians disproportionately affecting blacks. Given there is no apparent justification for such training deficiencies (e.g., the urgent need to deploy resources elsewhere) to that limited extent, one can fairly claim there has been, and in some locations may continue to be, systemic racism. But notice: the Department of Justice investigated and corrected the deficiencies in the BPD, as it has elsewhere. That is a further indication that at the nationwide level, the claim of systemic racism cannot be sustained. Systemic racism does not correct itself.

Besides police shootings, and the false claim of an epidemic of police killing black males, the one aspect of the criminal justice system that has drawn the most attention is the rate of incarceration of blacks, particularly black males. There is no question that for years, compared to general population figures, a disproportionate number of black men have been incarcerated. In federal prisons in 2022, about 38 percent of the inmate population was black;[201] statistics from 2018 for both state and federal prisons for inmates serving more than one year indicate that 33 percent of the prison population consisted of black inmates.[202] With respect to black men, there were 2,272 inmates for every 100,000 black men, indicating about 1 out of every 44 black men was serving time. This contrasts with the figure of 1 out of every 255 white men serving time.[203]

But this disparity disappears when we look at arrest rates, especially arrests for violent crime. In 2019, 51.2 percent of the arrests for murder and nonnegligent homicide were of blacks; blacks accounted for 52.7 percent of robbery arrests; for the general category of all violent crime, the percentage was 36.4 percent. In fact, the only crime categories in which the number of arrestees reflected the black proportion of the population were alcohol offenses (DUI and drunkenness).[204] Put simply, proportionally more blacks are serving time because proportionally more blacks—based on arrest records—commit crimes. The 33 percent of the prison population that is black matches almost exactly the 36.4 percent of violent crimes for which blacks are arrested.

Of course, arrest records cannot be paired with incarceration rates without qualification because not everyone who is arrested is also prosecuted, convicted, and sentenced to prison. In fact, the attrition rate is substantial. In the federal system, about 40 percent of arrestees are not prosecuted, for a variety of reasons (lack of evidence, technical deficiencies in the arrest requiring dismissal, mistaken arrest, prosecutorial priorities, and so forth); the conviction rate of those prosecuted is about 90 percent. Overall, two-thirds of those convicted were sent to prison; however, 92 percent of those convicted of violent offenses were imprisoned.[205] States vary widely in the percentage of charges that are prosecuted and convicted, but most states hover around 60 percent of charges that are prosecuted and convicted, a rate comparable to the federal rate.[206] In any event, although there is a significant attrition rate between arrest and prosecution, and a smaller attrition between conviction and imprisonment—much, much smaller for violent offenders—this attrition does not affect the correlation between the racial distribution of arrests and the racial distribution of incarceration. The correlation would be affected if it were the case that blacks were prosecuted far less often than whites, but were nonetheless imprisoned at a rate commensurate with their arrests. However, there is no evidence of that. If anything, the claim has been that blacks are prosecuted more often—but there is no persuasive evidence of that either.

Two other related issues can be addressed quickly. Some argue that blacks are unfairly arrested more often than whites, at least for certain offenses. This, in turn, could lead to higher incarceration rates which, if the arrests were racially motivated, could suggest a systemic problem. The offense most often mentioned is drug possession, specifically marijuana possession. An American Civil Liberties Union (ACLU) study indicates that, nationwide, blacks are more than three times as likely to be arrested for marijuana possession than whites, despite the fact that surveys indicate whites use marijuana as often as blacks.[207] But this comparison between use and arrests does not establish racism, systemic or otherwise. Police tend to be more present in black neighborhoods precisely because more crime is committed there. Therefore, they have more opportunity to witness drug offenses. Yes, there are undoubtedly some bigoted cops who may turn a blind eye to whites with weed while coming down hard on blacks; maybe there are even some scattered police departments where that is standard practice. But overall, the lower rate of arrests for whites simply indicates no cop is around to catch them with a couple of ounces. We could narrow the gap between marijuana arrests for black and whites were we to deploy substantially more police to white neighborhoods and, perhaps, college campuses, but that would deprive predominantly black neighborhoods of the police presence they need. That does not seem to be a prudent use of resources.

In any event, marijuana possession is not the main driver of incarceration, nor for that matter is drug possession in general. The majority of prisoners in state prison are violent offenders; 61 percent of blacks in state prison are serving time for violent offenses. A mere 3.2 percent of blacks are there because of drug possession—a lower percentage than the 4.5 percent rate for whites. Because of the types of crime that are under federal jurisdiction, a large number of inmates in federal prison are there for drug-related offenses, but 99 percent are there for trafficking, leaving a negligible amount, if any, imprisoned for simple possession.[208] In other words, with respect to the issue of incarceration, the ACLU study is largely irrelevant.

In addition to the alleged disparity in the overall rate of incarceration, some maintain there is also a significant racial disparity in the length of sentence given to those incarcerated, which, of course, is attributed to systemic racism. If true, because blacks would be unfairly serving more time in prison, this would contribute to their disproportionate share of the prison population. One study is often cited for the supposed fact that, on average, blacks receive longer sentences. Specifically, the study, which examined sentences in Georgia, is said to have established that blacks who were first-time felons received sentences 270 days longer than whites who had committed similar crimes.[209] But when one actually reads the study, one finds that the authors state that "it is important to note that a large part of the racial and skin color disparity in sentencing can be explained by legally relevant factors." In other words, the "270-day difference in sentences between blacks and whites is greatly reduced when factors such as crime type and severity are taken into account."[210] Similarly, an in-depth study of criminal case outcomes among indigent defendants in San Francisco found that apparent disparities in sentencing "almost completely disappear[ed]" when contextual factors were considered, particularly "criminal history and previous incarcerations."[211]

The fact of the matter is that there are proportionally more blacks in prison principally because proportionally more blacks commit serious crimes. The higher rate of crime by blacks should be no surprise given what we have already discussed concerning statistics relating to poverty and family composition. Sociologists, social psychologists, and criminologists have long recognized the correlation between socioeconomic status and criminal activity. One can pick up books from the 1950s and 1960s and see discussion of the high rate of crime among blacks and how the "close association between economics and recorded crime" as well as "broken families" explain this higher rate of criminal activity.[212] There has been some improvement in income for the black community since then, but otherwise, not much has changed, and, if anything, the percentage of single-parent families has increased, and so, not unexpectedly, the rate of criminal activity in the black community remains high. This high crime rate eventually translates into a high rate of incarceration. Crime, not systemic racism, results in blacks being imprisoned proportionally more than whites.

Let us close this review of the criminal justice system with a few comments on laws that were, at least in retrospect, arguably unjustified, and to some extent had an adverse impact on blacks. To begin, many claim that the war on drugs has been systemically racist. Punitive drug laws affected black communities more and led to a spike in the rate of incarceration for black men in the 1970s, 1980s, and 1990s. Two sets of legislation in particular, one at the state level and one at the federal level, have drawn particular attention.

New York's so-called Rockefeller Drug Laws, adopted in 1973, heralded a dramatic increase in the punishment meted out to drug offenders, with lengthy mandatory sentences even for possession of relatively small amounts.[213] It was not until 2009 that New York substantially revised these laws, eliminating most mandatory minimum prison sentences. The consensus of the legislature was that the laws had failed to curb drug abuse and had unnecessarily expanded the prison population, with a disparate impact on black males.[214]

However, what is too often overlooked in discussion of these laws is that in the late 1960s and early 1970s, calls for tougher drug laws in New York came from the black community. Middle-class blacks, fed up with increased drug use and associated crime in their neighborhoods, "lobbied aggressively" for an emboldened police presence; at town meetings in New York City, angry black residents reportedly confronted Governor Rockefeller over the drug problem in their communities.[215] Polls taken after the passage of the drug laws showed these tough measures enjoyed widespread support among blacks, with 71 percent of blacks favoring life sentences without parole for "pushers."[216]

The Rockefeller Drug Laws may have been unwise, and they had a disparate impact on the black community, but can one meaningfully claim they exemplify systemic racism when blacks themselves overwhelmingly supported this legislation? Not according to one scholar, who, although critical of the Rockefeller Drug Laws, concluded that black support for these laws shows that "the origins of policies that have created opportunities for inequitable administration of justice cannot be reduced simply to racism."[217]

Similar points can be made about the federal Anti-Drug Abuse Act of 1986, which imposed severe penalties for drug trafficking crimes involving crack cocaine, with much less harsh penalties for crimes involving powder cocaine.[218] Most noteworthy was the ratio between the amounts of crack cocaine and powder cocaine that would trigger mandatory minimum sentences. A mere five grams of crack resulted in a five-year minimum sentence, whereas one had to traffic five hundred grams of powder cocaine to receive the same sentence. At the time, the belief that crack cocaine was more addictive and dangerous than powder cocaine drove this distinction in punishment. Two years later, Congress came down even harder on crack cocaine, enacting a five-year mandatory minimum for mere possession of five grams of crack; no other drug possession offense had a mandatory minimum sentence.[219]

Less than a decade later, the U.S. Sentencing Commission had already determined that the 100-to-1 ratio between the amounts of crack and powder cocaine that would trigger mandatory minimums was unjustified—in part because crack cocaine is pharmacologically identical to powder cocaine—and that the law's penalty structure had a disproportionate impact on blacks as 80 percent of crack offenders were black.[220] Nonetheless, it took another decade before sentencing guidelines made any substantial reduction in minimum sentences for crack cocaine offenses, and it was not until the Fair Sentencing Act of 2010 that the ratio between the amounts of crack and powder cocaine triggering mandatory minimums was substantially reduced. Specifically, the act provided that twenty-eight grams of crack cocaine or five hundred grams of powder cocaine would trigger a five-year mandatory minimum, for a ratio of 18-to-1.[221] Subsequent legislation made the new ratio retroactive, resulting in a substantial reduction of prison time for current inmates through resentencing. Proposed legislation (the Equal Act) would eliminate the distinction between crack cocaine and powder cocaine entirely.[222]

From the foregoing, one can surmise that the currently prevailing consensus is that the harsher penalties for crack cocaine were unwise and had an unjustifiable disparate impact on blacks. Here again, though, it is important to recognize that a majority of the Congressional Black Caucus co-sponsored and supported the Anti-Drug Abuse Act of 1986. Their support reflected concerns voiced in black communities that use of crack cocaine was an epidemic that was fueling a wave of violent crime. A frequent complaint at the time was that the government was not taking drug-related crime seriously enough because the victims were mostly black.[223]

So, as with the Rockefeller Drug Laws, we have a situation where legislation is initially supported, if not demanded, by much of the black community, but, after a passage of time, is considered unnecessary and ill-advised and is condemned by some as racist in its effects. So, was the Anti-Drug Abuse Act of 1986 an example of systemic racism? An affirmative answer would entail the paradoxical conclusion that the black community can be systemically racist against itself. But such a paradox is perhaps what one should expect when basing claims of systemic racism solely on statistical disparities, without consideration of context and intent.

More could be said about the war on drugs, but the analysis and conclusions would not be materially different. There are legitimate differences of opinion about the wisdom of current laws governing the sale or possession of controlled substances. And some of our current laws might have a disparate adverse effect on the black community, but so too could the elimination of these laws. Using disparate impact as the primary tool for determining the wisdom of a drug law would likely produce an unstable and vacillating regime of drug laws. Although effects on a specific ethnic community are not entirely irrelevant, the touchstone for our laws should be whether for the entire country they ultimately reduce crime and drug abuse at a sustainable cost—cost not just in terms of dollars but also in terms of individual freedom—and reflect sound science on the harms of specific drugs.

To sum up our discussion of the criminal justice system: The criminal justice system at a national level is not systemically racist. Neither fatal encounters with police nor incarceration rates manifest racism, as disparities can be explained by non-racial factors. Some local police departments have had a pattern of treating black citizens and offenders more harshly, and this pattern may be explained by deficient policies, so, in that sense, their conduct can be considered a result of systemic faults. However, the cure for this problem is not a condemnation of the entire United States system as pervasively racist but rather a rigorous review of these local departments and insistence on the application of the norms of justice that prevail at the national level.

Conclusion on Systemic Racism

This chapter has considered key statistical disparities between blacks and whites that have been used as a basis for the claim that racism is embedded in the laws, policies, and practices of the United States, that is, that racism is systemic. Our review of the laws, policies, and practices that have been in place since the 1960s establishes that the "system" is not racist. Furthermore, our analysis of disparities in wealth, income, education, health, and criminal justice shows that these disparities do not result from systemic racism, but rather have other explanations. The dogma of systemic racism is just that: a doctrine derived from an ideological commitment, not evidence, and resting on the logical fallacy that unequal outcomes between the races necessarily reflect racism.

But what of our conclusion that the critical wealth gap can, in part, be attributed to the unequal starting position of many blacks following Emancipation? Reconstruction provided some assistance to blacks, principally through the educational efforts of the Freedmen's Bureau, but the assistance was too little and ended too quickly.[224] What, if anything, should be done now to remedy the shortfalls of Reconstruction?

This question naturally leads to consideration of reparations for slavery. Here, no position will be taken for or against reparations, principally because to do that topic justice would require a separate book. Certainly, the example of reparations for Japanese-Americans who were interned during the Second World War provides a precedent—sort of. The United States awarded $20,000 to surviving Japanese Americans; that is, the reparations went directly to those who had experienced internment.[225] And this points out why this payment represents only "sort of" a precedent. The payments went from the entity causing the harm, the United States government, to the persons who suffered the harm of internment. Roughly 160 years have passed since the end of slavery, and no one who was enslaved is alive today, nor are any of their children alive. Some may understandably argue that the passage of time, if anything, strengthens the case for reparations. Maybe. On the other hand, it sure does complicate calculations. How direct a descendant must one be? Is having one great-grandparent who was a slave sufficient? What process would we use to confirm degree of relationship? Are those who have both slavers and enslaved as ancestors disqualified? As reparations presumably need to be funded by taxes, should the taxes of first- and second-generation Americans be protected from any reparations-related increase, given that they had no connection to slavery? Would this answer be different for immigrants from Asian countries as opposed to immigrants from predominantly white European countries? Should any social welfare benefits provided during the last several decades be used as an offset to any reparations amount?

Another set of issues to consider relates to the policy goals we aim to accomplish through reparations. If the primary goal is to acknowledge and compensate for the injustice of slavery, then a recipient's income or wealth should have no bearing on their level of reparations. But if we are really aiming to reduce the wealth gap between blacks and whites, presumably there should be an income or wealth cutoff. And if the primary motivation for reparations is to narrow this wealth gap, there may be better—less expensive and possibly less divisive—ways to accomplish this than reparations. The Annie E. Casey Foundation claims that investments of up to $7,500 in "children's savings accounts could produce a significant reduction in the racial wealth gap."[226] The investment amounts would vary based on family income. This solution, of course, would require both unequal investments in the accounts of recipients and a generation to be effective. Whether that solution would be more politically acceptable than reparations is unclear.

What should be clear, though, is that the wealth gap issue should be addressed with an accurate understanding of its causes. As we have seen, the gap may be attributed in part to the legacy of slavery but is also due in large part to the predominance of single-parent households in the black community. If instead we are misled by the rhetoric of systemic racism, we will follow policy paths that are ineffective, counter-productive, and unjust—as the next chapter will show.

CHAPTER 3

The Misguided, Dystopian Goal of Equity

Standpoint theory is, essentially, a theory about the acquisition of knowledge, that is, an epistemological theory, to use a philosophical term. The doctrine of systemic racism is, at its core, a metaphysical theory, a claim about the fundamental nature of things tenuously based on a fanciful characterization of facts. With equity, we now come to a dogma in the realm of ethics.

Until recent times, "equity" and "equitable" were terms that largely reflected the moral or political views of the person using the terms. What was equitable to one person might not seem equitable to another. In this way, "equity" functioned much like the term "justice." (Is there any political leader who has ever claimed, "I'm in favor of injustice"? Stalin, Hitler, Pol Pot all favored justice.) To the extent "equity" had a shared, fixed meaning, it connoted fairness: an allocation of benefits and burdens that is appropriate under the circumstances, even though it might seem to be an exception to prevailing rules. In early Anglo-American law, an equitable remedy, such as specific performance of a contract, was a remedy not typically available under the law, but one a court could impose in its discretion.

With the advent of identity politics, however, "equity" has taken on, in most contexts, a specific meaning. Unfortunately, the gain in referential clarity comes at the expense of moral cogency.

The doctrine of systemic racism implies that racial disparities are intrinsically bad. If statistical disparities between blacks and whites represent an intrinsic evil, then it follows that it is an ethical imperative to eliminate these disparities. Hence, this is the principal goal of equity, as it is currently understood by many, including federal, state, and local government officials, university administrators, corporate executives, and their associated battalions of advisors and bureaucrats who specialize in "diversity, equity, and inclusion" (hereinafter "DEI"). To achieve racial equity, policies should be designed to ensure an equal outcome among blacks and whites—whatever category of life's circumstances are being measured, that is, whether we are considering income, wealth, educational achievement, health outcomes, or encounters with the justice system. Indeed, these categories are too broad as far as advocates of equity are concerned. We need to consider all possible subdivisions of these categories to ensure equal outcomes in all aspects of people's lives. It is not sufficient to equalize wealth; we should also equalize housing and access to transportation. Similarly, admitting racial groups to top universities in proportion to their percentage of the population is plainly inadequate for true equity. We must also ensure they graduate at the same rate, and if we are really serious about equity, we should make sure that all disciplines, including the sciences, have proportional racial representation. "Health" clearly is too general a category to permit us to determine whether all unjustified disparities have been eradicated. For example, even if life expectancy for blacks and whites is equalized, if blacks suffer more from certain diseases or receive less medical attention, surely, we must put an end to such disparities. Outcomes across the board must be the same. To quote Vice President Harris, "Equitable treatment means we all end up in the same place."[1]

If the reader believes I am reading too much into calls for equity, please consult Ibram Kendi's 2021 article complaining about the perceived disparate impact of COVID-19 and the lack of adequate data to track all relevant disparities (e.g., death rates, hospitalization rates, infection rates, test rates, vaccination rates).[2] Although the focus of the article is the pandemic, Kendi makes clear he believes the pandemic revealed a deeper problem with racial disparities in healthcare generally. To ensure we can combat these disparities, Kendi maintains we need not only universal access to healthcare, but also the collection and reporting of "every single variable of the identity of every single American every single time they receive medical care of any kind."[3] If whites over sixty-five are having their ears cleaned of excess cerumen more often than black seniors, we need to know that, and heaven help us if it turns out sildenafil is distributed more liberally to whites. Kendi's proposed comprehensive information collection program, given its size and intrusiveness, would be the envy of China—but it has the virtue of revealing the degree of oversight and control equity advocates crave to pursue their ambitious agenda.

Kendi's article also has the virtue of revealing that the equity agenda is not limited to eliminating racial disparities. Racial disparities between blacks and whites remain the priority, but disparities among other identity groups demand attention. Kendi expresses concern over the treatment of "Latino Americans," Asian Americans, Native Americans, Pacific Islanders, the elderly, and urban residents.[4] In this wider concern he is not alone. The Biden administration's "Executive Order on Advancing Racial Equity and Support for Underserved Communities Through the Federal Government" lists the following identity groups whose outcomes must be monitored to ensure equity: "Black, Latino, Indigenous and Native American persons, Asian Americans and Pacific Islanders and other persons of color; members of religious minorities; gay, lesbian, bisexual, transgender and queer (LGBTQ+) persons; persons with disabilities; persons who live in rural areas; and persons otherwise adversely affected by persistent poverty or inequality."[5] Quite a list. And this list governs all federal agencies in devising and implementing policies. They must "assess whether, and to what extent, [their] programs and policies perpetuate systemic barriers to opportunities and benefits for people of color and other underserved groups."[6]

The equity mandate, then, establishes as a criterion for a government program's success not whether the program is beneficial to most Americans overall, but whether the program has produced equal outcomes. So, for example, it is not acceptable if government economic policy boosts the income of the vast majority of Americans 4 percent a year for a decade if blacks, as a group, have experienced an increase of only 3 percent a year. The policy must be changed, and presumably, for the sake of equity, a policy that results in a 2.2 percent increase for everybody is preferable. We all must end up in the same place, with the "we" here referring not to individuals but to the collection of identity groups into which we are now divided.

Again, Kendi is instructive on this point. In discussing COVID-19 vaccination results, he laments that (as of April 2021), vaccination results were not exactly proportional to the population percentages of various identity groups, as "white Americans accounted for 67.4 percent of the fully vaccinated [but] they make up 61.2 percent of the U.S. population. By contrast, among the fully vaccinated, only 10 percent are Latino Americans and 8.4 percent are Black Americans, despite making up 17.2 percent and 12.4 percent of the U.S. population, respectively."[7] Kendi doesn't deem worthy of note the fact that government programs, first, resulted in the rapid production of effective vaccines in an unprecedented short period of time, and second, resulted in the percentage of Americans being vaccinated going from zero to over 56 percent in a period of just four months.[8] If we leave identity politics concerns aside, by any objective measure the federal government's vaccination program was a success.[9] By May 2021, when over 62 percent of the population was vaccinated, almost all Americans who wanted to be vaccinated had been vaccinated. Furthermore, the percentage of blacks who desired vaccination but had yet to obtain a shot was only 6 percent, a figure almost indistinguishable from the 4 percent of whites who desired vaccination but had not yet been vaccinated.[10]

The exact reason why there was some gap in vaccination rates for blacks and whites early in the rollout of the COVID-19 vaccines is subject to dispute. There is evidence that many blacks were vaccine-hesitant, taking a "wait-and-see" approach.[11] But Kendi and others deny this was the case. Let's assume, for the sake of argument, that the fault lay in difficulties blacks had in accessing vaccines. One study found that in ninety-four counties the percentage of blacks more than ten miles away from a facility offering vaccines exceeded significantly the percentage of whites in a similar situation.[12] So one policy alternative would have been to study the population density of black and white communities across the country and establish and staff a proportionate number of healthcare centers roughly equidistant for these two identity groups, all *prior* to offering any vaccines to the general public. This approach likely would have reduced any disparity between black and white vaccination rates, but at the cost of delaying vaccinations generally—possibly resulting in avoidable deaths. But as long as all identity groups suffer equally, isn't that better? Or at least the ethics of equity would so maintain.

But we may be understating the requirements of equity. Obtaining equal outcomes for blacks and whites ignores the historical advantages whites have enjoyed, correct? Enter the wisdom of Harald Schmidt, identified by the *New York Times*, as "an expert in ethics and health policy."[13] Early in the rollout of the vaccination program, when vaccines still were in short supply, there was a debate whether essential workers or the elderly should be vaccinated first. Legitimate arguments could be made for either group. We needed essential workers to provide healthcare, whereas the elderly had a greater risk of serious complications and death following infection. There was no need to inject race into this debate, but today's prevailing moral climate simply cannot leave race out of the picture. Schmidt maintained a key factor in any decision had to be the fact that proportionally more of the elderly were white—so we should not be so concerned about excess deaths among them: "Older populations are whiter ... Instead of giving additional health benefits to those who already had more of them, we can start to level the playing field a bit."[14] In other words, because whites had it better before, strictly equal outcomes aren't good enough: we need to rebalance matters between blacks and whites by allowing proportionally more whites to die. Welcome to the "playing field" of equity.

In this chapter, I will argue that the pursuit of "equity," as defined by its advocates, is problematic on several levels: it reflects a misunderstanding of the causes of disparities; it is ineffective, counter-productive and self-defeating; and it strives for a goal unobtainable except at the cost of our individual rights and freedom.

The Drive for Equal Outcomes Is Largely Based on the False Claim of Systemic Racism

As Kendi puts it: "Racial inequity is when two or more racial groups are not standing on approximately equal footing," such as when the percentage of whites who own homes is greater than the percentage of blacks or Latinos.[15] "Every policy in every institution in every community in every nation is producing or sustaining either racial inequity or equity between racial groups," and our choice is therefore between continuing with policies that have a disproportionate adverse impact on blacks or other disadvantaged racial groups or "temporarily assisting an under-represented racial group into relative wealth and power until equity is reached."[16] Statistical disparities are the key; if they disfavor historically disadvantaged groups, they are evidence of racist policies. The appropriate response is to eliminate these disparities by discriminating against favored groups until the disparity is eliminated, thus creating equity.

So goes the argument for equity, which, as one can tell, is predicated on the view that systemic racism is what causes disparities in all the various measures of well-being. But, as readers of the prior chapter are aware, the argument for systemic racism lacks support. There is no need to repeat the prior chapter's arguments here. It is sufficient to point out that the push for equity is misbegotten from the start. Without convincing evidence for current systemic racism, equity is a morally dubious goal pursued by the morally repugnant means of intentional discrimination against whites or whatever group (e.g., Asian Americans) the decision-makers of the day deem advantaged.

The prior chapter did conclude that a portion of the wealth disparity between blacks and whites can be attributed to the failure of Reconstruction to place blacks on anywhere near an equal footing with whites. But only a portion. Cultural factors, including family composition—a factor firmly within the control of black families—are major causes of the continuing wealth disparity as well. In any event, the fact that a plausible argument can be made for some level of reparations or investments in children's saving accounts to mitigate the wealth disparity does not imply we must eliminate disparities across the board. To the contrary, efforts to eliminate statistical disparities in all areas are not only unwarranted but also counter-productive.

The Misguided Goal of Eliminating Statistical Disparities

Equity in Education:
Proportional Representation in Courses, Schools, and Colleges

Let us consider the field of education first, where the pursuit of equal outcomes is arguably the most apparent—and where this pursuit is so clearly at odds with the fundamental purpose of education.

If we need to equalize results, the quickest and surest way to do this in the short-term (and for political reasons, education administrators and bureaucrats focus on the short-term), is to eliminate anything—tests, admission standards, course offerings, gifted programs, discipline policies—that might threaten to produce statistical disparities, especially in enrollment figures for honors courses, elite schools, or colleges. School systems and colleges are doing just that. The California Instructional Quality Commission proposed, in 2021, a revised Mathematics Framework, pursuant to which middle schools would abandon tracking in math courses—that is, they would stop offering different levels of math courses to students based on their abilities. The rationale for this proposed reform was that tracking resulted in "considerable inequities."[17] The draft framework also recommended postponing the teaching of Algebra 1 until the ninth grade, which would make it difficult for students to take a calculus course in high school given normal progression. The rationale here was that all students in middle school should be taking the same math courses. The draft framework cited in partial support of these proposed changes an accusation that tracking and course selection are hallmarks of "white supremacy."[18] Protests against the proposed new policy, as well as an extensive analysis of the draft framework which showed it was based on flawed research,[19] have resulted in California postponing implementation of the guidance until some point in 2023 pending further review.[20]

Many more similar examples could be given of how the drive for equity is curtailing or eliminating gifted programs or advanced course offerings. Seattle eliminated its middle school honors courses to achieve racial balance in the classrooms and ensure all students have the same courses.[21] Montgomery County, Maryland, also eliminated the distinction between regular and honors courses but tried to disguise this move by calling the combined classes "honors" classes. Again, the motivation was the felt need to engineer racial balance in classrooms.[22] A Long Island school district likewise ended tracking due to concerns over racial disparities.[23] Some observers have called this nationwide trend a "war on gifted-and-talented programs."[24]

Instead of eliminating specialized programs or schools, some school systems have changed criteria for admission, again with the goal of achieving racial balance. In Virginia, in 2020, the Fairfax County School Board changed the criteria for admission to Thomas Jefferson High

School, an elite school specializing in mathematics and science and considered one of the best in the country. Instead of basing admission primarily on the results of a test, the school would use a "holistic" approach, inviting eighth-graders with a GPA of at least 3.5, who are taking some higher-level courses, to submit an essay and a "student portrait sheet." Admissions officers would then evaluate these submissions, taking into account "experience factors," including demographic data.[25] The board was candid that the switch to the new criteria was designed to make the school's student population more closely resemble the percentages of the county's various ethnic groups. In an irony too little noticed by those who loudly proclaim "white supremacy" the ultimate source of racial disparities, the ethnic group most adversely affected by the change in admissions criteria was Asian Americans, who had constituted close to 70 percent of the school's students; the percentage of white students actually increased under the new criteria.[26] Concerned parents sued, and a federal district court ordered a stay to the new policy, finding it had been "infected with talk of racial balancing from its inception," but the court's stay was lifted on appeal and the case remains in litigation.[27]

Other school districts with elite schools have similarly modified admissions criteria with the aim of enrolling more blacks and Latinos. Boston changed its admissions criteria for three select high schools by dividing students into eight different socioeconomic groups and requiring admissions to be roughly equal from each group. Although students still take an entrance exam, their scores are no longer the decisive factor.[28] Chicago has actually gone through a series of changes to its admissions criteria for selective high schools, with the latest iteration reserving 30 percent of the slots to those with the highest test scores and dividing the remaining slots among four socioeconomic tiers.[29]

All these changes are being done in the name of educational equity. While it is apparent that the changes will result in a better match between student populations in various courses and selective schools and the percentage of a given racial or ethnic group in a school district, it is not at all apparent that they are serving a legitimate educational purpose. In fact, they may be harming, not helping students, whether white, black, Asian, or Latino. Watered-down honors courses will bore gifted students and will minimize, not maximize, their potential. On the other hand, placing students who are unprepared for more rigorous courses into a challenging environment will, in many cases, cause them to experience undue pressure and frustration. Some parents in the Long Island school district mentioned above have, in fact, demanded a relaxation of graduation requirements.[30] Mandating the same courses for everyone may lead, and has led, to poorer performance by everyone. District of Columbia schools, an equity pioneer, eliminated gifted and talented programs in 2005. Subsequently, in 2012, in part over concerns that the school system was not meeting the learning needs of high-performance students, the District of Columbia implemented a School Enrichment Model (SEM) program, whereby flexible group instruction would be offered to different groups within the same class. The results have been disappointing, with students at most SEM schools "more likely to perform below grade level than at or above it."[31] Furthermore, the achievement gap between black and Hispanic students and white students in the District remains wide, with white students outpacing black and Hispanic students on proficiency tests by 30 percent or more, both pre-and post-pandemic.[32]

Playing a numbers game by manipulating admission criteria or eliminating honors courses to achieve tacit quotas only masks differences in capabilities. Contrived proportional representation will help school administrators avoid accusations of racism—in the short term—but that may be all. If one truly wanted to assist students who may have underutilized potential, after-school tutoring programs should be offered free of charge, beginning early, certainly no later than fifth or sixth grade. Intensive assistance may help capable students catch up; imposing the same class structure on high school students with widely varying capabilities will benefit few, if anyone.

A similar solution could work to meet the oft-heard complaint that admission tests are unfair, because supposedly they just work to the benefit of wealthy families who can afford to pay for prep courses. To begin, this criticism ignores the many students who are able to do well on these tests without the benefit of prep courses: they do their homework regularly over the course of their school years and devote many hours to studying. Cramming via prep courses cannot beat the consistent and persistent accumulation of knowledge. But, in any event, if the issue is access to prep courses, then school systems can provide prep courses to all students who have a GPA above a certain cutoff point. Sure, this will cost money, but perhaps the budget for DEI trainers and bureaucrats can be cut to fund such a program. It would certainly do much more to help black students with underutilized potential than ritualized condemnations of white supremacy. In this regard, it is noteworthy that right before Fairfax County ditched its admissions test for Thomas Jefferson High School, it paid Ibram Kendi $20,000 for a one-hour Zoom lecture to school administrators and teachers and another $24,000 for multiple copies of one of his books.[33] Those funds would have paid for test prep for a significant number of minority students, and this would have been a more worthwhile investment than paying Kendi to reiterate the same overworked message one can find for free on YouTube.

Just as selective high schools have abandoned admissions tests, so too many colleges and universities have stopped using standardized tests, such as the SAT or ACT, to screen applicants, despite the fact that these tests are strongly predictive of academic success.[34] The primary concern is that use of these tests creates "inequities." For example, Worcester Polytechnic Institute (WPI) highlights on its website the fact that it has eliminated "SAT and ACT scores entirely from its admission process" because use of these scores creates "inequities and barriers to access."[35] Translation: we can't meet our racial quotas if we rely on these tests. WPI justified its decision in part by opining that scores can be "gamed through expensive test preparation courses and tutoring that provide an unfair advantage to wealthier students."[36] Again, this rationale elides the fact that many students do well without benefit of test prep courses—and a high test score may be the best way for a student with an otherwise run-of-the-mill GPA to show she has the skills required for college. And if WPI thinks test scores can be "gamed" more than grades, references, or student essays, it is engaged in self-delusion.

Colleges that forego use of standardized tests can, of course, point to the many critics of these tests as support for their decision. For example, the Brookings Institution asserts that because the average scores for blacks and Hispanics are lower than the average scores of whites and Asians, especially on the math portion of these tests, the tests "mirror and maintain racial inequity"; the lower average scores of blacks and Hispanics are the "likely result of generations of exclusionary housing, education, and economic policy."[37] Kendi, not unexpectedly, is much more vehement in his assessment, claiming that the "use of standardized tests to measure aptitude and intelligence is one of the most effective racist policies ever devised to degrade Black minds and legally exclude Black bodies."[38]

But the statistics presented by the Brookings study undercut its core claim. If "generations of exclusionary housing, education, and economic policy" are the explanation for lower average math scores, why then do Asian students consistently score higher on average than white students? In fact, the gap between the average scores for Asian students and white students (85 points) is not much smaller than the gap in average scores between white and black students (93 points).[39] If Asians have been victimizing whites for generations with respect to housing, education, and economic policy, this has somehow gone unnoticed. So, the suggested causal link between racially exclusionary policies and lower test scores is dubious. Furthermore, as the prior chapter already established, the most recent generations of blacks have not experienced systemic racism. While the racial gap in achievement may partly reflect differences in wealth, the wealth gap in recent decades has persisted in large part due to patterns in family composition, a circumstance within the control of black parents.

Kendi's claim relies on a classic straw-man argument. Contrary to his premise, the SAT and the ACT do not measure, and do not purport to measure, raw intelligence. That is not their purpose, nor is it how they are designed. They measure skill sets, the skills one needs to do well in college. A low math score is not "degrading"; it merely indicates one has not developed the skills necessary to do well in college-level math courses. Here again, the Brookings study inadvertently supports the validity of standardized tests. That study indicates that although the college enrollment gap between blacks and whites has decreased, the graduation gap remains; 45 percent of white students graduate within four years, whereas 21 percent of black students graduate within that time frame.[40] Brookings seems oblivious to an obvious possibility: many black students were admitted to college who did not have the skill sets necessary for academic success at the college level. There is a connection between test performance and success in college.

What is happening is that in the drive for equity—here meaning ending disparities in college admissions percentages—many colleges are accepting students who are not prepared for college. The short-term payoff for these colleges is that they can boast of the diversity of their student body. But there is a cost to the students themselves. Sure, some who are unprepared may find their footing and succeed. That does happen. But far too many will not. This development has effects beyond the frustration and misuse of time experienced by the students; it can have and has had long-term financial effects on them and others. The student debt problem is well-known. Less well-known is the fact that much of the student debt is carried by persons who have never graduated. Roughly 30 percent of all college students who are carrying student loans drop out before obtaining a degree; the percentage of black students with debt who drop out is higher, at 39 percent.[41]

Colleges that drop standardized tests as part of the admission process are not doing most prospective students any favors. The racial balance they temporarily achieve in their student populations primarily benefits the college's public relations, not the students. Just as with selective high schools, if the actual goal is to have more minority students prosper in their studies, the preparation for that must start before the students enter college, not while they are in college. Many colleges, especially community colleges, offer remedial courses, and there is nothing inherently wrong with that, but the data shows that for most who take these courses, it is too little and too late. A staggering 90 percent of students who take remedial courses at two-year community colleges fail to finish within three years. The statistics are not much better for four-year colleges, where 65 percent of students who take remedial classes fail to finish within six years.[42] If twelve years of schooling has not prepared one for college, for whatever reason, it is unlikely that a one-semester remedial course will remedy this deficit. Assistance for students who are lagging behind but show some promise must begin early, such as with after-school tutoring programs in elementary school or middle school.[43] Absent such programs, the push for racially proportionate admissions will cause more harm than good. True "equity" is not achieved by setting up unprepared students for failure.

But some colleges dodge the issue of whether they are benefitting students who are unprepared by denying that there is such a category of students. One critical task college-level DEI bureaucrats have shouldered is the policing of thought on campus, and one species of thought that must be extirpated is "deficit-mindedness." "Deficit-mindedness" is the unpardonable sin of thinking some students might actually lack college-level skills. Not true! That's as crazy as thinking the earth revolves around the sun. And like any respectable inquisitor, DEI monitors have compiled lists of "code words" used to convey or hint at forbidden thoughts, to enable us to be on the lookout for such thoughts. Fitchburg State University, for example, provides a useful guide to language that is *verboten*.[44] It warns that to guard against deficit-mindedness, these are the code words "to look for":

- Underprepared
- Underrepresented
- Minority
- Avoid words/statements of Universalism [sic]
- Achievement Gap
- Disadvantaged
- Unprivileged
- Underperforming
- At Risk
- First Generation

The booklet published by Fitchburg State University that contains this timely admonition is entitled "Policy Review with an Equity Lens." An apt title. When one uses the equity lens, problems that may cause one to question one's ideological commitment simply can't be seen.

But at least Fitchburg State has the decency to warn their professors about which terms must not be uttered. Some professors are not so fortunate, as an incident at Georgetown Law School illustrates.

The push for equal outcomes in admissions is not limited to high schools or colleges. It is also taking place in law schools and medical schools. Many law schools have made proportional admission of "underrepresented groups" a top priority,[45] with the result that they may be admitting some students who are not prepared for the demands of legal studies and struggle academically. But that fact must never be acknowledged—as two adjunct professors at Georgetown found out. In what she thought was a private conversation, Professor Sandra Sellers shared with fellow adjunct David Batson her "angst" over the fact that although she had some "really good" black students, a lot of them were ending up in the "lower" part of the class, and this happened "almost every semester," a result which made her "feel bad."[46] Batson mostly listened, but he at one point wondered whether an unconscious bias might affect his perceptions of students. When these remarks became public (they had been unintentionally recorded following a class recorded for future viewing), Georgetown Dean William Treanor fired Sellers and placed Batson on leave; Batson then resigned.

Treanor characterized Sellers' comments as "reprehensible" and "abhorrent," without explaining exactly what he found in her remarks that merited this harsh assessment and her summary discharge. Sellers did not admit to any bias in grading; she did not suggest in any way that blacks should not be attending law school; she stated she had taught some "really good" black students; she noted that many black students wound up in the lower end of her classes, but she added she was very concerned about this (she had "angst.")

There are only two possible explanations for Dean Treanor's reaction. One, he is of the opinion that the only reason a disproportionate number of black students might receive lower grades would be the bigotry of the professor. But he reported no investigation of Professor Sellers' grading, and, therefore, there seems to be no evidence of her bias apart from the fact of lower grades. In this case, the message to professors who desire continued employment is clear: the mandate of equal outcomes extends to grading. Two, he does not believe there should be *any* discussion on the issues of whether there might be racial gaps in academic achievement or the cause of such gaps. That kind of discussion might cast doubt on the wisdom of proportionate admissions, and such blasphemy cannot be tolerated. Significantly, in his message to the law school community, after going through a laundry list of initiatives designed to root out any conceivable bias, Treanor went to the bottom line: during his tenure as dean, he had "increased the percentage of students of color in our entering classes by 40%, including an entering class this year comprising 15% Black students—the highest proportion in the school's history by several percentage points."[47] Equal outcomes in admission accomplished—and damned be anyone who casts a shadow on this accomplishment by wondering whether all students actually benefit from this admissions practice.

In closing this discussion of the drive for equal outcomes within education, let me briefly address the one aspect of the issue most often referenced in discussions of this topic, and that is the discriminatory effect that admissions policies may have on students denied admission. I have not dwelt on this issue for a couple of reasons. First, it is already well known and it has been discussed at greater length and depth than I can provide here. Second, I wanted to emphasize how the drive for equal outcomes in admissions can harm those it is intended to help. In other words, regardless of any discriminatory effect, these policies may have, they are self-defeating. But it is important to note that the students most adversely affected by the discriminatory push for racial balance are Asian Americans, not whites. As a group, Asian Americans tend to do better than any other ethnic group, not only with respect to standardized test results but also with respect to academic achievement overall. To begin, this gives the lie to the claim that white supremacy is to blame for any imbalance between school or college populations and the population at large. Perhaps more important, it underscores the importance of one factor in academic achievement, and that is the cultural environment in which students find themselves. Asians are not inherently more intelligent than whites, just as whites are not inherently more intelligent than blacks. However, proportionally more Asian families may emphasize the importance of academics than white or black families. As discussed in the prior chapter, many black students consider being studious as "acting white." (Perhaps this meme should be updated to "acting Asian.")

This is a sensitive topic, and, of course, accepting the importance of cultural influences is at odds with the prevailing doctrine of systemic racism. But outside the fraught area of race relations, cultural influences on education are acknowledged with nary a voice raised in protest. For example, a recent study found that girls with a Jewish upbringing significantly outperformed girls from non-Jewish households.[48] This result aligns with statistics which for years have shown that children with at least one Jewish parent do better on standardized tests and have a greater probability of graduating from college than children from non-Jewish households. Contrary to what someone like Kendi would say, when confronted with these facts, we do not have to choose between saying Jews are inherently more intelligent or they are the beneficiaries of policies that discriminate against non-Jews. We simply have to acknowledge that in many Jewish households, parents have imbued their children with "educational and professional expectations of success."[49]

Assisting any student, including black students, to achieve their educational potential is a worthy goal, and more resources could and should be dedicated to this end. But insisting on proportional admissions at every level of schooling while refusing to consider the factors that may be causing some black students to underperform—indeed, refusing to even consider the possibility of underperformance—will turn our educational system into a Potemkin village, a system with a facade pleasing to bureaucrats and ideologues, but which fails to provide the best possible education for all.

Equity in Medical Care and Health: Race-Based Preferential Treatment

Unlike education, where a focus on disparities in enrollment provides a quick, superficially satisfactory response to the demand for equity, the complex factors that determine one's health make a speedy solution to perceived health disparities difficult. This fact has not prevented equity advocates from implementing or pushing for policies and practices which they view as essential for closing health equity gaps. As is the case with educational policies, however, some healthcare policies that aim for equity are misdirected and counter-productive.

To begin, though, we should reiterate key points from the prior chapter: health outcomes largely depend on two sets of factors, namely one's own conduct and one's socioeconomic situation. The relative prevalence of different behavior patterns in blacks (e.g., a greater predilection to obesity) and their relatively lower socioeconomic status account for much in the way of statistically different outcomes for various health conditions. Systemic racism is not the cause. Accordingly, equity policy initiatives which are predicated on the alleged causal effects of systemic racism are by their nature misdirected (which is not to say they can have no indirect beneficial effect).

The one policy change that would do the most to improve health outcomes for blacks would be universal health coverage because this would ensure that no one, even those who are economically challenged, would be denied medical care because it is unaffordable. There are arguments for and against universal health coverage, with those opposed focused principally on its costs. But the key point from an ethical perspective is that if the shift to universal health coverage is a good thing, it's because it's a good thing for most Americans, whatever their race or ethnicity. To argue that we should have universal health coverage because it would decrease health outcome disparities between blacks and whites is to elevate racial identity considerations over the greater good. Such an argument is not only ethically questionable but politically unwise. Opposition to universal health coverage is not likely to be overcome by insisting such a policy is necessary for racial equity.

As indicated, apart from major policy changes relating to healthcare coverage, the path to bringing about significant improvements in health outcomes lies principally in changes to individual behavior. For example, the leading risk factors for cancer (obesity, alcohol use, smoking) are all behavior-related.[50] Yet, incredibly, the American Medical Association (AMA), the largest professional organization for physicians in the United States, in its strategic plan for racial justice and health equity, expressly downplays attention to risky and damaging behaviors, despite their undeniable connection to health. Instead, the AMA advises physicians to move "upstream" to address the root cause of health inequities, which are white supremacy, racism, classism, sexism, homophobia, ableism, and xenophobia.[51] The AMA has committed itself and its members to working "with urgency" toward the achievement of health equity and the "shifting of the health outcomes narrative from the *cause*; solely from the individual and behavioral level to the *cause of causes*, the social and specifically the socioeconomic factors that influence the health narrative at the social and structural levels, [which] is a central priority in health equity work."[52] This radical shift from focusing on the circumstances and needs of the individual patient—remember, that person to whom the physician has a fiduciary duty—to some sort of ill-defined social and political advocacy represents a sea change in our understanding of the responsibilities of physicians. But don't worry. The AMA cites an unimpeachable authority in support of this dramatic shift, namely that renowned medical expert Ibram Kendi, who, in the quote attributed to him by the AMA, states that believing problems may arise out of the behavior of individual people is "racist" whereas an "anti-racist . . . locates the roots of problems in power and policies."[53]

Before proceeding to further criticism of the AMA and various other health and medical organizations, let me note that some of the initiatives undertaken in the name of health equity are uncontroversial if not laudable. Since 1990, the National Institutes of Health has had a division, the National Institute on Minority Health and Health Disparities (NIMHD), that has focused on health issues that particularly affect racial, ethnic, or other minorities.[54] By the way, the fact that NIMHD has been around for over thirty years by itself gives the lie to the claim that our health system is pervasively racist. In any event, NIMHD has sponsored a number of projects with the aim of addressing health issues which, although they affect everyone, have a special resonance for minority populations, such as research on lead poisoning in children and diabetes, obesity, and hypertension in adults. Similarly, many state and local health departments have given priority to projects that address problems that are particularly acute in minority communities. To cite just one example, the Minnesota Department of Health has had an "Eliminating Health Disparities Initiative," which, among other things, awards grants to organizations that provide health services, such as blood pressure screenings and immunizations, to "some of the hardest to reach populations."[55] Assuming it does not materially affect funding for more pressing health issues, improving access to healthcare for isolated populations is a good thing. Ideally, everyone would have access to needed healthcare services. These types of initiatives do not present any grounds for objection because they reflect traditional medical services, e.g., counseling patients about hypertension, and although they are prompted in part by concerns about disparities, the services are not conditioned on a patient's race. A white person who shows up for a blood pressure screening at a mobile unit in a remote area will not be turned away or told to wait until black or brown patients are served first.

Unfortunately, the AMA's strategic plan for equity both converts physicians from care providers into agents of political change and implicitly endorses race-based care. This plan constitutes a revolution in medicine, and not a good one.

The revolutionary nature of the AMA's plan is obvious from its language and tone, even without getting into the plan's details. The opening pages genuflect to the prevailing ideology, with a preamble that apologizes for using land previously used by indigenous tribes and for "the extraction of brilliance, energy, and life for labor forced upon millions of people of African descent for more than 400 [sic] years."[56] The plan document teems with references to the supposedly continuing, baleful influences of "white supremacy,"[57] which allegedly persists in part "by the way many whites ignore their whiteness to the point of invisibility [and] their role in a racial hierarchy" and in part by "the threat of violence."[58] There are ritual denunciations of capitalism[59] and meritocracy[60] and constant references to oppression.[61] One has the impression that the physicians who signed off on this screed are all graduates of the Che Guevara School of Medicine.

The AMA plan's strategies and proposed actions are themselves 90 percent rhetoric and 10 percent concrete tasks and objectives. But perhaps that is fitting because one of the plan's concrete objectives is to shape the way physicians (and the rest of us) talk. The AMA contends that we must rid ourselves of "malignant narratives." Among these malignant narratives are "a narrow focus on individuals; an historical perspective; [and]the myth of meritocracy."[62] It's not clear why the AMA finds "an historical perspective" troubling—unless the AMA fears people recognizing that all of us (white, black, Hispanic, etc.) are much better off in terms of living standards and opportunities than we were, say, a century ago, thanks in large part to the capitalism the organization denounces. Focusing on individuals—what a naïve patient might think physicians are supposed to do—is to be avoided because it takes our eyes off group equities. Meritocracy "ignores the inequitably distributed social, structural, and political resources that influence health and limit individual-level control or effort."[63]

Changing "narratives," changing how we talk about issues, is a common tactic of revolutionary movements. Habitual uses of certain language can influence our thoughts, and if you have trouble articulating a thought at odds with the revolutionary creed, so much the better. The weight the AMA places on health equity newspeak is indicated by the fact that one of the first projects the AMA undertook pursuant to its strategic plan was to issue, in collaboration with the Association of American Medical Colleges, a 54-page guide to "Language, Narrative, and Concepts."[64] (More will be said about this guide below.)

Another concrete goal is to reform medical school education. Specifically, the goal is to "[e]xpand medical school and physician education to include equity, antiracism, structural competency, public health and social sciences, critical race theory and historical basis of disease."[65] To begin, some of these subjects cover topics one should study, if at all, as an undergraduate. Second, there are only so many hours in a day. Necessarily, any time medical students are immersed in "critical race theory" is time they do not spend on, for example, distinguishing Crohn's disease from ulcerative colitis. But to complain that under the AMA model medical schools are preparing students for social activism at the expense of learning how to treat the individual patient misses the point that for the AMA, training for social activism is now the remit of medical schools. As the AMA's plan states, to pursue health equity we must "empower physicians and health systems to dismantle structural racism and intersecting systems of oppression."[66] Physicians are to be social reformers first, your caregiver second—if at all.

In the plan's section on "key actions," the priority given to social reform is made even more apparent. Pushing "upstream" is confirmed as essential and, in that connection, the AMA declares that physicians and healthcare systems must:

> Advance a new paradigm for health care as a key mover and driver of social and racial justice, by linking provider and health care system advocacy to other sectors, to effectively address both social and medical needs for populations and enhance understanding of and ability to detect and mitigate any unintentional worsening of inequities resulting from well-intentioned efforts.[67]

The "new paradigm" thus explicitly redirects physicians from care for individual patients to care for "populations," and the practice of medicine now embraces "social and racial justice," with "justice" presumably defined in terms of the critical race theory now endorsed by the AMA.

Medical schools have taken the AMA's guidance to heart. Besides inserting courses on equity into the already overcrowded medical school curriculum, some have replaced the traditional Hippocratic Oath recited by graduating med students with pledges by the students to uproot "structural violence" within the healthcare system. So, again, the focus is not on treating the individual patient, but on the pursuit of some ideologically motivated social goal. "Take two aspirin and *don't* call me in the morning; I'll be on the picket line." Weirdly, the oath recited by University of Minnesota med students also includes a pledge to "honor all Indigenous ways of healing that have been historically marginalized by Western medicine."[68] No doubt, over the centuries, through trial and error, indigenous people arrived at some methods of mitigating diseases and injuries. But if those methods, for the most part, are no longer used, it is not because they have been "marginalized." Rather it is because more effective methods have been developed, mostly through rigorous clinical studies. So, this part of the pledge either constitutes pointless virtue-signaling or a failure of the med students to understand how modern medicine works. Neither alternative inspires much confidence.

In sum, the medical establishment, with its focus on group identity, is expressly adopting a race-conscious approach to the practice of medicine. This will inevitably progress into a race-based approach, and indeed it already has.

But before discussing some examples of race-based medicine, let us return to the AMA's guide to "Language, Narrative and Concepts," as it provides important insights into the mindset of those now determining AMA policy, which in turn will clarify some of the consequences of the "new paradigm" of physicians being activists for "social and racial justice."

To begin, this language guide starts with an even longer apology for "genocide and forced labor" than the similar apology in the AMA's strategic plan. Strikingly, the apology states that "we carry our ancestors in us," essentially an assertion of collective guilt for the conduct of others that occurred generations ago.[69] The guide proceeds to decry the "dominant narratives" of individualism and meritocracy, which "must be named, disrupted and corrected."[70] When it comes to specific changes in language, two principles obviously govern: one, if some short and clear description can be replaced by a cumbersome circumlocution, then it must be so replaced—why use one word when four will do; and two, wording must always emphasize how oppression causes unfavorable situations. For example, instead of saying "workers who do not use PPE" one must say "people with limited access to (specific service or resource)."[71] But what if a worker has access to PPE but refuses to utilize it? Apparently, words fail in such a situation. "At-risk groups" is forbidden; instead, one must say "groups placed at increased risk."[72] Presumably, this means smokers are not at risk for lung cancer; instead, some unknown oppressive force—

white supremacy is a good bet—places them at increased risk. "Marginalized communities," itself already a euphemism, is to be discarded in favor of "groups that have been historically marginalized."[73] "Minority" is no longer acceptable because supposedly it means "less than" and is pejorative. "Historically minoritized" is the obligatory term as it emphasizes how groups have been made minorities "by dominant culture and whiteness."[74] So, a widely used term that simply and straightforwardly indicates that there are fewer blacks than whites, or fewer gays than heterosexuals (*not* less than, but fewer than), is now banned because it does not do enough to advance identity group ideology. And, of course, use of "white" or "black" as adjectives, e.g., "white paper," is discouraged because such usage supports white privilege.[75] Accordingly, make sure you catch yourself before you tell your physician you have a black eye; tell the doc instead that you have a "historically minoritized eye."

To assist physicians in understanding its recommendations, the AMA language guide also has a twenty-page glossary—crowded with the most tendentious definitions imaginable. "Class consciousness" is "the recognition by workers of their unity as a social class in opposition to capitalists and to capitalism itself";[76] "justice" describes "a future state where the root causes (e.g., racism, sexism, class oppression) of inequity have been dismantled and barriers have been removed";[77] "racial capitalism" is the notion that "racialized exploitation and capital accumulation are mutually reinforcing."[78] Next time you visit your physician, be prepared to be greeted with the salutation "comrade" and a raised fist.

But perhaps one is thinking that even if the language guide has some flaws, shouldn't physicians be sensitive to how their words are interpreted? Sure, but if one thinks the AMA's censors were merely trying to counsel physicians to be careful in their wording to avoid giving offense, their own description of the guide's purpose would quickly disabuse one of that notion. Following publication of the guide, several of the authors gathered for a recorded conversation to discuss the importance of language. In his remarks, David Ansell stated that he does not even like the term "equity." Instead, we should just talk about "racism." Ansell proceeded to clarify that "exactly the point of the guide" is to name the root cause of our ills, and that root cause is "white supremacism."[79] Fernando De Maio, who chaired the session, immediately thanked Ansell for his "insightful remarks" and seconded his observation about the guide's utility in revealing "root causes in systems of oppression."[80] Renee Canady then stated she appreciated Ansell's "clarification on that term equity, which is so problematic in so many spaces," and agreed that the focus should be on "racism" and "other forms of systemic oppression."[81] In short, the guide is an integral part of the AMA's plan to structure the practice of medicine around the dismantling of white supremacy, which will require giving priority to group outcomes over individualized care and treatment. Race-based medicine is the result.

Indeed, race-based medicine has already appeared. In 2021, Bram Wispelwey, a physician at Brigham and Women's Hospital in Boston (hereinafter "Brigham"), and Michelle Morse, formerly a physician at the same institution, published an essay in which they described a program they had developed for the hospital and the rationale for the program. To quote the authors, the program is "a preferential admission option for Black and Latinx heart failure patients to our specialty cardiology service."[82] In explaining why preferential treatment for black and Latinx patients was required, the authors first acknowledged their program might elicit legal challenges given "our system of colorblind law" (what a pity!), but then defended their approach, arguing that "given the ample current evidence that our health, judicial, and other systems already unfairly preference people who are white . . . our approach is *corrective* and therefore mandated."[83] The authors closed their essay by "encourag[ing] other institutions to proceed confidently on behalf of equity and racial justice, with backing provided by recent White House executive orders."[84]

After this program became known to the public, protests ensued. Morse claimed the protests caught them by surprise—despite their acknowledgment in their article that they expected legal challenges.[85] Brigham tried to downplay the preferential aspect of the program, stating on their website that the "program is not designed to create better or preferential care for some patients over others."[86] Of course, this assertion contradicts Wispelwey and Morse, who expressly proclaimed the goal was to provide preferential treatment. In any event, Brigham's description of how the program operates indicates it places a thumb on the clinician's scale and substitutes the hospital's race-based judgment for the clinician's assessment, regardless of the hospital's protests to the contrary:

For patients who self-identify as Black or Latinx, and present to the emergency department with heart failure, physicians will receive a prompt when a bed request is entered to admit the patient to the hospital's general medical service unit. The prompt will educate the clinician about the fact that, historically, this population has had inequitable access to specialized cardiology care and offer a recommendation to consider changing admission to the cardiology service. The notice does not restrict clinicians' individual judgment and decision-making in consideration of the best interest of the patient. Clinicians are always free to make judgements about appropriate triage based on illness severity, and there is flexibility to override the computerized recommendations *where there is a compelling rationale.*[87] (Emphasis added.)

So, clinicians can exercise their individual judgment and go against the hospital's recommendation "where there is a compelling rationale." Hardly reassuring, especially since Brigham will be monitoring all these decisions.

The kicker to this program of preferential treatment is that the justification for it arose out of a study of Brigham patients with heart failure, which actually showed no serious adverse effect from clinicians' decisions to refer black patients to general medicine service (GMS) as opposed to cardiology services.[88] The authors of the study, which included Wispelwey and Morse, emphasized that the data showed black patients with heart failure were less likely to be admitted to cardiology services than white patients—true, but the adjusted rate ratio was .91, not a huge difference.[89] (The difference for Latinx patients was more significant, with a rate ratio of .83). The study also showed black patients were more likely to be readmitted within thirty days, but again the difference was slight, with 26 percent of white patients being readmitted within that period compared to 29 percent of black patients.[90] The most revealing statistic was that, percentage-wise, *fewer* black patients died within thirty days of admission than white patients, 2 percent versus 4 percent.[91] This statistic cannot be explained if clinicians were ignoring the needs of black patients. (This statistic does not fit comfortably with the authors' predetermined conclusion, so they try to dismiss it by saying it is of "unclear significance.")[92] Furthermore, the overall percentage of all patients admitted to GMS who died within thirty days was equal to the percentage of patients admitted to cardiology services who died within thirty days (3 percent);[93] in other words, there was no difference in mortality between patients admitted to GMS as opposed to cardiology services. The most reasonable conclusion from these statistics is that clinicians referred patients to GMS because, in the clinicians' judgment, they were not as much in need of specialized cardiology services as other patients; race had nothing to do with their decisions. What this study shows is not that there was some disturbing racial inequity arising out of clinicians' treatment of black heart patients compared to white heart patients, but that medical researchers who operate under the prevailing dogma of systemic racism will draw conclusions to support that dogma, despite contradictory empirical evidence.

The move to race-based medicine is still in its early stages, but Brigham does not stand alone. The most noted use of race-based allocation of medical resources occurred midway through the pandemic, when several state health departments—in New York, Minnesota, and Utah—implemented race-based policies regarding the dispensing of treatments for COVID-19, such as monoclonal antibodies.[94] Because at the time demand was outrunning supplies, the health departments used scoring systems to determine which individuals had priority for receiving these medications. Some of the criteria, such as age and comorbidities such as diabetes or obesity, made sense. However, the health departments also gave points for being of a "non-white race or Hispanic/Latino ethnicity" despite the fact that there was no evidence that being black or Hispanic, by itself, made one more likely to catch COVID-19 or develop serious symptoms. As two researchers noted, after "controlling for other factors, such as income, education and residence [no study] shows clearly that Americans of Hispanic, African or Asian ancestry are at greater risk for severe Covid-19."[95]

There are a couple of noteworthy aspects regarding this use of race as a factor in determining priority for treatment. First, this use of race flies in the face of the efforts by many physicians and medical researchers to end what they consider race-based medicine, whereby various laboratory and clinical tests were assigned different significant values depending on the race of the patient. Perhaps the best-known example is the test for globular filtration rate (eGFR), a test to determine kidney function. Based on data from clinical trials which showed that people self-identifying as black tended to have higher levels of creatine in their blood, for years the significant level for eGFR was set higher for blacks than whites.[96] In recent years the argument has been made—typically by those who embrace the doctrine of systemic racism—that assigning a higher significant eGFR level to blacks could prevent blacks from receiving appropriate care for kidney disease in a timely fashion. This argument is usually coupled with the claim that "race" has no biological basis and, therefore, race cannot properly be used as an independent risk factor for any disease. However, one's ethnicity can be correlated with certain risk factors, as indicated, for example, by the much higher presence of sickle cell trait among those of African descent compared with other ethnicities. But we need not resolve the thorny issue of what biological differences there may be between different populations to see the inconsistency in maintaining that blacks do not have different risk factors for certain diseases while also maintaining that blacks qua blacks should receive priority for certain medications or treatments. Giving blacks priority for medications or treatments is either effectively claiming that being black *is* an independent risk factor for some diseases or just blatant race discrimination. Many health equity advocates will protest that practicing race-conscious medicine is not the same as practicing race-based medicine. But it is.

The other interesting aspect regarding the use of race as a factor for treatment priority is that some health equity advocates tacitly, if not expressly, admit that this practice constitutes race discrimination. And they have no shame about this. In their view, race discrimination against whites is fully justified because it constitutes a corrective to past injustices. As Camara Phyllis Jones, an epidemiologist and past president of the American Public Health Association, observed, when commenting on the priority some states gave to blacks and Hispanics for COVID-19 treatments, to achieve health equity "you must provide resources to rectify historical injustices."[97] As we have already seen, University of Pennsylvania ethicist Harald Schmidt argued that black workers should receive COVID-19 vaccinations before the elderly because most of the elderly are white and "[i]nstead of giving additional health benefits to those who already had more, we can start to level the playing field a bit."[98] Recall that the preface to AMA guide on "Language, Narrative and Concepts" solemnly assumed on behalf of people living today responsibility for the deeds of our ancestors, who "we carry . . . in us."[99] In other words, the mindset of many health equity advocates is that a rebalancing is required; whites received better treatment previously, so blacks should receive better treatment now. Put more bluntly, it is payback time. So, in the minds of these equity advocates, race is not an independent risk factor for any disease, but that does not matter because another rationale is at work. Kendi's mantra, that the "only remedy to past discrimination is present discrimination,"[100] applies to healthcare policy as much as it does to any other policy.

The drive for equity in healthcare is misdirected, as it is in other areas, because it rests on the unproven premise that there is continuing systemic racism. As a group, blacks do have statistically worse outcomes with respect to some health conditions, but this disparity is largely a result of lower socioeconomic status combined with behavioral factors. Moreover, the drive for equity is counter-productive for at least two reasons. First, the prevailing sentiment that physicians must become racial equity activists, as exemplified by the AMA's strategic plan, sacrifices the traditional practice of medicine in favor of advancing an ideology not shared by all Americans. Following the ideology's mandates works to degrade the treatment everyone receives; teaching med students about white supremacy will not help them diagnose appendicitis. In addition, turning physicians into racial equity activists will tend to undercut trust in physicians. There is already too much distrust, among both blacks and whites, with respect to healthcare providers, with adverse consequences for the health of many, as demonstrated by the recent pandemic. If patients begin to think, with some justification, that their physician sees them as a data point to be fit into some racial-outcomes chart, and not as an individual person, this distrust will deepen.

Finally, it is worth noting that there are race-neutral ways to achieve many of the goals health equity advocates seek. Access to healthcare is important for everyone, and race-neutral efforts to increase access make perfect sense and raise no ethical red flags, even though they may well benefit minorities more. Nothing wrong with that as long as no priority is given to any race. (For example, the policy should not be that no mobile vaccination unit goes to West Virginia or Wyoming until everyone in Harlem who wants to be vaccinated is vaccinated.) Focusing on improving healthcare for everyone will address real needs. Focusing on dismantling white supremacy will have physicians pursuing phantoms.

Equal Outcomes Are Unachievable Absent a Sacrifice of Freedom

The pursuit of equal outcomes is not limited to equal outcomes for racial or ethnic identity groups of students or patients. Equity advocates want equal outcomes in all areas of life for all identity groups. For example, mirroring the demand for equal admissions outcomes in schools and colleges, there is a push for equal outcomes in faculty hirings. Of course, to some extent, via affirmative action efforts, identity-based hirings have been going on for decades. The difference now is that what was implicit and unstated before—achieving a target percentage of minorities or women—is now made explicit. The racial reckoning of the last few years has emboldened equity advocates to be more candid about their aims. Thus, Texas A&M University has announced a program to increase the "presence of faculty of color" by setting aside a special fund for bonuses for "hires from underrepresented minority groups," including blacks, Hispanics, Native Americans, Alaskan Natives, and Native Hawaiians.[101] Whites need not apply. The program is designed to achieve "a demographic composition that represents the State of Texas." In other words, the aim is to have the percentage of blacks, Hispanics, and so forth on the faculty equal the percentage of the given minority group in the population. Equal outcomes.

As with hires in academia, so too with hires in government and private industry. The Biden administration, consistent with the commitment set forth in its Inaugural Day executive order to advance equity across the federal government, has hired more minorities and women for White House positions than any previous administration. Blacks make up 11 percent of the commissioned officers (assistants, deputy assistants, and special assistants) in the Biden White House, a figure close to the percentage of blacks in the general population (12.4 percent).[102] But that is not good enough for The Joint Center for Political and Economic Studies, which issued a report arguing this representation was insufficient because 22 percent of those who voted for Biden were black. The organization recommended this deficiency be remedied by appointing blacks to "vacant commissioned officer positions."[103] Here, we see how "equal outcomes" can have an elastic meaning. "Equal outcomes" implies the elimination of disparities, but how is the disparity calculated? For many, representation equal to a group's proportion of the general population may be enough to end the disparity, but others may use a different measuring stick. The Joint Center's use of the percentage of black voters supporting Biden to determine the size of the racial disparity in employment suggests it considers that only a racialized spoils system could achieve true equity. And because of the availability of different ways of calculating equal outcomes, we can be sure of one thing: whatever percentage of representation is achieved for a particular group, it will never be enough. The goalposts will keep receding.

As with hires, so too with layoffs, the other end of the employment scale. Companies in the last several decades have often considered the race, sex, and age of employees being laid off, to assist in avoiding, or at least defeating, claims of discrimination. However, they did this *sotto voce* because—well, because explicit use of race, sex, or age would be illegal. Under the new dispensation, employers feel free not only to be open about their plans but to boast of them. Thus, Twilio, a major communications company, proudly announced that in its 2022 layoffs, it would use an "Anti-Racist/Anti-Oppression Lens" to ensure its layoffs would have less "impact on marginalized communities."[104]

And the Minneapolis Public Schools District, in its latest collective bargaining agreement with the Minneapolis Federation of Teachers, committed to deviating from traditional seniority standards when laying off teachers. Instead of using a race-neutral seniority calculation, the school district will first lay off the least senior teachers who are not members of an "underrepresented" population, i.e., white teachers. The school district justifies this blatant race discrimination by claiming it is necessary to "remedy the continuing effects of past discrimination."[105] In other words, the school district maintains it is morally permissible, if not praiseworthy, to impose economic costs on individuals not because they have done something wrong, but solely because of their race. The new meaning of "equity."

Equal outcomes in employment is one thing, but obviously the push for equity must be much broader. Every policy, every decision must be analyzed to see if it advances equity. Thus, for example, in determining the location for a government facility, such as the new FBI headquarters, consideration should not be limited to whether the new location will be convenient for staff, enable security, and serve the underlying purposes of the agency, but whether it will promote racial equity.[106]

Promoting equity through relocation of government facilities will take time, however, and achieving equity is a priority *now*. To place equity on a faster track in several categories, members of Congress have proposed legislation that would mandate the Federal Reserve (hereinafter "the Fed") to "exercise all duties and functions in a manner that fosters the elimination of disparities across racial and ethnic groups with respect to employment, income, wealth, and access to affordable credit."[107] The House of Representatives passed the bill but it was not taken up by the Senate. Whether or not Congress ever approves the bill, it provides insight into the measures equity advocates want to take in pursuit of their goals—and how far-reaching and ruinous these measures might be.

The Fed currently has a dual mandate of price stability and full employment. "Full employment" does not mean no one is currently without a job; instead, it refers to the absence of deficit-demand unemployment. For example, people who are between positions may be unemployed, but they do not count against full employment. In any event, balancing these two objectives of price stability and maximizing employment is unquestionably challenging. However, many would maintain the Fed has done a reasonably good job over the last decade, with unemployment remaining at historical lows and with inflation kept in check until 2022. Equity advocates, though, would dissent from this assessment. Low unemployment and low inflation are not good enough if there exist racial disparities! Equity advocates have lambasted the Fed because the black unemployment rate has remained higher than the white unemployment rate.[108] Attributing this higher rate to a relative lack of job skills or education is, according to these advocates, a white supremacist dodge; the real explanation is a racist economic policy by which the Fed, at least until recently, achieved low inflation by sacrificing black jobs. Too often, blacks are the first to be laid off—so the claim goes—and, therefore, a tight monetary policy has more of an adverse effect on them. According to these advocates, the Fed must account for the "structural barriers" to black employment and "encourage job growth until that unemployment gap [between blacks and whites] closes, instead of pumping the brakes on the economy right at the moment the gap starts to close."[109]

But continually trying to fine-tune monetary policy to ensure the black and white unemployment rates are equivalent would almost surely produce at least two undesirable results: As equity advocates concede, monetary policy would have to be looser to close the gap between black and white unemployment, so a higher rate of inflation would be the likely result. And because those who are poorer suffer more from inflation, the higher inflation would likely have a disproportionate adverse impact on the black population. Furthermore, market conditions are dynamic. To maintain the equivalence in unemployment rates, adjustments would have to be made repeatedly and in short intervals, thereby producing economic instability, contrary to the Fed's mandate. Of course, in addition to these negative consequences, the entire effort would be misdirected, treating a symptom rather than the underlying cause of the unemployment gap, which is, for the most part, a difference in sought-after job skills. It would be like a plumber trying to fix a leak by repeatedly placing buckets under the pipe.

The proposed legislation would, as noted, broaden the Fed's mandate beyond full employment to eliminating disparities in "income, wealth, and access to affordable credit." So, the problems just mentioned with respect to trying to equalize unemployment rates would be magnified were the Fed to undertake these additional tasks. In addition, it is not clear what measures the Fed could take to achieve equal outcomes in income and wealth given the limited scope of its authority, which by itself is a cause for concern. Novel regulatory approaches are not a good fit for an organization that is supposed to promote financial stability. The Fed does have regulatory power over financial institutions, such as banks and savings and loan holding companies, and it does rate these organizations based on such things as risk management and financial condition.[110] Accordingly, perhaps it could give favorable ratings to institutions that provide a high percentage of loans to minority-owned businesses, even though, objectively, some of those loans would be risky. Similarly, it could reduce capital requirements for loans to such businesses. For individuals, underwriting standards could be adjusted to increase homeownership. All such measures would have to be extensive to affect income and wealth disparities, and the more extensive they are, the more they would undermine the Fed's mission of price stability. Such measures would increase systemic risk when the Fed is supposed to minimize systemic risk.

The Fed is but one governmental entity, albeit an important one.

In light of the Biden administration's commitment to a "whole-of-government equity agenda,"[111] other agencies can be expected to interpret their own missions to encompass elimination of disparities. In fact, it has happened already, although some efforts have encountered the problem that we still have a Constitution guaranteeing equal protection under the law. So, the Department of Agriculture's program to provide debt relief only to "socially disadvantaged farmers," that is, black, Hispanic, Asian, Pacific Islander, Native American, and Native Alaskan farmers, did not survive a court challenge.[112] The federal judge who enjoined the program pointed out that using race as the inflexible factor to determine eligibility for debt relief meant that a white farmer on the brink of foreclosure would not qualify, whereas a black farmer who enjoyed a prosperous year would qualify. This racially discriminatory denial of benefits was plainly unconstitutional. In August 2022, Congress refashioned the program so that it served a rational, nondiscriminatory purpose: debt relief was available to any distressed farmer, regardless of their race or ethnicity, and also to any farmer who suffered actual discrimination.[113]

Naturally, equity advocates lamented the court-ordered inclusion of whites in the debt-relief program.[114]

No doubt, more efforts will be made to funnel benefits to "socially disadvantaged" groups while excluding whites; as one observer noted, the government just needs to find "workarounds" to achieve the same result as racially exclusionary measures without using racially explicit language.[115]

Whatever the legal fate of such programs, the goal of eliminating disparities across the board, in all of life's circumstances, is unrealizable, and determined efforts to achieve that goal will result in curtailing personal freedom. Even if we hypothesize that for a time black, white, Asian, and Hispanic unemployment rates and income become equal, the dynamics of market conditions will inevitably disrupt that parity, one way or the other. What then? Repeated, endless government intervention in the economy is the only answer, unless the government tires of intervention and turns to direct supervision, instituting a command economy with control over employment and wages. That was, of course, how the Soviet Union tried to achieve equity; we know how well that worked out.

But however important income and employment are, there are also disparities to be eliminated in educational attainment, housing, access to transportation, healthcare, and health outcomes, and lest we forget, incarceration rates, police encounters, and all the other facets of the criminal justice system. What is the mechanism for permanently eliminating disparities in all these areas? No credible set of policies has been suggested. Sure, if we adopt the ethics of someone like Harald Schmidt and deny or delay various forms of healthcare to whites, then life expectancy for blacks and whites may quickly even out, but how then do we ensure these equal death rates endure? What if whites, having had their white supremacy diminished, turn increasingly in their despair to drugs, alcohol, and smoking, so their life expectancy falls significantly below that of blacks? Do we then curtail healthcare for blacks?

Note that the difficulty of permanently eliminating disparities has so far been understated. In this section, as is true for most of this chapter, the discussion of equity has concentrated on efforts to eliminate racial disparities. Racial equity is typically at the forefront of equity initiatives, and, therefore, it merits this level of attention. But we should not think we can eliminate racial disparities and then announce we are done. Consider another prominent set of equity concerns, and that is the disparities in various areas between men and women. Let us look at just one such disparity, and that is the wide differences between the numbers of men and women in various professions. For example, teachers and nurses are overwhelmingly women and engineers are overwhelmingly men. There are differences in compensation and working conditions attached to these professions, so the different career paths have significant economic consequences. I believe in epistemic humility, so I am not going to speculate why there are such stark differences in career choice, but the fact is that despite many initiatives to increase the percentage of women in engineering professions (less effort has been made to increase the percentage of men in nursing and teaching), not much has changed.[116] If this is a set of disparities that must be eliminated, and the prevailing doctrine of equity so instructs us, much more control needs to be exercised over the career choices of men and women, with adverse implications for individual autonomy. Again, one is reminded of the Soviet Union, where one's career path was often dictated by the needs of the people, not one's own preferences.

Thus far, we have discussed racial equity and touched on equity between the sexes, but it is important to bear in mind that for equity advocates, it is imperative to eliminate disparities that may adversely affect *any* underserved or marginalized group, and there are quite a few of these, as Biden's executive order confirms. Here we encounter the analog of the problem referenced in Chapter 1 when the difficulties posed by intersectionality for determining the precise epistemic advantage enjoyed by a particular identity group were shown to be insuperable. Similarly insoluble problems will confound any attempt to eliminate disparities in all areas of life between and among whites, members of religious majorities, heterosexuals, able-bodied individuals, persons who live in urban or suburban areas, "Blacks, Latinos, Indigenous and Native American persons, Asian Americans and Pacific Islanders and other persons of color, members of religious minorities, gay, lesbian, bisexual, transgender and queer (LGBTQ+) persons, persons with disabilities, persons who live in rural areas, and persons otherwise adversely affected by persistent poverty or inequality" (to quote the Biden executive order). Among other issues, there will be relentless confrontations among identity groups regarding what constitutes an equitable outcome. We have seen instances of this already, with disputes between Hispanics and blacks over immigration,[117] between Asians and blacks over school admissions, and between biological women and transgender persons over a broad range of issues. The racially inspired infighting among members of the Los Angeles City Council in 2021 revealed in blunt unmistakable terms how the supposed unity of "people of color" is a myth.[118] Perhaps they will show unity against those horrible whites, but once that presumed common enemy is subdued, do not expect the knives to be sheathed. Equal outcomes that satisfy all identity groups is nothing but a pipe dream, either that or a totalitarian dystopia in which the government exercises complete control over the economic and personal lives of everyone and directs everyone to be satisfied—or else.

Furthermore, no one has offered a convincing argument for the proposition that equal outcomes among identity groups is an overriding ethical imperative. Heretofore, the individual person has been the accepted unit of moral significance. We have recognized rights for individuals, not groups, as confirmed not only by the United States Constitution but by the Universal Declaration of Human Rights.[119] Subordinating individual rights to identity group goals will necessarily infringe on these rights. Individual persons are supposed to be ends, not means. Even the utopian fantasy of Marxism was phrased in terms of individuals: "From each according to his ability; to each according to his needs."[120] Marx didn't proclaim "Equal outcomes for all identity groups."

Shifting the locus of moral concern from individuals to identity groups will lead, and has led, to the erasure of individuality. People are not seen as individuals, but as exemplars of some identity group. People are lumped together even though they may share little in common other than their ethnicity, sex, or sexuality; sometimes, they do not even share that. The acronym LGBTQ+ is deployed in the Biden executive order as though all individuals who might fall in this broad class of classes have the same interests. They do not.

The ubiquity of antiracism seminars or trainings by DEI consultants, however well-intentioned, exacerbates this elevation of group identity over individuality. If we are trained to see people as members of groups, that is how we will see them. The DEI industry is huge, and it is growing rapidly, with expenditures for DEI work expected to reach $15.6 billion by 2026.[121] The obsession over group identity, especially racial group identity, has become a cash cow for this industry. Rare is the employee of any university, governmental entity, or corporation of any size who has not been required to attend a DEI antiracism training session. Too often, these antiracism sessions pit racial groups against each other, with "white supremacy" invariably being portrayed as the source of our evils. Sometimes, the trainers themselves express animosity against whites based solely on their race.[122] If a white person complains about the content of the training, their complaints will be condescendingly dismissed as manifestations of "white fragility"—if they are lucky.[123] When our problems are ascribed to the actions of white people, it is to be expected that sentiments of guilt, resentment, or outrage will be felt by many whites and hostility will be fostered in many nonwhites. Hardly a recipe for enhancing understanding or persuading people to put aside their differences and work for the common good.

In conclusion, the ethics of equity—as currently interpreted—places priority on an elusive, morally questionable goal, the pursuit of which would lead, among other things, to the disruption of our economy, the trampling of individual rights, and the balkanization of our society.

Indeed, the priority given to concern for identity groups has already produced a deleterious result in the important area of social science research. Equity advocates have committed to the willful suppression of research inconsistent with prevailing norms, as determined by "ethics experts and advocacy groups."

Censorship of Research in the Service of Equity

For some time now, any scholar who questions the prevailing orthodoxies, including the dogmas of systemic racism or the imperative of equity, has been subject to a storm of outrage, often culminating in a demand for the scholar's termination or discipline. Even when these scholars manage to retain their positions, they are often ostracized, intimidated into silence, or cowed into abject apologies.[124] Today's Red Guards will not tolerate dissent. Obviously, these incidents have the intent and effect of limiting any questioning of these orthodoxies.

Now, though, matters have proceeded further. *Nature Human Behavior*, a heretofore well-regarded social science research journal, has announced that it will refuse publication of any article that contains content "that undermines—or could reasonably be perceived to undermine—the rights and dignities of an individual or human group on the basis of socially constructed or socially relevant human groupings."[125] The rationale offered for this restriction is that although "the pursuit of knowledge is a fundamental public good, considerations of harm can occasionally supersede the goal of seeking or sharing new knowledge, and a decision not to undertake or not to publish a project may be warranted."[126] The editors of this journal try to justify their new censorship policy by analogizing it to restrictions placed on studies that use human subjects, such as drug trials. This analogy is inapposite, to say the least. Trials involving human subjects present the direct and immediate risk of bodily harm to individuals, and in most such cases, there are established standards for how these risks are to be assessed. By contrast, the worry that some research may "undermine" the "dignities" of a "human group" provides editors with an open-ended license to suppress any research that is inconsistent with their ideological commitments.

It is important to emphasize that this editorial policy authorizes the suppression of well-designed research with empirically supported claims. Academic journals have always had the policy of rejecting works exhibiting sloppy research or unsupported conclusions (although, as Chapter

1 indicates, some journals publish gibberish). So, the only reason for this new policy is to provide a basis for rejecting valid research. The editors are openly taking the position that sound science must be subordinated to ideology.

The editors attempt to obscure the significance of their policy by claiming they will utilize the policy "cautiously and judiciously, consulting with ethics experts and advocacy groups."[127] This is not reassuring. Who is an ethics expert? The aforementioned Harald Schmidt, who thinks white lives must be sacrificed to "level the playing field"? Which advocacy groups are authorities on social science? Black Lives Matter? Advocacy groups by definition are pursuing a specific agenda, so all the editors' caution amounts to is an admission that they will require scientific research to defer to prevailing political norms. The same could be said for research done in any totalitarian regime.

Although *Nature Human Behavior* may be the first academic journal to expressly adopt a policy censoring valid research on the ground that it may undermine the "dignities" of a "human group," various academic bodies and professional groups have implemented similar policies rejecting or disfavoring research or presentations that do not conform to prevailing notions of social justice. For example, the Society for Personality and Social Psychology, a large and influential professional association, has adopted a policy requiring those wishing to present at their annual meeting to explain how their presentation advances the "equity and antiracism goals" of the organization.[128] The ideal of academic researchers devoted to seeking the truth, whatever its implications, has given way to the demand that academics become advocates for the prevailing ideology.

As indicated, the suppression via intimidation of those with views contrary to the ideology of identity politics has been taking place for some time now. But the brazen trumpeting of official policies of censorship marks a significant and ominous step. Just as organizations now feel free to be candid about race-based preferences, so too do academics now openly embrace and promote dogma over evidence. Ideologues are not just blind to facts; they want to blunt everyone else's vision.

The Ethics of Equity and Transgender Athletes

This willful obscuring of facts features prominently in the next and final topic in this chapter, which deals with issues arising out of the phenomenon of transgender men and women, a phenomenon largely unknown until the mid-twentieth century and one that gained widespread public attention only in the twenty-first century, when the pace of people transitioning skyrocketed. "Equity" is used in a somewhat different sense in discussions about policies relating to trans men and women because, given the relatively low numbers of trans men and women, statistical disparities do not form a key part of the discussion (except with respect to suicide rates, discussed below). Nonetheless, the thread that connects claims about equity regarding transgender individuals with claims about equity regarding other groups is the decisive weight given to group identity. As will become apparent, this commitment to identity politics results in the failure to address and resolve properly conflicts between transgender individuals and others. Such conflicts should be adjudicated through empirically grounded, individualized assessment, but instead, the identity Left dismisses these conflicts by the expedient of denying objective reality.

Among other controversies regarding the policies and practices that should be adopted with respect to transgender persons are disputes about pronoun usage, bathroom access, housing of prisoners, consequential alterations to the bodies of minors with drugs or surgery, and participation of transgender athletes in athletic competitions. As indicated by the section heading, our discussion will focus mostly on this last-named dispute.

Objective factual analysis is critical for all these controversies, but let us use an ethical principle as a starting point. This approach will clarify matters and take some issues off the table. If, in accordance with liberal tradition, we respect autonomy, then there is a strong presumption that adults should be free to structure their lives and bodies as they see fit and pursue whatever activities they deem appropriate, provided this causes no harm to others. This presumption is not irrebuttable, and for those who demand limb amputations on the grounds that they suffer from "bodily integrity identity disorder," perhaps the presumption may not hold.[129] But gender transitioning adults are not anywhere near as seriously self-disabling as those who desire to be legless or armless. So, sure, if an adult biological male wants to be considered a woman or an adult biological female wants to be considered a man and they take whatever steps they think appropriate to "transition," our default attitude should be one of benign indifference. Except in certain contexts, their decision does not materially affect us.[130] Furthermore, because, unfortunately, not everyone shares this ethical outlook, transgender individuals have been and continue to be victims of discrimination, so legal protections against discrimination in employment, housing, and public accommodations are warranted.

The foregoing comments dispose of a substantial portion of the potential controversies surrounding transgender individuals. One would think that recognizing the right of adults to transition and agreeing that legal protections are appropriate would insulate one from being called "transphobic." Not in today's environment. Other controversies remain, and unless one adheres without deviation to the prevailing orthodoxy, one stands condemned as a transphobe. Herewith is my quick take on four such controversies, followed by a longer discussion of athletics, which is the controversy most revealing of the dogmatism of identity group ideology.

Pronouns

Just as there is a presumption that adults should be free to structure their lives and bodies as they see fit, there is a presumption that we should address and refer to people as they like. Using someone's preferred pronoun does not imply approval of them or their lifestyle choices; it is merely polite behavior. So, if a transgender woman wants to be referred to as "she," go ahead. No concession is being made any more than one concedes an ignoble judge is honorable by addressing the judge as "Your Honor."

That said, the proliferation of pronouns has reached the point of absurdity, with schoolchildren now being encouraged to choose just about any word they want as a pronoun, including "tree."[131] Even the more widely used ones, such as "ze," "co," "en," "ey," require charts to navigate.[132] Some standardization is called for lest pronouns lose their utility. Pronoun usage naturally evolved in almost all languages because pronouns avoid the cumbersome repetition of names and enable an identifying reference to individuals when no name is known. The statement "The person who stole my wallet—he went that way" indicates that a male-appearing person is the thief we should look for, whereas "ze" or "co" does not provide much identifying assistance and "tree" only induces bewilderment. It implies no disrespect to persons to limit nominative case pronouns to three choices: he, she, and they (for non-binary).

Bathroom Access

Regarding bathroom access, I do not see this as presenting a substantial question in most contexts. Those identifying as a woman can use the bathroom for women or a gender-neutral bathroom, and a similar protocol can apply for those who identify as a man. Yes, this means transgender women who have not had genital-altering surgery will be using the same facilities as biological women, but stalls provide privacy, and, in any event, catching a glimpse of an inadvertently displayed flaccid penis does not seem likely to cause trauma. The only possibly significant issue is the safety issue: a trans woman assaulting a woman in the bathroom for women. To date, this has not been a significant problem, with, to my knowledge, only one putative case—and this is of doubtful relevance.[133] Policy can be reevaluated if assaults multiply.

Housing of Prisoners

Once we turn to the housing of convicts, matters become more serious and nuanced. The primary consideration for housing should be the safety of inmates. After all, this is the primary reason why we have separate facilities for male and female prisoners. The best approach is an individualized approach, meaning prison officials should determine where housing the prisoner would be the safest option for both the prisoner and the other inmates. A transgender woman with a history of violent offenses against women should not be placed in a facility for women. On the other hand, a trans woman who is a nonviolent offender may have a high risk of being raped or assaulted if placed in a facility for men. The Obama administration recommended such an individualized approach, but unfortunately, both the Left and the Right have propagated demands for blanket approaches.[134] Granted, blanket approaches would provide ease of administration, but the safety of prisoners requires careful, individualized consideration.

Medical Treatment for Minors

If we believe gender dysphoria, that is, distress over a felt incongruence between one's sense of identity and one's biological sex, is traceable to a treatable mental disorder, and if we believe this condition can be reliably diagnosed, and if we believe treatment beyond counseling, such as puberty blockers or surgery, can reliably treat this disorder, and if we believe minors can provide informed consent to such life-altering treatment, then medical gender treatment of minors may be warranted. (I intentionally refrain from using the term "gender-affirming" treatment; this is question-begging.) However, it is not clear whether any of the last three conditions is satisfied, and the first is not free from doubt either.

Unless one believes in immaterial souls or minds, we are physical beings. Labeling a disorder as "mental" is an indirect way of saying we do not really understand it very well. Yes, the psychiatrists who compile the Diagnostic and Statistical Manual of Mental Disorders have concluded that gender dysphoria is a mental disorder.[135] Their predecessors previously assured us that homosexuality was a mental disorder, and the history of psychiatrists' conclusions about mental diseases and disorders is rife with conclusions driven by cultural or ideological assumptions. Some caution with respect to gender dysphoria is warranted.

Moreover, the process for diagnosing a child with gender dysphoria too often begins with a parent noticing what the parent considers gender non-conforming behavior, effectively resulting in a person's stereotypes about male and female behavior as the initial basis for medical consultation. Reliance on such stereotypes runs counter to the modern view that there is no essentially male or female behavior. A boy's expression of interest in dolls does not imply a desire to switch genders. (What is a G. I. Joe "action figure" but a doll with a rifle?) It is especially concerning that parental judgments are sometimes made when the child is very young—three or four years old.[136]

Proponents hail medical treatment for gender dysphoria as not only effective in reducing distress but also lifesaving; opponents question its efficacy and, when the treatment is given to minors, condemn it as child abuse. To date, a solid majority of those adults and adolescents who have undergone treatment, whether puberty blockers, cross-sex hormones, or surgery, appear content with the results, but an increasing number of individuals who have undergone medical treatment have detransitioned, with some firmly contending they never should have transitioned in the first place.[137] One problem with assessing the effectiveness of medical treatment of adolescents is that such treatment has become generally accepted only within the last decade and regret over a transition may take several years to manifest. Regarding the alleged "lifesaving" character of medical gender treatment, there are divided opinions. Interestingly, there is "some evidence that testosterone reduces distress and suicidality in females," but there is also "evidence that estrogen increases suicidality in males and that puberty blockers offer no benefit."[138]

The emphasis on the alleged lifesaving value of medical treatment is motivated by the much higher rate of suicidal ideation and depression among adolescents with gender dysphoria.[139] But it is not clear whether these mental health issues are always caused by untreated gender dysphoria or are simply co-occurring mental health problems. In any event, the existence of mental health problems among many of the adolescents who seek medical treatment compounds the problem of assessing a minor's capacity to give informed consent to treatments that can have lifelong consequences. We consider juveniles to have reduced capacity for decision-making in most areas; this is the rationale, for example, for treating them differently within the criminal justice system. The age of consent for sexual activity ranges from sixteen to eighteen in the United States. It seems incongruous to allow fourteen-year-olds to decide to undergo treatment that will have permanent consequences, including consequences to their sexual expression, while also maintaining that these minors cannot legally consent to a single sexual act. A final complicating factor is the unexplained exponential rise in the number of children and adolescents declaring they are transgender. Although only 7.6 percent of the U.S. population is between 13 and 17, this age group now makes up a stunning 18 percent of transgender persons.[140] Many schools have been inundated with books and other teaching materials which discount the significance of biological sex and counsel that how one feels is what one is.[141] As a character says in one popular book: "I don't *feel* like a boy. I *am* a boy."[142] Although these materials may have the worthy purpose of promoting acceptance of transgender persons, they may also persuade children who do not conform to gender stereotypes that they must be transgender. Children and adolescents are notoriously susceptible to suggestion.

The foregoing does not necessarily imply that states should ban body-altering treatment of minors for gender dysphoria. It does indicate that more caution is called for. Ideally, this issue would be studied by a neutral commission—one which does not include practitioners who are invested in medical treatment or right-wing ideologues who are adamantly opposed to treatment under any circumstance. Sadly, the prospects of convening any such commission are dim. The battle lines are drawn, and that is even more readily apparent on the issue of transgender athletes.

Transgender Athletes

Women have participated in games and sports for pleasure for millennia, but it is fair to say that organized athletic competitions for women were rare until modern times, due in part to stereotypes regarding appropriate conduct for women.[143] Even after organized competitions were started (women first participated in the Olympics in 1900), athletic opportunities for women were limited. The situation has improved in recent decades, although true parity still has not been achieved.

In any event, women's sports have almost always been women's sports—that is, they have been sex-segregated. The principal reason for separate women's and men's competitions is that women would not have equitable opportunities to participate in sports were all sports unified, e.g., if there were just the National Basketball Association and not the National Basketball Association (NBA) and the Women's National Basketball Association (WNBA). No doubt the players in the WNBA are very talented and could outperform most men, but they could not outperform the professional athletes in the NBA. So, were there no separate league for women, most of them would have no professional career. This difference in relative abilities is reflected at every level of athletic competition, from secondary school onward.

The reason for this difference is biology. There are several biological differences between men and women, which become most obvious following puberty and its cascade of hormones. Men, on average, develop broader shoulders and larger hands and feet, more upper body muscles, more fast twitch muscles, lower body fat, greater height, and so on. The key hormone is testosterone. Men have more testosterone, on average, than women. Testosterone provides a significant advantage in most athletic competitions, as indicated by, among other things, the fact that doping with testosterone and its synthetic analogs is banned by almost all athletic associations.[144] Given these biological differences, there is, understandably, an athletic performance gap between men and women.

The relevance of these biological facts was accepted by nearly everyone until the advent of transgender athletes, in particular transgender women. Then for some proponents of equity, ideology took precedence over biological reality.

Trans women who have gone through puberty as males tend to have the same athletic advantages that men have over women. Not unexpectedly, when trans women athletes compete with biological women, they often come out on top.[145] The case of Lia Thomas, a competitive swimmer at the college level, perhaps best illustrates the advantages that some trans women will have. Ms. Thomas, when competing as a man, was a good collegiate swimmer, but not great. She ranked 462nd in the United States as a man. When she switched over to competing against women, she won a collegiate championship, breaking records in the process.[146]

Cases like Thomas's have sparked a heated debate over whether trans women should be permitted to compete with women. Partisans on both sides of this debate are prone to exaggeration when arguing for their respective positions. Those who favor banning trans women have claimed that failure to do would effectively mean the end of women's sports. Hardly. Only about a couple dozen trans women have competed at the collegiate level in the past decade.[147] Women's sports can survive.

On the other hand, those who argue that trans women must be included typically play the suicide card; they use the scare tactic of claiming exclusion would push trans athletes into deep depression or even suicide. "Offering inclusion to some of our most vulnerable young people who are at great risk for depression, drug abuse, and suicide, ought to be the mission of every educator and every other thinking and loving human being."[148] A skeptic might point out that if someone is mature enough to decide to transition, that person should be mature enough to understand the competitive advantages that may accrue to her and how those without the same biological advantages may justifiably feel cheated of opportunities. And why are we to be concerned about the mental health of the transgender only? How about the depression induced in a woman who has trained for years for competition only to be bested by a person who was considered a mediocre athlete before she switched genders?

Reality is messier than the extreme positions staked out by partisans. No, women's sports will not collapse, but there are only so many positions on the track team and, for many competitions, only one person can win an event. It is no answer to the grievances of female athletes beaten out by a trans athlete to say there is no guarantee they would have won or made the team in the absence of transgender competitors. They would maintain they had legitimate expectations that they would be competing against women with substantially similar hormonal histories. If a bunch of middle schoolers trying out for soccer were informed a couple of eighteen-year-olds would also be competing against them for spots on the team, one could not dismiss their complaints with a hand wave and the observation that not all of them would have made the team anyway.

But it is also understandable why transgender women want to participate in women's events. It is an important part of their identity. Moreover, banning them from women's sports effectively means they would be required to give up competitive sports, in many cases after devoting years to their sport.

So, what is the answer? There may not be one right answer. Arguably each sport, at the national or international level, should establish its own guidelines. For example, the governing body of a sport might use a presumption that trans women can compete after X number of years of hormone therapy, with rights of appeal by any affected party. Individualized assessment is more likely to result in fair competition than blanket rules. But I am less concerned here with providing a solution to this knotty problem than in pointing out how identity group ideology results in denial of facts.

"Trans women are women. Period." This is the battle cry of the ideologues. And the message is clear: no debate allowed. If one questions the right of trans women to compete in women's sports, one is transphobic. Can't be any other explanation. And the distinct biological development of men and women? Not relevant. Greatly exaggerated. One of the bizarre aspects of the ideologues' position is that the very same people who deny that testosterone has any meaningful effect on one's competitive ability are also the ones who argue that hormone therapy is essential for those with gender dysphoria. For one issue, hormones might as well be water, but for the other issue, hormones are a critical component of transitioning. Only dogma can magically transform a substance from inert to potent.

Of course, those who adhere to dogma must divert attention from relevant facts if they have any hope of persuading others. The ACLU, once a stalwart defender of free speech and other fundamental freedoms, is now a prisoner of identity group ideology, requiring it to put forward inane arguments, claiming that any difference in athletic abilities between biological males and females is illusory, supported only by "myths."[149] The ACLU's arguments against these alleged "myths" consist of a series of falsehoods, fallacies, and irrelevancies. The ACLU claims no women are harmed by the inclusion of transgender athletes. This is news to all the female athletes who have protested or sued over inclusion of trans women in athletic competitions.[150] The ACLU also states exclusion of trans athletes will reinforce stereotypes about women being weak. Absurd. No one thinks women athletes are weak, and no doubt many women athletes could out-compete men in many sports. But at each level of competition—high school, college, professional sports—the average woman athlete will be at a disadvantage compared to the average male athlete. Otherwise, why do we even have separate women's sports? The ACLU, summoning its mind-reading powers, then segues into the farcical argument that the dispute over trans women athletes is really based on a nefarious desire to "exclud[e] trans people from yet another public space." An assertion of this kind is a standard tactic of those who have no real argument: ascribe sordid motives to your opponent. The ACLU continues by stating that trans women cannot have any advantage in sports because they are harassed in school. This is an obvious non sequitur. It is highly regrettable whenever trans women are harassed, and steps should be taken to prevent such harassment, but that has nothing to do with their athletic abilities.

There is no need to run through all of the ACLU's claims. Not one of them deals with the key issue: is it true or not that male hormones tend to provide men with physical characteristics different from those of women that can be advantageous in many sports? The answer to this question is obvious; the ACLU pretends not to see it.

Conclusion on Equity and on Left-Wing Dogmas

The ACLU's adamant refusal to acknowledge biological reality is a consequence of their commitment to identity group ideology. For them, as for other ideologues, this commitment to dogma determines what counts as a fact. We have seen this willful refusal to acknowledge reality already, for example, in the failure of educators to acknowledge the possibility that some minority students may be unprepared for college and in the refusal of academic journals to publish research that contradicts prevailing dogmas, and in the failure of proponents of systemic racism to acknowledge that family composition has a role in sustaining the wealth gap between blacks and whites, and in the failure by adherents of standpoint theory to recognize that there is an objective reality for all individuals, no matter what their identity group. What unites the various dogmas examined in the first part of this book is the notion that group identity is paramount. Group identity determines what we can know, if anything. My "truth" is different than your "truth." Policies supposedly based on group identity explain the various disparities between blacks and whites; the aggregate decisions made by individuals have nothing to do with these disparities. Equity can be achieved only by eliminating disparities between and among all identity groups, whatever the cost to individual rights. And any factual evidence that undercuts these claims is dismissed if it is even acknowledged.

The identity group ideology that now grips much of the Left, and, indeed, many of the key institutions of the United States, threatens to nullify the Enlightenment principles that have provided the basis for the progress humanity has accomplished in the last couple of centuries. Fundamental to liberal democracy are protections for individual rights, a robust culture of free speech, the recognition that no group can claim special authority, and political association premised on shared interests, not identities. Just as Marxism once aimed to replace liberal democracy with a society born of class consciousness, identity group ideologues now aim to replace liberal democracy with a society born of caste consciousness.

But there is yet another detrimental consequence of identity group politics, and that is its reinvigoration of extremes on the Right. It is to an examination of dogmas on the Right that we now turn.

CHAPTER 4

Christian Nationalism: Imposing a Religious Identity on the United States

The Left is not alone in its focus on identity. The Right has its own versions of identity politics. The most prominent form of it relates to the identity of a nation as opposed to any racial or ethnic group.

Christian nationalism maintains the United States is a Christian nation, not in the sense that most Americans are Christians—a claim that grows increasingly more tenuous—but in the sense that the United States was founded on biblical precepts and the Founders intended the nation to remain faithful to these precepts. Continued adherence to these precepts is central to the nation's identity. Christian nationalists strive through their actions, political and otherwise, to align American culture and laws with what they perceive as the correct Christian viewpoint. Although there are differences among Christian nationalists regarding which political tactics and what specific laws would best restore the United States to its true Christian character, there is a rough consensus that abortion, same-sex marriage, and pornography should be banned and teacher-led prayer and Bible readings in public schools should not only be permitted but required. Recognizing that not all Americans share these views, Christian nationalists use their historical claims to lend legitimacy to their political agenda. According to them, they are not trying to impose alien norms on the American people; instead, they seek to reinstate the norms that are consistent with America's original Christian character. Christian nationalism is, thus, a blend of a historical thesis and a politico-religious commitment, with this commitment based in large measure on the historical thesis.

The foregoing sets forth the central beliefs of Christian nationalists. Apart from these core tenets, Christian nationalists diverge in some of their theological beliefs, and in some cases, these differences may affect the precise wording they use to describe the religious nature of the United States and its founding. For example, some Christian nationalists refer to "Judeo-Christian" principles as providing the foundational structure for the United States.[1] This phrasing may be simply a diplomatic nod to Judaism, though, as invariably the emphasis is on alleged Christian principles. In any event, some Christian nationalists strenuously object to use of the term "Judeo-Christian" to describe the nation's founding principles, arguing, not unreasonably, that Christianity and Judaism are "distinct, incompatible, and irreconcilable religions" and, less reasonably, that "Christianity alone is the true biblical religion."[2] Similarly, some Christian nationalists believe that the United States is especially favored by God (at least as long as it adheres to biblical precepts) and has been entrusted with carrying out some divine mission. This is a view commonly referred to as American exceptionalism, although, of course, secular forms of American exceptionalism also exist. Meanwhile, other Christian nationalists expressly disavow American exceptionalism, rejecting the claim that the United States is uniquely favored by God. On this view, the Founders freely chose to align the country with God's will for all nations and any beneficence that God aims America's way is earned—and can be lost.[3]

In addition, there are differences among Christian nationalists with respect to how they view the "end times" and the eventual return of Jesus Christ. A significant number of Christian nationalists are premillennial dispensationalists—that is, they believe that after a period of tribulation, Jesus Christ will return to defeat the Antichrist and rule the earth, bringing about an era of peace and harmony (the "millennium"), but not all Christian nationalists share this belief.[4] Some, but far from all, Christian nationalists subscribe to "Dominionism," the view that, prior to the return of Jesus Christ, Christians have a divine mandate to reshape American culture and law to reflect Christian values, and that the means for doing this is to seize control of the "seven mountains" of family, religion, education, media, entertainment, business, and government.[5]

These internal differences need not concern us; the key point is that all Christian nationalists claim that the Founders established the United States as a Christian nation and that, to remain true to the Founders' intent, the laws and culture of the United States should continue to reflect Christian precepts (meaning the Christian nationalists' understanding of Christian precepts).

The historical claims of Christian nationalism are properly classified as dogmas, as they are held tenaciously despite the paucity of supporting evidence. As will be shown, the Founders deliberately rejected the model of a confessional state. The foundational document of the United States, the Constitution, is a secular document establishing a secular government.

Were Christian nationalists some obscure, small sect, any analysis of their claims would be unnecessary and inconsequential. However, Christian nationalists form an important part of the MAGA coalition. They do not constitute a majority of the coalition, but they are a vocal, motivated element, and Republicans could not hope to win office in many areas of the country without their support. Estimates of their numbers vary, but they probably constitute around a quarter of current Republican voters;[6] furthermore, they are loyal supporters of those candidates they perceive to be sympathetic to their views. In fact, surveys indicate that those who endorse the cardinal beliefs associated with Christian nationalism (e.g., the federal government should advocate Christian values, the federal government should allow teacher-led prayer in public schools) were the most likely supporters of Donald Trump, in both 2016 and 2020.[7] Moreover, although open Christian nationalists are not anywhere near a majority of Republican politicians, many adopt the rhetoric of Christian nationalists and some Republican office-holders and candidates for office explicitly identify as Christian nationalists.[8] Even Trump himself, not a person noted for piety in his pre-presidential years, has donned the mantle of a defender of the faith and has stated that the United States has an essentially religious identity, although he has stopped short of asserting an expressly Christian identity.[9] Whether Trump's late-in-life religiosity is sincere or calculated is irrelevant. The point is he recognizes he can tap into an important source of support by endorsing claims dear to the heart of Christian nationalists.

In fact, the catchphrase for the Trump political movement, "Make

America Great Again," captures nicely the mindset and ambitions of Christian nationalists. They seek what they contend is a restoration of America's Christian orientation and values—a return to a past where America was great precisely because it embodied Christian precepts. They maintain that "secular humanists" or "socialists" or "liberals" have maneuvered the nation away from its Christian foundations, relentlessly forcing changes in laws and policies that have led to the nation's decline. Only a return to the nation's Christian roots, they argue, can arrest and reverse this decline. A call to reclaim past glory is a common feature of reactionary movements, but the curious thing about the Christian nationalist movement is that, as we will see, they seek a return to a past that is simply a product of their imagination.

In arguing against the dogmas underlying Christian nationalism, I am going to focus exclusively on historical claims. In other words, I am not going to argue that the core doctrines of Christianity itself are false. That debate would take us too far afield and is not necessary to refute Christian nationalism. Likewise, I am not going to argue against the political positions of the Christian nationalists, however ill-advised or repugnant they may be. Again, that exercise would take us off topic, which is the dogmatism of their historical claims.

With respect to the historical claims, we can divide them into three analytically distinct components: 1. All or almost all the Founders were devout Christians; 2. The Founders intended to establish the United States as a Christian nation, as shown by the founding documents; 3. The structure of the American government embodies Christian precepts.

Although these are analytically distinct claims, Christian national-ists often conflate them. For example, they devote an inordinate amount of attention to the religious beliefs of the Founders and then use their claims about these beliefs as supposed proof of the Founders' intent to establish a Christian nation. But as a matter both of logic and historical fact, a person can be devoutly religious and still believe that the govern-ment should be secular. Indeed, it is tempting not to discuss the Found-ers' religious beliefs at all on the ground that their beliefs are not relevant to the central issue of whether the United States is foundationally a Christian nation, but not addressing that topic could be interpreted as trying to avoid what some maintain, albeit mistakenly, is key evidence for the Christian nation thesis. So, reluctantly, I will address this issue.

The Founders' Religious Beliefs

One term that merits clarification at the outset is "Founder." There are several plausible ways to determine who belongs to the class of Founders. Certainly, the thirty-nine individuals who participated in the Constitutional Convention and approved the draft of the Constitution should be included. But what of the sixteen individuals who attended the Constitutional Convention but refused to sign the draft? How about all those who attended the state ratifying conventions, or at least those who voted to approve the Constitution? And how do we deal with those who participated in the debates in Congress and the states over the Constitution's first ten amendments, what we now know as the Bill of Rights? Depending on how one defines the class of "Founders," the term could refer to a few dozen or to more than a thousand individuals.

Although this is an interesting question, I submit that precise boundaries are not required. All we need are some reasonable limits. For example, a class of no less than those who approved the draft of the Constitution and no more than all those who participated in an official capacity in the debates over the Constitution, including the Bill of Rights, or were invited to provide advice to those who participated in such debates, would be a reasonable class. Such a flexible definition cannot be criticized as designed to support predetermined conclusions. However, it does exclude ridiculously expansive outcomes. For example, not everyone who picked up a musket to fight for independence is a "Founder." One reason a flexible definition is sufficient is that at the end of the day, it is the text of the Constitution and the Bill of Rights that should be our primary guide regarding the secular or religious character of the United States, not the personal beliefs of any Founder. As Christian nationalists should appreciate, the Founders' purpose is best known through their fruits. (See Matt. 7: 15–20.)

One position regarding membership in the class of Founders that should be taken, but rarely is taken, is that being a signatory to the Declaration of Independence does not by itself make one a Founder. The Declaration is not a founding document; it did not give shape to the government of the United States. It severed a connection with Great Britain; it did not organize a nation. Reading the Declaration makes its limited purpose clear. It largely consists of an exposition of the reasons why the united colonies decided to break with Great Britain. As the preface states, the Declaration provides this explanation because a "decent respect to the opinions of mankind requires that they [the united colonies] should declare the causes which impel them to the separation."[10] Granted, some of the political principles alluded to in the Declaration obviously informed the structure of the federal government subsequently established by the Constitution. The United States is a representative democracy in which the government derives its authority from the "consent of the governed." But it was the Constitution, not the Declaration, that integrated this principle into America's governmental structure. The primary reason Christian nationalists tout the Declaration as a foundational document is that they read the Declaration's reference to a "Creator" as evidence that the nation is founded on Christian principles. This reference cannot carry the weight the Christian nationalists place upon it, for the reasons discussed below.

But let us return to the subject of the Founders' religious beliefs. One of the favorite tactics of authors who promote the Christian nationalist viewpoint is to list quotations containing religious references from putative Founders and then infer from these quotations that the Founders intended to establish a Christian nation. David Barton, who has created a book publishing empire largely based on this tactic, is perhaps the best-known practitioner of this maneuver, but there are several others.[11] Obligingly, the organization Barton founded, Wallbuilders, has a website where one can peruse some of the quotations that Barton maintains show the Founders were staunchly Christian. Interestingly, many of these quotations come from wills, the type of document where one might expect believers to make a reference to God. For example, one quotation featured on the website reads as follows: "In the name of God, Amen. I, Daniel of St. Thomas Jenifer . . . of disposing mind and memory, commend my soul to my blessed Redeemer."[12] (St. Thomas Jenifer was a Maryland delegate to the Constitutional Convention.) What this quotation shows other than that St. Thomas Jenifer's thoughts turned to God as he contemplated death is unclear.

This battery of quotations, and similar ones, aim at a non-existing target. Barton argues that his quotations provide "abundant evidence to refute any notion that the Founding Fathers were atheists, agnostics, or deists."[13] But no reputable historian claims that the Founders were atheists or agnostics. No one denies that most of the Founders were religious in the sense that they believed in a personal God; many were also Christian. These quotations show nothing about the intent of the Founders to base the nation on Christian principles. In fact, by omission, these lists of quotations manifest the weakness of the argument that the Founders intended to establish a Christian nation. Glaringly absent from all these compilations is any express statement from a Founder that they intended to establish a Christian nation. Why the silence on this critical point if that was their overriding purpose? Evidence that many Founders were Christian does little, if anything, to advance the Christian nation thesis.

Furthermore, one must be cautious with using the label "Christian" in referring to the Founders for a couple of reasons. First, although it is true that many late eighteenth-century Americans used this term to describe themselves, the term "Christian" was often secondary to a more specific designation of a person's religious affiliations. Denominational differences among Protestant Christians were more significant at that time than they are today. It is important to bear in mind that many who flocked to the colonies were dissenters from the Church of England; moreover, they were dissenters because of very specific objections to the rituals and doctrines of the Church of England. They may have considered themselves Christian, but their primary identification was as a Baptist, a Congregationalist, a Presbyterian, or a Friend (Quaker). And, of course, there were those in the colonies who belonged to the Church of England, which, after independence, became the Episcopal Church. Disputes among these sects were common and impassioned.[14] Thus, it is anachronistic to blend all these various denominations together under the label of "Christians." The deep denominational differences that existed in the late eighteenth century by themselves cast significant doubt on the claim that the Founders intended to establish a "Christian" nation. Exactly whose understanding of Christianity was being established?

In addition, just as today there are people who are culturally Christian or Jewish or Muslim without necessarily accepting the doctrines of these religions, likewise, some Founders attended church, celebrated Christian holidays, or perhaps engaged in some religious rituals, such as prayer, without accepting key Christian doctrines, such as the divinity of Christ, original sin, or the redemptive quality of Jesus' death. In fact, influenced by the Enlightenment, many Founders were rationalist in their approach to religion—that is, they rejected revelation as a guide to religious truth, which, of course, meant they did not rely uncritically on the Bible. "The Founders thought that people should be free to seek religious truth guided only by reason and the dictates of their consciences ... [This] did not make the Founders irreligious, nor did it make most of them anti-Christian. But the new ideas caused them to question much of orthodox Christianity."[15]

This rationalism existed on a spectrum, which is one reason disputes persist about whether a given Founder was a Christian or a deist. Some of these disputes are verbal in nature, meaning they turn on how one defines "Christian" and "deist." If to be a "deist" one must reject all religious ritual and view the deity as nothing more than the proverbial first cause of the universe, then few if any of the Founders were deists. However, if a "deist" is someone who limits his religious beliefs to what can be established by reason, rejects miracles and revelation, and participates in religious rituals as a matter of custom and not out of a sense of worshipful devotion, then more than a few Founders, including some of the more prominent Founders, such as Washington, Franklin, and Jefferson, were deists.[16] They believed in a God, but not the Redeemer God of Christianity. Furthermore, they looked askance at religious fervor. In the words of one historian, they considered themselves "free of the prejudices, parochialism, and religious enthusiasm of the vulgar and barbaric."[17] It is highly unlikely that influential individuals such as these, who regarded orthodox Christianity as just a step removed from superstition, would have countenanced turning the nation they had struggled to establish into a Christian bastion.

Some Christian nationalists have attempted to argue that Washington and Franklin were not deists (Jefferson is usually conceded), but their arguments range from meritless to frivolous, often relying on expansive definitions of "Christian" or unsupported inferences. Yes, Washington occasionally attended church services, but so do many skeptics even today. Richard Dawkins, perhaps the most prominent contemporary atheist, sings Christmas carols.[18] Being culturally Christian does not an orthodox Christian make. With respect to documentary evidence, the Wallbuilders website features a letter from Franklin to Thomas Paine in which Franklin urges Paine not to publish the manuscript that was to become Paine's notorious *Age of Reason*, the quintessential deist work of its time. The inference Wallbuilders apparently wants readers to draw is that Franklin objected to Paine's deism. But actually the letter indicates that Franklin had no disagreement with Paine's views regarding the nature of God. Instead, Franklin questioned the wisdom of publishing the work because of the effect it might have on "weak and ignorant men and women . . . who have need of the motives of religion to restrain them from vice."[19] Here Franklin was expressing the view, common among the educated elite of the time, and still mistakenly held by some today, that the uneducated need the threat of divine punishment and the promise of divine reward to motivate them to act virtuously. The conduct of non-religious people the world over, more numerous today than they were in Franklin's time, proves Franklin wrong, but this point need not be debated. What is clear is that this letter casts no doubt on Franklin's own rejection of the Christian God.

I deliberately left Madison out of the list of rationalists/deists even though some historians include him in that group. Coming to a firm conclusion about Madison's religious beliefs is difficult because he was reticent about disclosing them. That said, some of his early writings, including his letters, indicate he subscribed to some of the tenets of orthodox Christianity. But, if anything, Madison's arguable status as a devout Episcopalian weighs heavily against the Christian nation thesis. There was no stronger advocate for the total separation of church and state than Madison.

Madison, along with Jefferson, was instrumental in securing religious freedom for Virginians. Their collaboration began in 1779 when Jefferson, then governor, introduced a bill which provided, among other things, that all persons would be free to express their opinions on religious matters, no one could be compelled to support, through taxation or otherwise, religious bodies, and no one's civil rights could be diminished or enlarged as a result of their religious views. The bill did not pass at first; in fact, it took seven years before it was enacted, and Madison was the primary legislator responsible for ensuring its eventual passage. (Jefferson was in France from 1785 through most of 1789.) As one historian has noted, although "Jefferson is almost entirely responsible for . . . composition [of the Virginia Statute for Religious Freedom], James Madison was the most potent force in securing its adoption."[20]

What eventually pushed support for the Statute for Religious Freedom over the top was a bruising battle over proposed legislation, sponsored by Patrick Henry, which would have imposed taxes for the purpose of supporting Christian clergy. To minimize opposition to the measure, Henry's bill provided support for all Christian denominations, with proceeds from the taxes even going to support costs of worship for Quakers and Mennonites, denominations that had no clergy. In 1784, the House of Delegates approved the bill in principle, and it was submitted to committee for final drafting. At that time, Madison began in earnest to organize opposition to the bill.[21] Among his efforts was the anonymous writing of a petition entitled "A Memorial and Remonstrance Against Religious Assessments," which was then circulated among Virginians. This petition is worth reading in its entirety as it is an eloquent and robust defense of the freedom of conscience and of the necessity of the strict separation of church and state. To summarize its essence, though, the petition argued that government had no competence in matters of religion, history showed religious interference in government matters always had harmful consequences, and freedom of conscience was a natural right and inviolable. The petition galvanized opposition to the assessment measure, and proponents of the assessment allowed the measure to die.[22]

In addition, with the legislators now focused on the issue of religious freedom, and with the tide of opinion running his way, Madison reintroduced Jefferson's bill for religious liberty. His sense of timing proved accurate. In 1786, the legislature approved the bill and the Virginia Statute for Religious Freedom became the first major piece of legislation in the world to protect freedom of conscience with respect to any religious viewpoint. This legislation was enormously influential, helping to persuade many of the necessity of keeping government out of religion and vice-versa. As one scholar noted, "[O]wing to the political leadership of Virginia at this formative period in our history, and the high standing of her statesmen in the Federal Constitutional Convention, the document had a very great influence on establishing religious freedom in this country."[23]

Madison, of course, was a key player at the Constitutional Convention and was the representative in the First Congress who introduced the amendments that were to become the Bill of Rights. His role in both cases, which will be discussed further below, strengthen the argument that being a Christian does not in any way imply support for a government based on Christian precepts or religious precepts in general. But Madison's conduct in the battle over religious assessments and in the struggle to pass the Statute for Religious Freedom by itself removes any doubt that a Christian can support strict separation of church and state.

So, to summarize the argument on the Founders' religious beliefs: no one disputes that almost all the Founders believed in some version of God and that many Founders were Christian, but there is no explicit statement from any of the Founders that they intended to establish a Christian nation, which is inexplicable if the Founders were committed to that goal. Moreover, more than a few Founders, including several influential ones, did not accept Christian doctrine, which is a further reason to conclude that their support for a Christian nation is highly unlikely. Finally, the case of Madison, arguably a Christian, shows that Christians could be and were stalwart supporters of church-state separation. The religious beliefs of the Founders, by themselves, do not in any way lend support to the claim that they intended to establish a religious state.

The Founders' Intent as Shown by the Nation's Founding Documents

In truth, the above subchapter heading should refer to the nation's founding "document," because there is only one document that provides the structure for the government of the United States, and that is the Constitution. But Christian nationalists would accuse me of begging the question were I to take that approach. As discussed below, Christian nationalists typically rely most heavily on the Declaration of Independence and a slew of documents from the colonial era—that is, documents dating to a time before there was a United States.

Curiously, the one other document that arguably could be said to be another founding document is usually ignored by Christian nationalists, namely the Articles of Confederation. The Continental Congress adopted these articles in November 1777 and their provisions went into effect on March 1, 1781, and they stayed in effect until March 9, 1789, at which time they were superseded by the Constitution. This was the first official document to proclaim that the name of the new nation would be "The United States of America," and it was through the Articles that the states became one nation.[24] Perhaps one reason the Articles often escape mention is that the government they established is recognized as a failure: Congress had no power to tax or to regulate interstate commerce; there was no executive branch; there was no proportional representation in Congress, with each state having one vote. These deficiencies, of course, explain why within a few years there was a movement to supplant the Articles.

Another reason, though, why Christian nationalists do not focus on the Articles is that their wording does not provide support for the claim that the United States is a Christian nation. There is no statement to that effect in the Articles, nor do the Articles cite any biblical precepts as a basis for any of its provisions. That said, there is a passing reference to a deity in the closing paragraph, which begins with this valedictory statement: "And whereas it hath pleased the Great Governor of the World to incline the hearts of the legislatures we respectively represent in congress, to approve of, and to authorize us to ratify the said articles of confederation and perpetual union . . . "[25] This formulaic allusion to a nondescript deity is too thin a reed to provide any sustenance to the claim that the Founders created a Christian nation.

But even this conventional reference is absent from the Constitution. The document which truly established the government of the United States contains no reference to Jesus Christ, the Judeo-Christian or Christian God, or any deity anywhere in the body of the document.[26] This was no oversight. The Founders were familiar with the constitutions or charters of the various states and colonial governments, most of which contained references to God or Jesus Christ. The Founders deliberately chose not follow this example when they were establishing a government for the new nation.

Moreover, there is no statement in the Constitution suggesting in any way that its provisions derive from the Bible or Christian principles. Nor is there any hint that the government should collaborate with or support religious bodies. Article I, sec. 8 of the Constitution enumerates the powers of Congress. Nowhere in that list is any reference made to the authority of Congress to support religious bodies or to conform legislation to religious beliefs or doctrines. Similarly, Congress has no authority to enforce religious doctrines. Religion is simply not a concern of the government. Furthermore, the Constitution makes clear that the government derives no authority from a deity. Authority is derived from the consent of the governed, not the grace of God. As stated by the Preamble, "We the People" have established the government.

The complete absence of any reference to God or Jesus Christ or Christianity in the body of the Constitution substantially undermines the Christian nation thesis.[27] If the Founders wanted to ensure a government based on Christian precepts, why is not God or Jesus or Christianity invoked plainly and repeatedly in the text of the document? Indeed, forget repeated references—why isn't there at least one such reference in the body of the Constitution? The authors of the Constitution could have easily ensured that their intent to create a Christian state would be understood by adding a few words to the Preamble. They could have worded the opening clause in the Preamble to include the phrase "in order to found a more perfect union *based on Christian principles*." It would have taken little effort to include these four words. Christian nation advocates want us to believe Christianity was of central importance to the Founders, and they wanted the new nation to be based on Christian principles, yet the Founders could not be bothered to make any reference to those principles in the Constitution.

Significantly, this omission of any reference to God, Jesus Christ, or Christian principles did not go unnoticed or uncriticized. Indeed, one remarkable aspect of the claims of today's Christian nationalists is that their understanding of the Constitution is contradicted by their counterparts' protests in the late eighteenth and early nineteenth centuries. Many devout Christians were outraged by the Constitution's omission of any reference to God or Christian principles. As one historian has noted, many religious Americans were concerned that the "Constitution affirmed no faith, recognized no church, pledged loyalty to no God, [and] placed itself on no transcendent foundation."[28] These critics complained about this omission vociferously, with some proposing amendments to the Constitution to remedy this perceived defect. For example, at the Connecticut ratifying convention, delegate William Williams proposed that the Preamble be modified and enlarged to make explicit that the government's authority derived from God.[29]

Moreover, for those who wanted a government grounded on Christianity the failure to reference God, Jesus Christ, or Christianity was not the only problem in the Constitution. The one provision in the Constitution that does mention religion unambiguously confirms the disassociation of the government from religion. Article VI of the Constitution expressly prohibits any religious test for public office: "no religious test shall ever be required as a qualification to any office or public trust under the United States." This clause drew significant opposition. In New Hampshire, during the ratification process, an opponent warned, correctly, that the absence of a religious test meant "a Turk, a Jew, a Roman Catholic, and what is worse than all, a Universalist, may be President of the United States."[30] In Virginia, there was a proposal to amend Article VI to state "no other religious test shall ever be required than a belief in the one only true God."[31] It failed.

These immediate efforts to alter the wording of the Constitution to deprive it of its secular nature had no success, but laments about the godlessness of the Constitution and efforts to amend or modify the Constitution continued for generations. In 1811, prominent minister Rev. Samuel Austin, later president of the University of Vermont, cited the Constitution's lack of connection with Christianity as its one principal defect.[32] In 1812, a time of peril for the new nation, the president of Yale College, Rev. Timothy Dwight, feared that the United States had offended God because:

> We formed our Constitution without any acknowledgement of God; without any recognition of His mercies to us as a people, of His government or even of His existence. . . . Thus we commenced our national existence under the present system, without God.[33]

Grumbling turned into action amidst the distress and tensions generated by the Civil War. Some argued that the South's secession and the carnage of the war were recompense for the nation's affront to God. Only if God received proper acknowledgment would the bloodshed cease and the nation heal. In 1863, a number of clergy banded together to create the National Reform Association, whose purpose was to lobby for an amendment to the Constitution that would explicitly acknowledge the Christian God—not the people—as the source of authority for the government. The amendment would have changed the Preamble to read:

> We, the people of the United States, humbly acknowledging Almighty God as the source of authority and power in civil government, The Lord Jesus Christ as the Governor among the Nations, and His revealed will as of supreme authority, in order to constitute a Christian government . . . do ordain and establish this Constitution for the United States of America.[34]

The National Reform Association failed in its attempt to amend the Constitution, but one must give them credit for persistence. The organization still exists today and has the same goal, although the wording of its proposed amendment has changed slightly.[35]

According to today's Christian nationalists, all these individuals and organizations who protested the Constitution's exclusion of God and failure to provide homage to the Christian religion were engaged in a pointless exercise. The Founders had already established a Christian nation, although they apparently did it *sotto voce*.

The reality, of course, is that these protestors read the Constitution correctly: the document is totally secular, with the only reference to religion being the negative reference in Article VI stipulating that no religious test could ever be required for a federal office. Whatever one may think of the merits of these protestors' complaints, at least they had the intellectual honesty to recognize the Constitution for the secular document that it is—an intellectual honesty that today's Christian nationalists sadly lack.

Consideration of the Bill of Rights, the first ten amendments to the Constitution, which were proposed and ratified a little over two years after the effective date of the Constitution, confirms the secular nature of the United States government. With respect to the relationship between the government and religious beliefs and institutions, the First Amendment is, of course, key. That amendment provides, in pertinent part, "Congress shall make no law respecting an establishment of religion, or prohibiting the free exercise thereof." In other words, Congress is not supposed to do anything that supports or promotes religion, or inhibits religion, nor is it to interfere with how believers express their beliefs. Government is to keep its distance from religion.

Perhaps the most ridiculous claim that has gained currency among some Christian nation advocates is that the Constitution does not provide for separation of church and state because the phrase "separation of church and state" is not itself in the Constitution. What these persons fail to understand is that it would have been redundant to include such a phrase either in the body of the original Constitution or in any of its amendments. The document as a whole embodies the view that the government is not to meddle in religious matters. The federal government is given very specific, limited powers only over various secular matters. It has no powers relating to religion. The government is secular both in its origin—being expressly founded on the consent of the governed, not the authority of God—and its function. The government and religion have nothing to do with each other. It was Jefferson who coined the phrase "wall of separation between church and state" in his 1801 letter to the Danbury (Connecticut) Baptist Association.[36] That letter provides a succinct, cogent explanation of why he employed that metaphor. In the letter, he stated that he revered the Constitution because it embodied the principles that "religion is a matter which lies solely between man and his God, that he owes account to none other for his faith or his worship, [and] that the legislative powers of government reach actions only; and not opinions." When religion is a matter *solely* between a man and his god, there is no place for government. Necessarily, it follows that government operates in a different realm entirely from religion. Government deals with matters of *this* world; religion with other-worldly matters. To insist that the Constitution does not mandate separation of church and state because it does not contain that exact phrase is more preposterous than a person who is not named as a beneficiary in a will making a claim on the estate on the ground that the will does not specifically exclude him by name.

Another position sometimes put forward by Christian nationalists, and one that has found favor among some Supreme Court justices, is that the establishment clause prohibits only the preferring of one religion (or, for some, the preferring of one Christian religion) over another. It does not prohibit support of religion in general. This is the so-called "nonpreferentialist" interpretation of the establishment clause of the First Amendment. Pursuant to this interpretation, the government can support religion, even financially, provided the government does not favor or prefer one religious denomination over others. A major weakness of this argument is that it is contradicted by the evolution of the wording of the First Amendment during its consideration by the First Congress. A review of the House and Senate proposals regarding the wording of the First Amendment reveals that one specific proposal rejected was a draft amendment that limited the First Amendment to a prohibition on Congress giving preference to one religion over others and interfering with the rights of conscience. In other words, the First Congress considered a nonpreferential version of the First Amendment but declined to adopt it.

Madison introduced the proposed Bill of Rights in the House of Representatives on June 8, 1789.[37] His proposed amendments included one that specified: "The civil rights of none shall be abridged on account of religious belief or worship, nor shall any national religion be established, nor shall the full and equal rights of conscience be in any manner, or on any pretext, infringed." After some debate and modification of the proposed language, the House sent to the Senate a draft version of the religion clauses of the First Amendment similar to the version ultimately adopted: "Congress shall make no law establishing religion or prohibiting the free exercise thereof, nor shall the rights of conscience be infringed."

What happened to the language thereafter is important for resolving disputes about the meaning of the First Amendment. Unfortunately, neither the debates in the Senate nor in the subsequent meetings of the House-Senate conference committee were recorded. However, there is a record of the proposals that were considered, and that record is all that is needed.

The first motion in the Senate presented what today we would call the "no preference" position. The motion was to strike out from the House proposal "religion, or prohibiting the free exercise thereof," and to insert, "one religious sect or society in preference to others." The motion passed. The proposal on the floor then read: "Congress shall make no law establishing one religious sect or society in preference to others nor shall the rights of conscience be infringed." If this proposal had ultimately carried the day, those who claim the First Amendment prohibits only the preference of one religion over another obviously would have a strong case.

But the proposal did not prevail. The proposed language changed a couple more times, in a bewildering fashion. The Senate first broadened the scope of the amendment considerably and then narrowed it almost beyond recognition. First, it accepted a proposal not dissimilar from the final language of the amendment: "Congress shall make no law establishing religion or prohibiting the free exercise thereof." However, a week later, for reasons unknown to us, the Senate changed its mind and produced a version of the amendment that expressly limited the government's powers over religion only in a few specific areas: "Congress shall make no law establishing articles of faith or a mode of worship, or prohibiting the free exercise of religion." This was the language the Senate returned to the House, along with the Senate's versions of the other amendments.

The House agreed to the Senate's language on most of the other amendments but would not accept the Senate's version of the First Amendment, necessitating a joint conference committee to resolve the differences between the two chambers. The language that emerged from the conference committee was the language that was adopted and eventually ratified. "Congress shall make no law respecting an establishment of religion or prohibiting the free exercise thereof."

There are a couple of noteworthy aspects to this final language. The clause prohibits any law "respecting," that is, regarding or relating to, an establishment of religion. Thus, not just laws that explicitly establish religion are forbidden, but also laws that tend to establish religion, through support or endorsement. In addition, the clause's prohibition is not limited to establishment of *a* religion but rather extends to anything respecting "establishment of religion" in general. That is, a law does not have to favor one particular religion to violate the First Amendment; it merely has to favor religion in general.

Given this legislative history, it is implausible to maintain that the establishment clause merely requires the government to be neutral among religions. Congress considered and rejected language that might have allowed for support of religion in general. Therefore, to insist that the First Amendment permits such support is akin to arguing that a proposed sales price for a house is binding on the seller even when that price was explicitly considered and rejected during contract negotiations. As one constitutional scholar has observed, restricting the reach of the establishment clause to a prohibition on preferential aid "requires a premise that the Framers were extraordinarily bad drafters—that they believed one thing but adopted language that said something substantially different and that they did so after repeatedly attending to the choice of language."[38]

Interpreting the religion clauses of the First Amendment as reinforcing the Constitution's placement of religious matters outside the purview of government also has the virtue of making the establishment clause and the free exercise clause consistent. Unfortunately, modern legal scholarship, including decisions by the Supreme Court, has too often referred to an alleged tension between the two clauses, as if those who proposed and adopted the amendment somehow neglected to notice they were giving effect to two provisions that were at odds with each other.[39] If there is a tension, it is one created by court decisions which have expanded and distorted the free exercise clause so that it no longer merely protects people from government interference in their mode of worship and religious expression, but also gives them rights to government largesse.[40] Properly interpreted, the two clauses support each other: they instruct government not to favor or disfavor religion in general in any way and to allow people to hold and express any religious views without penalty. Again, the amendment is a means of ensuring that government maintains its distance from religion.

We should consider one final argument regarding the significance of the Constitution offered by Christian nationalists, and that is the argument that the First Amendment limited the actions of the federal government only, and, by implication, indicated the Founders had no objection to the laws and practices in some states which allowed government support of religion.[41] Massachusetts, for example, supported Protestant religious bodies with tax funds until 1833.[42] Of course, the Bill of Rights originally applied to the federal government only. The Constitution set forth the structure of the federal government, and the first ten amendments to the Constitution clarified the limits on the power of the federal government. It was not until the twentieth century that the Supreme Court ruled, through a series of cases, that most of the Bill of Rights had been "incorporated"—and thus made applicable to state governments—via the due process clause of the Fourteenth Amendment (ratified in 1868).[43] However, it is plainly an illegitimate inference to conclude that because the First Amendment initially applied to the federal government only that somehow the Founders approved of the religious-friendly policies of some states. In fact, there is evidence to the contrary. Franklin, in commenting on Article 3 of the Massachusetts Constitution of 1780, which provided support for Protestant churches, expressed disappointment about this provision, but also stated his hope that given progress in the views of the inhabitants of that state—in its early days the Massachusetts Bay Colony brutally enforced religious conformity—this provision would eventually be revised:

> Though the people of Massachusetts have not in their new constitution kept quite clear of religious tests, yet, if we consider what that people were a hundred years ago, we must allow they have gone great lengths in liberality of sentiment on religious subjects; and we may look for greater degrees of perfection when their constitution, some years hence, shall be revised.[44]

The Constitution, including the Bill of Rights, belies any claim that the Founders established a Christian nation.

Before taking leave of the Constitution, however, we need to consider one final play by the Christian nationalists—and one, superficially, that appears to be an ace in the hole. Joseph Story, an associate justice of the Supreme Court, was a noted jurist and an author of a work many in the nineteenth century considered authoritative: his three-volume *Commentaries on the Constitution*, published in 1833. In this work, Story claimed that Christianity was part of the common law (that is, judge-made legal precedent distinct from statutory law) and that, moreover, not only did government have the right to encourage Christianity but it also had the duty to do so.[45] With respect to the First Amendment specifically, Story contended:

> The real object of the [First] amendment was not to countenance, much less to advance, Mahometanism, or Judaism, or infidelity, by prostrating Christianity: but to exclude all rivalry among Christian sects, and to prevent any national ecclesiastical establishment which should give to a hierarchy the exclusive patronage of the national government.[46]

Christian nationalists place great weight on Story for obvious reasons, but this reliance is misplaced.[47]

Whatever his qualities as a jurist, Story played no role in the founding. He was born three years after the Declaration. He was ten when the Constitution was adopted. His analysis of the Constitution, then, is not based on first-hand knowledge, but represents a projection of his own views onto the document. Story even conceded that his analysis of the First Amendment clashed with Jefferson's.[48]

Furthermore, it is instructive that when the time came for Story to apply his view that Christianity is part of the common law, he qualified it considerably. The 1844 case of *Vidal v. Girard's Executors* dealt with the interpretation of a will that left funds for the establishment of a school for orphans but prohibited clergy from teaching in the school. In his opinion for the Court, Story repeated the adage that Christianity is part of the common law, but also stated that this observation needed to be "qualified": Christianity was part of Pennsylvania common law only in the "qualified sense" that "it is not to be maliciously and openly reviled and blasphemed against."[49] Story's four-decades removed commentaries on the Constitution do not alter the conclusion that the Constitution provided the foundation for a secular state.

Let us turn now to documents that Christian nationalists find more congenial to their views, namely the Declaration and various documents from the colonial era.

Christian nationalists typically argue that the Declaration is at least as important a founding document as the Constitution; occasionally they maintain it is even more important than the Constitution. Barton compares the relationship between the Declaration and the Constitution to that between a corporation's articles of incorporation and its bylaws, and he goes on to argue that the Declaration, not the Constitution, is "*the* foundational document in our Constitutional form of government."[50] The comparison is inapt as articles of incorporation provide at least a skeletal form of governance for a corporation; the Declaration provides no outline for a government. As to the argument that the Declaration is "*the*" foundational document, Barton's evidence for this is the ceremonial reference to the year independence was declared in the dating of documents. For example, George Washington dated a document by stating that it was given under his hand "and the seal of the United States, in the city of New York, the 14th day of August, A.D. 1790, and in the fifteenth year of the Sovereignty and Independence of the United States."[51] This reference on official documents to the year independence was declared has been done innumerable times since 1776; it is standard on many official federal documents. My certificates of admission from the Supreme Court and the U.S. Court of Appeals for the District of Columbia Circuit contain similar references. Reference to 1776 serves as a convenient dating system, tied to a singularly important event, well-known to almost everyone in the United States. This custom betokens nothing about the governance of the country, other than the United States continuing to be a sovereign nation. Barton's evidence is plainly insufficient.

Why such a desperate effort to raise the profile of the Declaration? The Christian nationalists believe the three references to a deity in the Declaration—the "separate and equal station to which the Laws of Nature and Nature's God entitle" an independent people; individuals "endowed by their Creator" with unalienable rights; and the signers' "firm reliance on the protection of divine Providence"—show that the government of the United States is "*not* secular since in numerous references [the Declaration] invoked God and His principles into civil government."[52]

How to respond? For starters, three references are not appropriately described as "numerous." More importantly, these references to a deity lack the significance Christian nationalists attribute to them. They do not indicate the United States had a religious foundation, much less an explicitly Christian one. These deific references presumably were acceptable to the Christians among the Founders, but they are more expressive of a rationalist/deist viewpoint; we should not forget that Jefferson was the primary author of the Declaration. (And it is also true that his primary collaborators, Franklin and John Adams, were not orthodox Christians.) The consensus of historians is that "Nature's God" in the Declaration is not a Redeemer God, but a God who establishes an order to the universe, which allows us to understand how things work through application of our reason and the categories of cause and effect.[53] Moreover, through use of our reason, we can discern not only the physical order of things, but also the moral order—the natural laws governing conduct. Put another way, as the Declaration asserts, key moral truths are "self-evident." The Creator has endowed us with certain rights through the way in which this deity has organized the world. No human is inherently superior to any other human ("all men are created equal"), and therefore no human or group of humans is entitled to direct the conduct of others without their consent (governments derive their just powers "from the consent of the governed").

Whether one agrees with the natural law views set forth in the Declaration, it is apparent they owe nothing to Christianity. Christianity is a revealed religion. Revelation, not reason, is the source of its wisdom.[54] Its core precepts are set forth in the Bible, which is a collection of writings allegedly inspired by God, including accounts of numerous miracles, which, by definition, are occurrences that cannot be explained by the laws of nature. Core doctrines of orthodox Christianity, such as the Trinity and the Incarnation, are candidly described as "mysteries," inexplicable and unfathomable by reason alone. Moreover, the Declaration is plainly not a covenant with God. Legitimate political authority arises from the will of the people; it is not based on the grace of God.

This last point warrants elaboration because the Declaration's understanding of the basis for political authority contrasts sharply with the arguments of Loyalists who wanted to maintain allegiance to the British crown; the Loyalists' contentions were primarily based on overtly religious grounds. God had ordained George III as the rightful ruler of Great Britain and its colonies, and it was incumbent upon Christians to render obedience to this divinely authorized monarch.[55] Although it would be inaccurate to characterize the Declaration as anti-Christian, its reasoning was definitely at odds with a popular Christian argument of the time.

So much for using the Declaration as justification for maintaining the United States is a Christian nation. We now come to the last set of documentary evidence for this view, and in this case last also means the least. A number of Christian nationalists point to various charters and constitutions from the colonial period as evidence that the United States is a Christian nation.[56] Prominent among these cited colonial-era documents are the Mayflower Compact (from 1620) and the Fundamental Orders of Connecticut (from 1639). The former was, of course, the rules for self-governance the Pilgrims adopted out of necessity when they failed to land in the territory they had been assigned. The latter provided the framework for government in the colony of Connecticut and is considered by some to be the first written constitution for an English colony in North America. Both documents can plausibly be interpreted as stating that a principal goal of each settlement was to promote the Christian faith. The Mayflower Compact provided: "We, whose names are underwritten, the Loyal Subjects of our dread Sovereign Lord King James ... Having undertaken for the glory of God and advancement of the Christian faith ... a Voyage to plant the first Colony in the northern Parts of Virginia ... combine ourselves into a civil body politic."[57] The Fundamental Orders provided: "[W]e the Inhabitants and Residents [of Connecticut towns] ... enter into Combination and Confederation together, to maintain and preserve the liberty and purity of the Gospel of our Lord Jesus which we now profess."[58] The triumphant tone of the Christian nationalists who mine and then display these historical gems is best exemplified in this passage:

> Anti-Christian historians *never* draw attention to the fact that there had been Christians who founded *explicitly Christian* colonies in America since 1585, when the first Roanoke colony was attempted. Yes, the colonies that were founded 200 years before the constitution was ratified were founded as Christian nations. Anti-Christian scholars and "experts" can balk all they want at "Christian nationalism" but the historical record is as clear as the noonday sun on a cloudless day— the American colonies were not founded as secular, pluralistic, nations where there was absolute religious freedom, but as *Christian* nations for *Christian* people governed by *Christians* where they would have freedom to practice the *Christian* religion.[59]

But this is a perfect example of what logicians call *ignoratio elenchi*—a misdirected argument that succeeds, if at all, in establishing irrelevancies only.

To begin, none of these documents founded a nation. As The Mayflower Compact clearly indicates, the colonists considered themselves loyal subjects of the King of England. As such, they continued to be bound by English law. The Compact and the Fundamental Orders, as well as similar documents, merely set forth practical rules that were needed for organizing the colonies given the distance to the Mother Country.

More important, these documents were written 130 to 150 years before the colonies declared independence and set about establishing a nation. Today's Christian nationalists blithely ignore this multigenera-

tional passage of time, as if nothing of cultural and intellectual importance transpired over this long period of time and the Founders necessarily held the same philosophical and political beliefs as the Pilgrims.
To assume that Washington, Franklin, Jefferson, Hamilton, Madison,
and their contemporaries had the same mindset as the Pilgrims is obviously unwarranted. Consider: do Americans today hold the same beliefs
and attitudes as Americans living in 1870?

Moreover, it is not merely the passage of time that casts doubt on the
assumption that the Founders held the same beliefs as the early colonists.
There is positive evidence that many of the Founders were influenced by
Enlightenment thinkers, especially John Locke. "Locke was the great
seventeenth-century English philosopher whose writings most shaped
the intellectual and political world view of Americans in the eighteenth
century. . . . All the important figures of the founding generation, including John Otis, John and Samuel Adams, James Madison, Thomas Jefferson, Patrick Henry, and Benjamin Franklin were disciples of Locke."[60]
In Locke's view, as articulated in his seminal work *Two Treatises of Government*, political authority derives from the people's consent.[61] Government is a product of a social contract among the people; it is not
the result of God anointing a ruler. Moreover, government's primary
purposes are to protect the rights of individuals, in particular, the rights
of life, liberty, and property, and maintain order. Government does not
have the function of promoting morality or religion. Put another way,
Locke rejects the notion of a Christian state.

Locke provided more details on his views regarding the government's relationship with religion in his essay *A Letter Concerning Toleration*, perhaps one of the most important works on the relations between
church and state ever written.[62] Locke argued that the people have in-
stituted government to protect their "civil interests," so government authority is limited to protecting "things belonging to this Life"; it does
not extend to "the salvation of souls."[63] Government is not competent to
make judgments about theological matters. Therefore, the government
has no right to compel people to accept any religious doctrines, "including articles of faith, or form of worship, by the force of [its] laws."[64]

Separation of government from religion was not only necessary as
a matter of political philosophy, but as a practical matter as well. Locke
was well aware of the sanguinary religious conflicts that had devastated

Europe since the 1500s. The only way to prevent continued strife was to allow people to make their own decisions about what to believe—it was their souls on the line anyway.

By taking these positions, Locke was implicitly repudiating the views held by some of the early colonists, especially those in Massachusetts. The Puritans of Massachusetts Bay Colony consciously set out to establish a repressive government, with rigorous rules governing conduct and religious belief unmatched in the contemporary world outside of Iran. The Puritans' "Holy Commonwealth was not intended for everyone, not even for all Christians."[65] Religious dissenters, such as Quakers, were banned from the colony, and those who did not adhere to this ban were hanged.[66] This was the "Christian" commonwealth today's Christian nationalists claim laid the foundation for the United States. The reality, of course, is that the Founders decisively rejected this model for the United States.

No need to belabor this point. Documents from the early colonial era have relevance to the governing principles of the United States only in the sense that they illustrate what the Founders were reacting against. In no way do they support the contention that the United States is a Christian nation.

The Principles Underlying the Structure of American Government

A final argument by Christian nationalists avoids reliance on direct evidence about the Founders' religious beliefs or their intentions. Rather it asserts that biblical precepts are reflected in the fundamental values that shaped the institutions of American democracy. On this view, the Founders did not have to make explicit their intention to create a Christian nation. The government they organized and the legal system they implemented manifests their Christian (or Judeo-Christian) values.[67]

This argument is typically coupled with the claim that these values are now eroding. The United States is in moral and social decline. In conjunction with this argument, one typically finds citations to charts or tables that purport to show that over the last few decades there has been an increase in violent crime and birth rates for unwed mothers and a decrease in educational attainment. The Christian nationalists attribute these trends to the courts' unjustified separation of church from state, the alleged promotion of secular humanism in our schools, and so forth. Sometimes they pinpoint the beginning of decline to a set of specific events, typically the 1962 and 1963 Supreme Court decisions that prohibited teacher-led Bible readings and prayer in public schools during class time.[68]

This argument is unsound in every possible way. The values that support American democracy have no connection to biblical precepts, which, if anything, support anti-democratic institutions. The American legal system aspires to providing justice, but only in the broadest possible sense can this be said to bear any relation to Christian or Judeo-Christian notions of justice. As to claims of American decline, first, the statistics cited by Christian nationalists are sometimes wrong or out-of-date and, more important, when one compares American society today with American society of the 1950s—when women were routinely denied opportunities, blacks and other minorities routinely suffered discrimination, states were still resisting integration, and the social safety net was more like a frayed sieve (e.g., there was no Medicare)—the contention that the United States has been in moral and social decline is revealed as highly dubious.

Let us start our analysis by identifying the principles underlying American democracy. That government authority derives from the consent of the governed is an obvious one. The separation of powers is also fundamental, as shown by the very structure of the Constitution. That government authority over the lives of individuals is limited is another. That government has the obligation to protect the people's lives, liberty, and property can be added to the list. And, of course, the rights set forth in the Bill of Rights must be respected by the government. This list, even if incomplete, is sufficient for our purposes.

So, is Christianity the source for these principles? Well, Christian nationalists saturate their writings with claims about how Christianity is a bulwark for freedom: "From Martin Luther, to the Puritans, to the Founding Fathers, Bible-believing Christians have and always will be crusaders and defenders of freedom."[69] Such claims are the product of staggering ignorance or Orwellian redefinition. To begin, Christianity did not begin with Martin Luther (although he was no advocate for freedom either; see below.) Christianity is an outgrowth of Judaism— indeed, one cannot accept Christian doctrine without also accepting the

Old Testament as divinely inspired—and the Old Testament reports that the ancient Israelites had no trouble accepting monarchical or oligarchical governments. Moreover, Leviticus expressly authorizes enslavement of non-Jews (Lev. 25: 44–46). Individual freedom was not a cornerstone value in ancient Israel.

Respect for individual freedom did not exactly surge once Jesus appeared on the scene. According to the New Testament, no word condemning slavery passed his lips, although he had plenty to say about the evils of fornication. The apostle Paul referred on several occasions to slavery without condemning the practice. Regarding democratic government, Jesus was also silent; implicitly, he condoned Rome's authoritarian rule by advising to render to Caesar those things that are Caesar's (Matt. 22: 21).

That those in charge of the state had been ordained by God and were entitled to obedience was a key element of Christian political thought from late Roman times forward. Monarchs ruled by divine right; they were anointed by God. This anointing took on concrete form through coronation ceremonies in which representatives of the Catholic Church or Orthodox Church (in the Byzantine Empire) placed holy oil on the ruler.

This alliance between Christianity and monarchs and other divinely appointed rulers did not end with the Reformation. Luther notoriously allied himself with the German princes and nobility during the Peasants' Revolt of 1525.[70] Among the demands of the peasantry were abolition of serfdom, reduction of compulsory services, and the right of people to choose their own pastors. Apparently, these demands were too much for Luther. Luther not only opposed the peasants but also urged the nobility to crush the revolt savagely, encouraging them to "cut, stab, strangle" the rebels.[71]

And Protestant rulers in the sixteenth and seventeenth centuries exercised authoritarian power just as jealously and avidly as their Catholic counterparts. Henry VIII and Elizabeth I in England had views on the divine right of kings similar to those of Philip II of Spain despite their religious differences.

The notion that governmental authority legitimately derives only from the consent of the governed arguably had some limited historical precedents before the Enlightenment—think of ancient Athens and the

Roman Republic—but its fully developed theoretical justification is a product of the Enlightenment. It certainly owes nothing to Christian political philosophy.

With respect to the separation of powers, its lack of direct association with Christian precepts should be apparent. All the monarchs over the centuries who ruled with the approval of the Catholic Church, the Orthodox Church, or later Protestant religious leaders ruled, for the most part, absolutely, combining executive, legislative, and judicial functions. The only limit religious leaders tried to impose on the rulers' power related to the perceived prerogatives of religious bodies.

Remarkably, however, some authors endeavor to argue that the separation of powers is peculiarly a Christian notion. The claim is that the Founders wanted to avoid the concentration of power in any one individual or group because they were influenced by Christian views on the sinful nature of humans.[72] That humans are inherently flawed and, therefore, it is prudent to have some checks on the exercise of power by government officials is consistent with some Christian beliefs—and no doubt some Founders held such beliefs—but this in no way establishes that Christian beliefs were the source of the Founders' separation of powers principle. Such a claim is an implausible reconstruction of the Founders' reasoning.

The most extensive contemporary treatment of the actual reasons supporting the Constitution's separation of powers appears in *The Federalist*, the collection of essays written by James Madison, Alexander Hamilton, and John Jay during 1787 and 1788 to persuade New Yorkers to support the then-pending Constitution. When one reviews *The Federalist*, one finds numerous references to the faults shared by many humans—overweening ambition, partiality, venality, and so forth—but there is no biblical or doctrinal reference to support these observations. Rather Madison, Hamilton, and Jay repeatedly base their observations on "experience, the least fallible guide of human opinions."[73] *The Federalist* is packed with discussions of historical events as illustrations of what can go wrong when government power is not appropriately limited; there is no appeal to original sin, Adam's fall, or any other biblical notion. In addition to relying on experience, the authors of *The Federalist* do cite some thinkers as support for the principle of the separation of powers. But no, they do not cite Augustine, Aquinas, or Calvin; they cite

Montesquieu, the French political philosopher of the Enlightenment.[74] The principle of the separation of powers has no direct connection to Christian doctrine or belief.

Turning to other foundational principles of American government, the principle that governments should protect the lives and property of their subjects or citizens is of ancient pedigree. If Christian governments followed this principle, in theory, then so did governments before the advent of Christianity. There is little point to a government unless it protects people from domestic violence and foreign invasion.

But matters stand differently with respect to the principles that government has limited authority and that one of government's principal obligations is to protect the liberty of its people. After Christianity became the official religion of the Roman Empire and through the Middle Ages up into Early Modern Europe, the prevailing understanding was that government had the obligation to ensure its subjects lived in accordance with God's law, as then interpreted. Consistent with that obligation, the government had the right and duty to direct the lives of its subjects, including actively promoting their spiritual health and not allowing them to fall into theological error, lest they endanger their immortal souls and the souls of others. As Thomas Aquinas argued when justifying the death penalty for heretics, the government, in alliance with the church, had an obligation to protect the faithful from eternal damnation. He explained, "it is a much graver matter to corrupt the faith, which quickens the soul, than to forge money, which supports temporal life."[75]

Again, the Reformation did little to change this political philosophy. The notion that the government had an affirmative obligation to guard against heresy, and in doing so the authority to restrain the freedom of its people, persisted after the Reformation. Protestant states condemned heretics to death as surely as Catholic states, although perhaps with less regularity; they lacked the bureaucratic machinery of the Inquisition.

The view that the government had a duty to guard against religious error carried over into some early American colonies. As one historian noted:

> There is no way to deny—and as far as I can see, no use in denying—
> that the Protestants coming to this country in the seventeenth century
> were almost unanimous in their conviction that toleration was a dan-

gerous and heathen notion. . . . If you believe, as men believed in that era, that you are altogether on the Lord's side, and that your enemies are and must be entirely on the devil's, you can see no virtue in the idea of tolerating them.[76]

Massachusetts Bay Colony, in particular, "frankly employed the civil power to compel all inhabitants to conform and contribute."[77] As already noted, the Puritans "viewed their mission as divine," and to further that mission, the state had to have "coercive power sympathetic to the Puritan goal."[78] Instead of "extending toleration to those of different religious convictions, the Puritans persecuted dissenters in their midst just as they had been persecuted as English Dissenters." In Massachusetts, "religious freedom was defined as freedom from error."[79] So much for the argument of Christian nationalists that "Puritans [were] crusaders and defenders of freedom."

Moreover, it is informative and striking that some Christian nationalists today openly advocate a return to a Puritan-style regime. Stephen Wolfe, in presenting the case for Christian nationalism, contends that a Christian state has the authority to punish any external expression of "false religion," whether by teaching, writing, or simply saying something heretical or blasphemous.[80] The rationale is that such expressions risk injury to the souls of true believers (shades of Thomas Aquinas!). In true doublespeak fashion, Wolfe then argues that Christian nationalists respect freedom of conscience because the state would not punish people for their private beliefs.[81] Yes, one is free to think anything—as long as one keeps one's mouth shut. Just like their Puritan exemplars, today's Christian nationalists have no respect for individual freedom.

With respect to the Bill of Rights, there is no need to go through the various rights *seriatim*. From the above discussion, it is apparent that the rights to freedom of religion, freedom of the press, and free speech have no distinctively Christian roots. Similarly, the same conclusion holds with respect to the rights to assemble peacefully and to petition the government. Many rights recognized in the first ten amendments involve legal processes, and although several of these rights (e.g., right to trial by jury, right to confront one's accusers) had origins in English common law, Christianity was not their source. Special mention should be made of the Eighth Amendment's prohibition of cruel and unusual punishments. This, too, had English precedents, as a similar provision had been part of the 1689 Bill of Rights, but it also showed the influence of Enlightenment thinkers such as Cesare Beccaria, whose writings on criminal punishment were familiar to many of the Founders.[82] Significantly, in the mid-1700s, Christian nations, such as France and Spain, still imposed gruesome, horrific punishments on convicted criminals, including death by prolonged public torture.[83] It was not Christian doctrine that ended such practices; it was a rational assessment by Enlightenment thinkers of the purposes of criminal punishment.

To sum up, there is no evidence that Christian doctrines, principles, or values provided the foundation for America's constitutional democracy. To the contrary, nations that had governments charged with promoting Christian values had shown themselves to be hostile to the freedoms valued by the Founders, and the Founders were aware of this unhappy history.

Let us turn now to the American legal system, beyond the specific provisions in the Bill of Rights. Here one must concede that, at least in the popular imagination, Christian nationalists have secured a partial victory. A significant portion of the American populace believes that "Judeo-Christian" precepts, in particular the Ten Commandments, are the foundational source for American law. This view is perhaps best summarized in the explanatory placard that was used in a Ten Commandments display in a Kentucky courthouse—a display found unconstitutional by the Supreme Court in a narrow 5-4 decision. That placard stated that the "Ten Commandments have profoundly influenced the formation of Western legal thought and the formation of our country.... The Ten Commandments provide the moral background of the Declaration of Independence and the foundation of our legal tradition."[84] Christian nationalists make this claim, but so do many others, including assorted judges, legislators, state legislatures, and the U.S. House of Representatives.[85] As further support for the view that Judeo-Christian precepts provide the foundation for American law, Christian nationalists cite judicial decisions from the nineteenth century which state that Christianity is part of the common law.[86] Nonetheless, despite the widespread acceptance of the claim that the United States legal system is founded on Judeo-Christian or Christian principles, a critical examination of the claim reveals it to be erroneous.

Before examining the claim as it relates to the Ten Commandments, let us first leave aside some obvious complicating issues for anyone familiar with relevant biblical passages, namely that the numbering of the commandments God gave to Moses is unclear, as is the content of the "Ten Commandments." The original set given to Moses on stone tablets had no assigned numbers, and Catholics and some Protestants number the commandments differently, with Catholics relying on the numbering system devised by Augustine, the early Christian bishop and theologian.[87] Moses destroyed the original stone tablets. (Ex. 31: 15–19.) When God gave him replacement tablets, the commandments were strikingly different, consisting principally of cultic instructions, concluding with the notorious command not to "boil a kid in its mother's milk." And it is with respect to this latter set that the term "ten commandments" first appeared in the Bible. (Compare Ex. 20: 2–17 with Ex. 34: 1–28.)

But to delve into these issues would drag us into swirling theological waters. Moreover, if what we are considering is the influence of the Ten Commandments on American law, issues concerning the "real" content of the Ten Commandments are irrelevant. Myths and inaccuracies can have influence as much as reality—as any political propagandist can confirm. So it is sufficient if we consider the generally accepted content of the Ten Commandments, regardless of whether this content reflects the Bible accurately.

Using Augustine's numbering, we have, with some modification in wording:

1. You shall not have other gods before me.

2. You shall not use the name of God in vain.

3. Keep the Sabbath holy.

4. Honor your parents.

5. You shall not kill.

6. You shall not commit adultery.

7. You shall not steal.

8. You shall not bear false witness against your neighbor.

9. You shall not covet your neighbor's wife.

10. You shall not covet your neighbor's goods.

Commandments 5, 7, and 8 are reflected in some fashion in American law, past and present. Adultery, prohibited by Commandment 6, was at one time a criminal offense in most states; some states still have laws on the books criminalizing adultery, but the legal consensus is that such statutes are now unenforceable. However, adultery is still a recognized ground for fault divorces. It is unclear what Commandment 4 requires, other than enjoining respect for one's parents, which is not a legal requirement. It could perhaps be interpreted to imply a duty to support one's parents in old age, something probably very relevant to Bronze Age societies, but whatever moral weight this guidance has today, it has not influenced American law. Commandments 9 and 10 are not, and have not been, reflected in American law, either criminal or civil. There is no punishment or penalty for desires in and of themselves; we have no thought crimes.

Turning to Commandments 1–3, that is the commandments with a clear religious content, Commandment 1 has had no influence on American law, even if one interprets the commandment broadly. At the federal level, freedom of conscience has been the rule. At the state level, there was for a period of time government support of religion in some states, but no prohibition on holding any particular belief. It is a different matter with respect to Commandments 2 and 3. One could plausibly argue they did have some influence on English common law, and English common law provided the basis for American law until such time as common law precedents were abrogated or superseded by statute. The extent of this influence will be discussed further below.

But we return to Commandments 5, 7, and 8, which are the ones most people think of when they allude to the Ten Commandments providing the foundation for legal systems. Sure, murder, stealing, and material falsehoods, including perjury, are subject to criminal punishment and civil penalty. However, all this shows is that these commandments are, in a broad sense, consistent with American law, not that they are the source of American law. This confusion between consistency and causal connection is exacerbated by the centuries-long pronouncement by church leaders of the foundational role of the Ten Commandments and the amplification of this message through repetition by believers, including some judges and jurists, and the various elements of popular culture. The message has become deeply ingrained.

A few moments of critical reflection, however, should suffice to show the key flaws in this claim. First, consider what human societies did before the Ten Commandments. Did they condone everyone constantly killing, stealing, and deceiving in a Hobbesian war of all against all? Had that been the case, human society would not have survived. No, moral anarchy did not engulf the globe before Moses climbed Mt. Sinai. Human societies followed what ethicists refer to as the common morality.[88] The common morality consists of core norms accepted by all cultures for the simple reason that they are necessary for human social groups to survive. For humans to live together in peace and prosper, the humans in a group need to follow norms such as don't kill, don't steal, tell the truth, keep your commitments, and so forth. Every human society also has had norms regulating sexual conduct, although the content of those norms differs from group to group. That said, most societies have had norms prohibiting betrayal of a sexual commitment. "[I]njunctions against violence, deceit, and betrayal . . . are familiar in every society and every legal system. They have been voiced in works as different as the Egyptian Book of the Dead, the Icelandic Edda, and the Bhagavad Gita."[89]

Of course, these core norms governed conduct only within one's group. The widespread acceptance of the notion of universal human rights is a fairly recent occurrence, dating to the eighteenth century.[90] During much of human history, outsiders were considered fair game to wage war upon, to kill, to enslave. The Ten Commandments did not change that. The ancient Hebrews were as in-group oriented as any other ancient peoples, as confirmed by the total, remorseless warfare carried out by Moses and his successors against the Midianites, the Canaanites, and other out-groups. (Ex. 23: 20–33; Num. 31: 9–18, 33: 50–56; Deut. 7: 1–5, 20: 16–18.)

The pre-biblical moral norms governing conduct in early human societies were reflected in the first law codes. For example, the law code of the Babylonian king Hammurabi, who reigned perhaps 700 years before Moses lived (the dates for Moses, who may be a legendary figure anyway, are disputed), punishes murder, theft, false allegations, and improper sexual conduct.[91] The Ten Commandments are not unique as a moral code or as a basis for legal prohibitions.

One possible counter-argument would be that even though the secular components of the Ten Commandments are hardly unique, nonetheless, in terms of causation, the Ten Commandments have had more influence on the American legal system than other possible competing sources of legal principles. Ultimately, this counter-argument is unpersuasive if the point of the contention is to show the Ten Commandments have had substantial influence on American law, but to arrive at this conclusion requires us to follow the convoluted development of English law before American independence. It is convoluted, in part, because England developed three concurrent systems: common law courts (the Court of Common Pleas for civil cases and the King's Bench for criminal cases), ecclesiastical courts, and the Chancery Court, that is, the court of equity.

During the early Middle Ages, English law encompassed vestiges of Roman law commingled with the customs of Germanic tribes.[92] Apart from some local courts, such as manor courts, the interpretation and application of the law depended largely on the will of the king or his designates. The real beginnings of common law—which is just another way to say customary law applied in a common fashion throughout the kingdom—occurred when Henry II reformed the English system by creating permanent courts that could administer justice without the king or a designate being present.[93] These courts decided cases based on precedent, that is, how customary law had been applied in the past, with the occasional statute modifying precedent. There is nothing to indicate the portions of the Ten Commandments addressing secular offenses had any significant role in shaping common law precedent, with the possible exception of adultery.

Under the late Anglo-Saxon kings, adultery was recognized as a serious legal wrong, which may reflect the increasing influence of Christianity and its teachings.[94] But the state imposed no penalty; instead, adultery excused the cuckolded husband in the event he killed the interloper. Following the Norman Conquest, jurisdiction over matrimonial matters, including adultery cases, was ceded to ecclesiastical courts, which also had jurisdiction over matters involving clergy (the nub of the dispute between Henry II and Thomas Becket) and testamentary matters.[95] In these courts, adultery was considered a transgression punishable by imposition of some penance. In general, these ecclesiastical courts purported to apply Christian doctrine, which included at least passing reference to Mosaic law.

Beginning in the 1300s, the English chancellor began to receive numerous petitions seeking relief that for whatever reason—sometimes technical ones—could not be obtained in common law courts. (The position of chancellor was a key administrative position under the king.) For example, common law courts were limited to awarding damages, whereas the chancellor could demand specific performance of a contract or grant an injunction. Over time, a bureaucracy developed around the chancellor and a separate court system, the Court of Chancery, came into being.[96]

Then with the coming of the Reformation, and an increase in attention and deference to the Bible, Chancery Court opinions began to be sprinkled with citations to Mosaic law as a partial rationale for the court's decisions, although interestingly it was the rare case that referred to the Ten Commandments specifically.[97] Instead, reference was usually made to one of the many other laws or directives attributed to Moses. A good example is the historic Earl of Oxford's Case, decided in 1615.[98] Like the evolution of the Chancery Court itself, the case is convoluted, but essentially it was a dispute over real property between the plaintiff, who had a claim based on a presumed exception to a statute and who had constructed houses on the property, and the defendant, who claimed the property years after the houses had been built on the basis that the statute had voided the plaintiff's claim. The Chancery Court decision cites Deuteronomy 28:30, a verse which forms part of a series of curses on those who do not follow God's law. One curse is that those who disobey God will build a house but not dwell in it. Somehow the Lord Chancellor interpreted this curse as favoring the plaintiff's case. However, the decision also noted that the common law requirement of consideration to make a valid contract similarly supported the plaintiff's case, as the defendant could not possess property made valuable by the plaintiff without offering just compensation.[99]

Legal historians note the Earl of Oxford's Case mostly for the prolonged jurisdictional dispute it sparked between common law courts and the Court of Chancery. Without getting into irrelevant details, the outcome of the dispute was the acknowledgment that the Court of Chancery had the authority to fill in gaps left by the common law.[100] In carrying out this interstitial role, decisions of the Court of Chancery during the seventeenth century referred to what conscience required, and conscience was sometimes informed, in part, by biblical teachings. This phenomenon was not unusual given the religious fervor of the times.

After the United States was founded, no separate equitable system was created at the federal level. Instead, federal courts were empowered to apply both common law principles and equitable principles,[101] with the latter by the early nineteenth century having been solidified into a body of precedent as binding as the precedents of common law. Many states, at first, had separate law courts and equity courts. Over time, with a few exceptions, states consolidated these courts into one system, while maintaining the distinction between legal and equitable relief. In any event, whether applying legal or equitable principles, American courts, from the time of their founding until the present day, have, with infrequent exceptions, based their decisions on statutory law or precedent, not perceived dictates of the Bible generally or the Ten Commandments specifically.

Of course, judicial decisions, whether in the nineteenth century or today, have sometimes cited scripture, for rhetorical effect, for historical background, or as a guide to wisdom. Law review articles have collected dozens of American judicial decisions citing some biblical verse; nearly all these biblical citations play no role in the actual disposition of the case.[102] If they did play a substantive role, at least under contemporary jurisprudence, they would be subject to constitutional challenge. Moreover, almost all these biblical citations are to passages *other* than the Exodus verses referencing the Ten Commandments.

What happened to the case law developed by England's ecclesiastical courts? The United States has never had a parallel system of ecclesiastical courts, which would be plainly impermissible given the Constitution's separation of church and state. That said, the notion that adultery was a serious wrong did carry over into the criminal codes of many states.

Much ground has been covered in the last few paragraphs, so it is appropriate to pause and take stock. Neither the Ten Commandments nor Mosaic law in general had any significant influence on the development of English common law. Mosaic law influenced some decisions of the Chancery Court, in the seventeenth century in particular. This was at a time when biblicism had gripped English intellectual life.[103] That said, the Ten Commandments did not receive more deference than other biblical directives. In a parallel line of authority, ecclesiastical courts did rely in part upon the prohibition of adultery in the Ten Commandments as justification for imposing penalties on adulterers. With respect to United States law, the commandments regarding killing, stealing, and bearing false witness have had no discernible impact on the law; they have not been cited as a reason for having laws dealing with such actions, nor have they provided the rationale for judicial decisions regarding such actions. On the other hand, the prohibition on adultery did influence the criminalization of adultery in many states.

The influence of the commandment prohibiting adultery on early American law hardly provides proof that the Ten Commandments constitute the "foundation" of American law. American law was influenced overwhelmingly by secular considerations.

How then do we explain the observation made by various judicial decisions, including some early U.S. Supreme Court decisions, that Christianity is "a part of the common law"?[104] To some extent, this issue was addressed during the previous discussion of Justice Joseph Story's commentaries on the Constitution, but it is appropriate now to provide further background as to the English roots of this adage. The seminal case was the 1675 decision in *Rex v. Taylor*, in which the defendant was tried for, among other things, calling Jesus Christ a "whoremaster" and declaring religion "a cheat."[105] These comments were not well received in England during the 1600s. In his opinion, Chief Justice Hale concluded that blasphemy, hitherto a matter relegated to ecclesiastical courts, was punishable under the common law as "the Christian religion is a part of the law itself."[106] This assertion was thereafter cited in subsequent blasphemy cases, in both England and the United States. However, although Christian nationalists today invoke these cases as supposed additional proof that the United States is a Christian nation, as we have seen, these cases do not carry the significance attributed to them. Justice Story, in his decision in *Vidal v. Girard's Executors*, emphasized that the maxim that Christianity is part of the common law needed to be qualified as it meant only that Christianity "is not to be maliciously and openly reviled and blasphemed against."[107] Under this analysis, if any commandment influenced American law, then it was Commandment 2's prohibition on sacrilegious speech. Furthermore, an 1890 law review article surveying

American court decisions shows that by that date either the claim that Christianity was part of the common law had been repudiated or it had been confined in its application to blasphemy cases or cases involving Sunday closing laws.[108] In the twentieth century, following the Supreme Court's decision that the free speech clause of the First Amendment applies to state goverments,[109] courts began to dismiss blasphemy charges as an unconstitutional restraint on speech, so even this limited influence of Christianity on American law had lost its effect.

Speaking of Sunday closing laws, such laws do suggest the influence of Commandment 3, as well as custom. In a 1961 case in which employees of a Maryland retail store challenged their conviction for selling goods on a Sunday, the Supreme Court acknowledged that Sunday closing laws, also known as Blue Laws, "indisputably" had a religious origin, which could be traced to Commandment 3's directive to keep the Sabbath holy.[110] Nonetheless, the Court upheld the law in question, reasoning that the law had a secular motivation of mandating a day of rest from labor and that this secular motivation now predominated. Of course, Sunday closing laws are now largely a thing of the past, so again, even this limited effect of one of the commandments has become irrelevant.

In conclusion, the claim that the Ten Commandments provide the foundation for American law is, to put it generously, greatly exaggerated. Most commandments had no effect whatsoever on American law. Prohibition of acts such as murder, theft, or perjury would have happened even if paganism had triumphed over Christianity. All human societies have such prohibitions. There are only three commandments that could be said to have influenced American law: the prohibitions on taking God's name in vain, keeping the Sabbath holy, and prohibiting adultery. But this influence was limited, and even this limited influence dissipated some time ago. Similarly, as indicated, any claim that Christianity, as a whole, undergirds our legal system lacks sufficient evidence. The few judicial references to Christianity being part of the common law related to a very specific, narrow range of cases, and developments in the law over the last century have made even these references outdated.

The foregoing argument does not imply that the religious views of the electorate and their representatives never influence which laws are proposed and enacted. Of course, that happens. For example, although one can theoretically make a secular argument in favor of restricting abortion, those opposing abortion are for the most part motivated by religious views regarding the moral status of zygotes, embryos, and fetuses. But acknowledging that religious views have influenced and can influence which laws get adopted is quite different than maintaining the United States was founded as a Christian nation. The United States has the constitutional and legal structure of a secular republic.

A Few Words About White Nationalism/White Supremacism

As stated at the outset of this chapter, Christian nationalism is the most prominent form of identity politics on the Right. However, there are also white nationalists and white supremacists who maintain that whites have a unique identity that distinguishes them from other races in various significant ways and that, in some fashion, the laws and policies of the United States should protect or promote whites. (The terms "white nationalist" and "white supremacist" are often treated as interchangeable, but logically they are distinct. A white nationalist could believe that whites deserve special status or protection, perhaps even to the extent of having their own country, but may not necessarily believe that whites are superior to other races. Whether white nationalists and white supremacists recognize this logical distinction themselves is questionable.)

I decided not to address at length the beliefs animating these groups principally for two reasons: one, their beliefs do not merit careful examination, and two, their influence on American politics is negligible. Yes, because of their greater predilection for violence, they do pose a threat of domestic terrorism, as the FBI has concluded,[111] but their willingness to resort to violence only confirms their inability to attract widespread popular support.

Of course, the identity Left characterizes "white supremacy" as a cause of many of our societal ills, but for all the reasons set forth in chapters 1–3, this claim lacks merit. This claim is an assertion driven by ideology and unsupported by fact.

Conclusion on Christian Nationalism

The Christian founding of the United States is a "just-so" story, a myth that cannot withstand scrutiny. Nonetheless, despite its lack of factual support, a significant portion of Americans hold fast to this belief. Misleading historical claims help sustain the myth of a nation originating in Christianity, but its appeal also lies in the fact that it reflects what many want to be true. A historical thesis may underlie Christian nationalism, but the historical claims are shaped by the ideology. The Christian nationalist understanding of history lends a patina of legitimacy to the efforts of Christian nationalists to advance their policy agenda. They are not trying to bend the country to their will; they merely want to restore the country to its Christian foundation.

There have been religious right-wing movements before at various points in United States history, with Jerry Falwell's Moral Majority of the 1980s being the most recent prior example. Why is Christian nationalism experiencing a recrudescence now? Because some see it as an answer to the identity politics of the Left. Indeed, some Christian nationalists explicitly maintain their agenda is the required response to beat back the "woke."[112]

In this belief they are mistaken. The reality is that both the identity Left and the Christian nationalist Right share a common outlook, namely hostility toward Enlightenment values. This affinity between the identity Left and the Christian Right, and the danger it poses, will be discussed in this book's conclusion.

CONCLUSION

The Enlightenment Values Threatened
from the Right and the Left

Despite the animosity that left-wing identity politics ideologues have toward members of the MAGA coalition, and vice-versa, these adversaries share a common antagonism toward Enlightenment values. This is a matter of grave concern. I submit that the values of the Enlightenment have been indispensable for the advancements in science, material well-being, personal autonomy, and respect for human rights that the West, and the world, have experienced over the last two centuries.

What are the values that the Enlightenment has bequeathed to us?[1] At the core of Enlightenment thought was the rejection of the claims of special authority claimed by the church. Truth was determined through empirical evidence and sound reasoning, not through revelation. Because no institution or person can claim special authority, no statement made by anybody has any more validity than the reasoning and evidence offered in support of it. The Enlightenment notion that truth is available to all, provided they have sufficient support for their assertions, had further implications. One, it placed a value on empirical inquiry, giving further impetus to the scientific revolution that was already underway. Two, it placed a value on a culture of free speech. If no one is in a privileged position to discern the truth, then criticism of knowledge claims must be open to everyone. Three, it lent support to democratic government. Again, if no one has a position of special authority, then everyone should have a say in decisions about governance, and political authority is derived from the people through their consent.

Three other Enlightenment values are also significant. Religious dogma had insisted on the notion of absolute truth. Enlightenment thinkers accepted the idea of probabilistic truth and were prepared to live with uncertainty. This idea fostered greater tolerance for diverging opinions. Enlightenment thinkers placed value on personal freedom, at first principally with respect to religious and political freedom. However, once the value of personal freedom was recognized, the scope of personal autonomy increased over time. Many people today have more say over the direction of their lives—what career to pursue, whether and whom to marry, whether to stay married, whether to bear children—than any other sizeable group in human history. Along with the value of personal freedom, the Enlightenment thinkers promoted the notion of universal human rights, a notion alien to almost everyone prior to the eighteenth century. These rights were natural and equal—held by all and held by all equally, as reflected in the Declaration of Independence, an article of Enlightenment values.

Let me pause here to address one obvious objection to my overview of Enlightenment values, and that is that equal rights for Enlightenment thinkers meant only equal rights for white male property owners, as indicated by the continuation of slavery in the United States and the continuation of the subordination of women throughout the Western world. Moreover, some Enlightenment thinkers held racist views, with support from "scientific" racial classifications. This is one reason some on the Left disparage Enlightenment values as merely an expression of white supremacy.[2] But this criticism fails on two counts: it fails to distinguish between ideals and the flawed individuals who advanced these ideals, and it fails to give sufficient weight to the fact that science is always a work in progress. Anthropological science, if one can even call it that, was in its infancy in the 1700s, and given limited data and existing prejudices, it is not surprising that some thinkers arrived at incorrect conclusions. And, yes, it would have been lovely if slavery had ended immediately at the time of the Declaration, but longstanding institutions and practices do not necessarily come tumbling down overnight. Slavery had existed from time immemorial in almost all human societies, in the Americas, Africa, Europe, and Asia. Apart from some isolated, sporadic musing by some philosophers through the ages, slavery was almost everywhere accepted.

Jesus did not denounce it; Moses, Confucius, and Mohammed all advocated it. The slave trade to the Americas in the 1500s, 1600s, and 1700s depended on African sellers as much as European buyers. Organized opposition to slavery only began to materialize—that's right, in the late 1700s, in Europe, that is, at the time of the Enlightenment.[3] The tension between the ideals of the Enlightenment and the existence of slavery was not resolved in the United States until the Civil War, but it was resolved, in favor of freedom. Had it not been for the Enlightenment, slavery may well have continued, as indicated by its stubborn persistence in various nations that were untouched by the Enlightenment. Saudi Arabia did not ban slavery until 1962.[4]

Similarly, with women's rights, recognition of their equal standing was delayed by the endurance of the ages-old belief that women are in some sense inferior to men, especially with respect to reasoning ability. It took time to overcome this prejudice—time and willingness and opportunity to question and challenge this prejudice. Again, Enlightenment values facilitated this process. It is hard to imagine anything like the 1848 Seneca Falls women's rights conference taking place in Asia, Africa, or the Middle East.

The two greatest moral revolutions in the history of humanity were the abolition of slavery and the emancipation of women. Neither would have happened absent the Enlightenment.

The importance of Enlightenment values for human progress and happiness is why the dogmas on the Left and Right pose such a danger. Christian nationalists, of course, reject the core Enlightenment principle that no one has special epistemic authority. Christianity, as is true with most religions, is predicated on the notion of revelation. Under orthodox Christian doctrine, God has spoken to a special cognitive upper class of prophets, and the rest of us just must accept these prophets' pronouncements as absolutely true. From the Left, we have the claim that the oppressed have special insight and we must defer to them when they speak from their lived experience. Lived experience is simply the identity Left's version of revelation. And just as clergy preach the need to accept revelation, today's practitioners of priestcraft, our DEI bureaucrats and trainers, demand obeisance to lived experience.

In part, because neither the identity Left nor the Christian nationalists on the Right accept the Enlightenment view that no statement made by anybody has any more validity than the reasoning and evidence offered in support of it, they do not support a culture of free speech. They already possess The Truth. They do not need to hear from anyone else, and they certainly do not want to hear from you if you challenge their dogmas. If you are not fully committed to the doctrine of systemic racism, good luck finding an academic position or any job of importance in a corporation, and, of course, you are not going to be invited to speak on campus. Moreover, the announcement by some academic journals that they will not publish articles deemed harmful is just the Left's version of the Christian nationalist position that error has no rights and heretical views must be suppressed because they can harm the believer. And not unexpectedly both the identity Left and the Christian nationalist Right are avid censors; the identity Left does not want high school students to read *To Kill a Mockingbird*, *Of Mice and Men*, and *The Adventures of Huckleberry Finn*, and Christian nationalists object to *Beloved*, among many other books.[5] The curious thing is that according to most mainstream media, only the Right favors book banning—but that misleading reporting is itself an example of how facts can be suppressed.[6]

Neither the identity Left nor the Christian/authoritarian Right are friends of science. The animosity of the latter group is obvious. They deny any scientifically established set of facts that conflict with their religious tenets, e.g., evolution. The identity Left's opposition to science is more subtle, but just as pernicious. As indicated, the identity Left wants to circumscribe scientific research so it does no harm to their version of social justice. Any study that might call into question the doctrines of the identity Left must be suppressed. Furthermore, by declaring that objective, rational thinking, cause and effect reasoning, and emphasis on the scientific method are all attributes of "whiteness," the identity Left deprecates the scientific enterprise, which has given us material well-being unimaginable to prior generations. In place of the "white" scientific enterprise, the identity Left apparently wants to substitute insights derived from lived experience, narratives, and *cuentos*. Instead of objective truth, there is "my truth." Try developing a vaccine based on "my truth."

But perhaps the most troubling, disheartening, and ironic assault on Enlightenment values is the identity Left's rejection of the universality of rights. That development is ironic because, as stated above, the identity Left excoriates Enlightenment thinkers for their failure to implement their ideals fully, with "universal" in practice meaning "white men." Yes, it has taken some time for the Enlightenment ideal of universal rights to reach fruition, but it happened by the early years of the twenty-first century, with equal rights largely achieved for gays and lesbians, on top of the equal rights already recognized for racial minorities and women. But it is precisely when social and legal significance are no longer attached to one's group identity that the identity Left wants to turn the clock back and reinstate social and legal significance to group identities. When policy is expressly designed to deny equal benefits to individuals because of their race—and this is what the identity Left's racial equity means in practice—then the ideal of universal human rights has been abandoned.

By elevating group identity over universal human rights, the identity Left is also erasing the individual. When human rights are truly universal, one's group identity does not matter; each person is regarded as and treated as an individual. By classifying people based on their group identity, the identity Left seeks to impose a rigid conformity on individuals. They claim, for example, that there is a "voice of color." But there is no uniform voice of color. Black individuals and Hispanic individuals are just like white individuals; they have a range of opinions about various public policy issues. To deny this reality, the identity Left exiles dissenting black and Hispanic individuals to the realm of "whiteness." Only the identity Left could come up with the paradoxical neologism "multiracial whiteness."[7] And successful Asians who provide embarrassing counterexamples to notions of oppressive "white supremacy" are dismissed as being "white adjacent" or "white equivalent." The identity Left thus relies on bewildering gibberish masquerading as profundity all with the aim of dismissing opposing views without engaging with them.

It is obvious, of course, that the Christian Right also denies universal rights. They are candid about this at least. One of the principles of Christian nationalism is "the primacy of Christian peoplehood" which entails that certain viewpoints must be excluded from the public square, including "political atheism," anything tending to subvert Christianity, opposition to Christian morality, "heretical teaching," and anything tending to promote the political and social influence of non-Christian religions.[8] The Puritan commonwealth updated for the twenty-first century.

So, both the identity Left and the Christian/authoritarian Right threaten the Enlightenment values that have provided people in the

United States, specifically, and the West, in general, with more political and religious freedom, protections against discrimination, personal autonomy, and prosperity than anywhere else in the world. Immigration to the United States and Europe is a problem in the sense that it needs to be managed better, but it is a problem that attests to the success of Enlightenment values. People of all races and ethnicities risk their lives to get into the United States and Europe; they are not beating down the doors to get into Russia, North Korea, Iran, Cuba, Venezuela, or China.

Were Christian nationalists to gain control of the United States, that would be a catastrophe for our democracy. But because most Americans recognize the obvious danger in this prospect, the likelihood that a takeover by the authoritarian Right would happen is small, although not negligible. The only way this could possibly happen is if enough Americans see the authoritarian Right as the only way to resist the identity Left. Much more likely is the slow rot to our democracy that will follow the further entrenchment of the tenets of the identity Left as it secures control over universities, corporations, and the government. Equity will triumph over equality of opportunity, merit will be discarded as a basis for selection or advancement, public policies will be expressly tailored to promote the interests of this or that "marginalized" group regardless of whether this serves the interests of the public as a whole, allegedly harmful and offensive speech will be denied any public platform, scientific research will be limited to conform to the prevailing ideology, and every conceivable aspect of culture and public life will be inspected to see if it is tainted with "whiteness."

However, this is not inevitable. Furthermore, the answer to the identity Left is not to seek refuge in the equally pernicious nostrums of the authoritarian Right. We cannot save liberal democracy from the identity Left by destroying it. Liberalism, the liberalism that is based on universal rights and other Enlightenment values, can still be saved; however, it needs vocal defenders. Those who recognize the importance of Enlightenment values need to speak up. They need to speak up at school board sessions, at meetings with politicians, at corporate DEI trainings, at chats among friends and colleagues. Sure, doing so is and will be uncomfortable, and one must be prepared to be called a "racist" or accused of shedding "white tears" or labeled a "multiracial white" if one is a person of color; challenging dogmas is not easy or pleasant. But remaining silent is to acquiesce in these divisive dogmas and be a mute witness to the nation's self-destruction. The choice is stark: we can either have a liberal democracy that allows us to transcend our differences or a fractured nation where our group identities define and divide us.

NOTES

Introduction

1. Abby Goodnough and Jan Hoffman, "The Elderly vs. Essential Workers: Who Should Get the Coronavirus Vaccine First?" *New York Times*, Dec. 5, 2020, www.nytimes.com/2020/12/05/health/covid-vaccine-first.html (quoting Harald Schmidt, a health policy "expert," who argues workers who are disproportionately minorities should have priority over the elderly for vaccines because "Older populations are whiter," and "Instead of giving additional health benefits to those who already had more, we can start to level the playing field a bit.").

2. American Medical Association, "Organizational Strategic Plan to Embed Racial Justice and Advance Health Equity, 2021-2023," 2021, esp. pp. 8, 19, 36–41, www.ama-assn.org/system/files/2021-05/ama-equity-strategic-plan.pdf.

3. Executive Order no. 13985 of January 20, 2021, "Executive Order on Advancing Racial Equity and Support for Underserved Communities Through the Federal Government," *Federal Register* 86 (January 25, 2021): 7009–7013.

4. A captivating, comprehensive account of the Chinese Cultural Revolution, in all its gruesome detail, can be found in Yang Jisheng, *The World Turned Upside Down: A History of the Chinese Cultural Revolution* (New York: Farrar, Straus and Giroux, 2021).

5. On or about August 28, 2020, Northwestern University law faculty engaged in a ritual of self-denunciation at a town hall meeting, calling themselves racist. See Carly Ortiz-Lytle, "Northwestern University's Interim Dean Admits to Being a 'Racist' During Digital Town Hall," *Washington Examiner*, Septem-

ber 1, 2020, www.washingtonexaminer.com/news/northwestern-universitys-interim-dean-admits-to-being-a-racist-during-digital-town-hall.

6. That the video-recorded killing of George Floyd ignited a racial reckoning which, in turn, resulted in widespread acceptance of the doctrine of systemic racism, has been noted by a number of different commentators. See, for example, Silvia Foster-Frau et al., "Floyd's Death Sparked Prolonged Concern for Race and Racism, But It's Still Unclear What That Means," *Washington Post*, April 20, 2021, www.washingtonpost.com/national/floyds-death-sparked-prolonged-concern-for-race-and-racism-but-its-still-unclear-what-that-means/2021/04/20/ . Floyd's slow-motion death, captured in a gruesome video, was unquestionably disturbing. Still, why his death in particular had such a tremendous impact is a worthy subject for study, although any dispassionate analysis may have to await a significant passage of time.

7. Ibram X. Kendi, *How To Be an Antiracist* (New York: One World, 2019), p. 19.

8. Others share this viewpoint. See, e.g., William A. Galston, "Right-Wing Populism May Rise in the United States," *Wall Street Journal*, September 27, 2022, www.wsj.com/articles/right-wing-populism-may-rise-in-the-u-s-giorgia-meloni-italy-europe-immigration-working-class-college-educated-11664277816?mod=itp_wsj&mod=djemITP_h.

9. Craig Simpson, "Decolonise Your Ears as Mozart's Works May Be an Instrument of Empire, Students Told," *The Telegraph*, May 7, 2022, www.telegraph.co.uk/news/2022/05/07/decolonise-ears-mozarts-works-may-instrument-empire-students/.

10. For example, the United Kingdom established a commission to examine, inter alia, the claim that there was systemic racism in that country. See The [Sewell] Report, [U.K.] Commission on Race and Ethnic Disparities, March 2021, assets.publishing.service.gov.uk/government/uploads/system/uploads/attachment_data/file/974507/20210331_-_CRED_Report_-_FINAL_-_Web_Accessible.pdf.

11. Those interested in the extent to which the cultural revolution in the United States is mirrored in other Western democracies should consult Douglas Murray's *The War on the West* (New York, Broadside Books, 2022), which provides a worthwhile overview of some of the common cultural trends affecting Western democracies.

12. For my overview of the tenets of critical race theory, I rely principally on Richard Delgado and Jean Stefanic, *Critical Race Theory: An Introduction*, 3rd ed. (New York: New York University Press, 2017), esp. pp. 8–11.

13. Under the one-drop rule, any amount of black ancestry made one black. For discussion of this absurd rule, see F. James Davis, *Who Is Black? One*

Nation's Definition, 10th anniversary ed. (University Park, PA: Penn State University Press, 2001).

14. "The Battle Over Critical Race Theory," *The Takeaway*, WNYC Studios, New York Public Radio, broadcast June 21, 2021 (see esp. comment of host Melissa Harris-Perry: "Is Anybody Teaching Critical Race Theory in Third Grade?"), www.wnycstudios.org/podcasts/takeaway/segments/battle-over-critical-race-theory.

15. See, e.g., Zach Goldberg and Eric Kaufmann, "Yes, Critical Race Theory Is Being Taught in Schools," *City Journal*, October 20, 2022, www.city-journal.org/yes-critical-race-theory-is-being-taught-in-schools; Nicole Ault and Megan Keller, "How Teachers Are Secretly Taught Critical Race Theory," *Wall Street Journal*, September 2, 2022, www.wsj.com/articles/if-students-dont-learn-critical-race-theory-why-do-teachers-pacific-educational-group-school-board-administrators-students-class-11662150413; and Marisa Iati, "What Is Critical Race Theory and Why Do Republicans Want To Ban It in Schools," *Washington Post*, May 29, 2021, www.washingtonpost.com/education/2021/05/29/critical-race-theory-bans-schools/.

16. Nicole Hannah-Jones, et al., "The 1619 Project," *New York Times Magazine*, August 14, 2019, www.nytimes.com/interactive/2019/08/14/magazine/1619-america-slavery.html.

17. The claim regarding the colonists' motivation was modified in a later version of *The 1619 Project* so that it applied only to some colonists. See Timothy Sandefur, "The 1619 Project: An Autopsy," CATO Institute, October 27, 2020, www.cato.org/commentary/1619-project-autopsy; "Twelve Scholars Critique The 1619 Project and the New York Times Magazine Editor Responds," History News Network, January 26, 2020, historynewsnetwork.org/article/174140.

18. Donna Cassata and Michael Scherer, "Trump Drops His Support for Rep. Mo Brooks in Alabama Senate Race," *Washington Post*, March 23, 2022, www.washingtonpost.com/politics/2022/03/23/trump-brooks-alabama-senate/.

Chapter 1

Standpoint Theory: Objectivity as a White Male Delusion

1. Peggy McGlone, "African American Museum Site Removes Whiteness Chart After Criticism From Trump Jr. and Conservative Media," *Washington Post*, July 17, 2020, www.washingtonpost.com/entertainment/museums/african-american-museum-site-removes-whiteness-chart-after-criticism-from-trump-jr-and-conservative-media/2020/07/17/. Note the implication of the headline that it was only "conservatives" who took issue with the

chart.

2. Nancy C. M. Hartsock, "The Feminist Standpoint, Developing the Ground for a Specifically Feminist Historical Materialism," in *Feminist Social Thought: A Reader* ed. Diana Tietjens Meyer (New York: Routledge, 1997), pp. 462–483.

3. Ibid., p. 474.

4. Nancy W. Brickhouse, "Embodying Science: A Feminist Perspective on Learning," *Journal of Research in Science Teaching* 38(3) (2001): 282–295, 284. Harding's argument regarding the male bias in the natural sciences may be found in many works, but the best source may be *Whose Science? Whose Knowledge? Thinking from Women's Lives* (Ithaca: Cornell University Press, 1991), pp. 77–102. Let me take this opportunity to mention that when some of the feminist literature uses the word "gender," I will typically use the word "sex." For example, I will refer to sex differences as opposed to gender differences. Especially with the advent of disputes regarding transgender individuals, "gender" might be confused with "gender identity."

5. Chanda Prescod-Weinstein, "Making Black Women Scientists Under White Empiricism: The Racialization of Epistemology in Physics," *Signs: Journal of Women in Culture and Society* 45(2) (2020): 422–447, 426.

6. Ibid.

7. Sandra Harding, "Rethinking Standpoint Epistemology: What is 'Strong Objectivity'?" *The Centennial Review* 36(3) (1992): 437–470, 459.

8. I note that Harding, among others, has argued that standpoint theory does not actually deny the possibility of objective knowledge. Instead, she claims standpoint theory only challenges objectivity as traditionally understood. She contrasts the traditional understanding of objectivity as value-neutral with "strong objectivity," which she argues can be achieved only by starting knowledge projects from the lives of the oppressed and incorporating their insights. Ibid., pp. 444–445, 458–461.

9. Sandra Harding, "Standpoint Theories: Productively Controversial," *Hypatia* 24(4) (2009):192–200, 192–193.

10. Emily Margaret Pelland, "Nuanced Narratives: Reporting with Critical Race and Feminist Standpoint Theories," (2019). *Graduate Theses, Dissertations, and Problem Reports*. 3804. p. 2, researchrepository.wvu.edu/etd/3804.

11. As indicated, how the proletariat actually achieve the requisite level of class consciousness to see things as they are and to undertake revolutionary action is a subject of debate within Marxism. Lenin famously argued that the working classes by themselves can only develop "trade-union" consciousness. They need the assistance of revolutionary socialist intelligentsia—people like Lenin—to guide them. See V. I. Lenin, *What Is To Be Done?* (New York:

International Publishers, 1969), esp. pp. 29–34. Marx himself appears not to have resolved the issue of how the proletariat actually achieves appropriate class consciousness. Some early writings suggest revolutionary consciousness is something that develops automatically, whereas other writings suggest either that social struggle raises consciousness or a scientific understanding of social-ism possessed by a revolutionary vanguard provides the necessary impetus. See Michael Levin, "Marx and Working-Class Consciousness," *History of Political Thought* 1(3) (1980): 499–515. This a parochial dispute within Marxism, but it does cast a light on some analogous problems within standpoint theory. Unless women automatically develop better insight as a function of their oppressed status, there must be some mechanism which coverts their oppression into a vehicle for better insight. This issue will be discussed below.

12. Harding, *Whose Science?* p.121.

13. Ibid., p.124.

14. Ibid., p.126.

15. Ibid., p.127.

16. Harding, "Rethinking Standpoint Epistemology," p. 459.

17. Charles Mills, "Ideology," in *The Routledge Handbook of Epistemic Injustice,* ed. Ian James Kidd, Jose Medina, and Gaile Pohlhaus, Jr. (New York: Routledge, 2017) (hereinafter "RHEI"), p 108.

18. Peggy McIntosh is credited for launching the concept of privilege in her essay "White Privilege: Unpacking the Invisible Knapsack," *Peace and Freedom* July/August (1989): 10–12. For an exhaustive, and at times humorous, summary of the various ways in which the concept of privilege has been de-ployed and weaponized, see Phoebe Maltz Bovy, *The Perils of "Privilege"* (New York: St. Martin's Press, 2017).

19. Interestingly, Harding has a different explanation of how the social situation contributed to the resistance to heliocentric theory, observing that Ptolemaic astronomy had a better "fit" with the "hierarchical social structure of the Catholic Church and feudal society." Harding, *Whose Science?* p. 135. This explanation strikes me as forced—looking for a more profound explanation when a simpler, straightforward one is available.

20. H. Tristram Engelhardt, Jr., *The Foundations of Bioethics* (New York: Oxford University Press, 1986), p. 160.

21. American Psychiatric Association, *Diagnostic and Statistical Manual of Mental Disorders*, 2nd ed. (Washington, D.C.: American Psychiatric Associ-ation, 1968), p. 44. By resolution in 1973, the APA removed this designation from its manual.

22. Daniel Solorzano and Tara J. Yosso, "Critical Race Methodology: Counter-Storytelling as an Analytical Framework for Education Research,"

Qualitative Inquiry 8 (2002): 23–44, 26.

23. Ibid.

24. "Demarginalizing the Intersection of Race and Sex: A Black Feminist Critique of Antidiscrimination Doctrine, Feminist Theory and Antiracist Politics," *University of Chicago Legal Forum* 1989(1): 139–167, 149.

25. Ibid., p. 140.

26. "Mapping the Margins: Intersectionality, Identity Politics, and Violence Against Women of Color," *Stanford Law Review* 43(6) (1991): 1241–1299, 1242.

27. Ibid., p. 1245.

28. Harding, "Standpoint Theories: Productively Controversial," p. 194.

29. Patricia Hill Collins, "Intersectionality and Epistemic Injustice," in RHEI, p. 115.

30. Ibid., p.119.

31. Stephanie Shields, "Gender: An Intersectionality Perspective," *Sex Roles* 59 (2008): 301–311, 302.

32. Ibid.

33. Ibid., p. 303.

34. Harding, *Whose Science?* pp.155–156. I should note that although the quoted text obviously addresses an issue posed by intersectionality, the text is from a passage in which Harding discusses the issue of whether standpoint theory is committed to relativism (a topic I will address later). However, when, in other works, Harding has specifically addressed how intersectionality meshes with standpoint theory, she uses similarly vague language. See Harding, "Standpoint Theories: Productively Controversial," pp. 193–194 (gender relations are always "positioned" in other social hierarchies, just as "agents in those other hierarchies are locatable on the maps of gender relations").

35. Sirma Bilge, "Intersectionality Undone: Saving Intersectionality from Feminist Intersectionality Studies," *Du Bois Review* 10(2) (2013): 405–424, 420.

36. Ibid., p. 412.

37. Lou Ferreira, "LGBT People Globally Are Not Waiting for 'White Saviours' To Rescue Them," *Open Democracy*, June 8, 2021, www.opendemocracy.net/en/5050/lgbt-people-globally-are-not-waiting-for-white-saviours-to-rescue-them/.

38. Adam Fitzgerald, "Time for Cis-Gender White Men To Recognize Their Privilege," *Thomson Reuters Foundation*, May 2, 2019, news.trust.org/item/20190502130719-tpcky/.

39. Damon Young, "Straight Black Men Are the White People of Black People," *The Root*, September 18, 2017, www.theroot.com/straight-black-men-are-the-white-people-of-black-people-1814157214.

40. Collins, "Intersectionality and Epistemic Injustice," pp. 119, 120.

41. Harding, *Whose Science?* p. 147.

42. Ibid., p. 146.

43. Nancy Tuana, "Feminist Epistemology: The Subject of Knowledge," in RHEI, p. 125.

44. Harding, *Whose Science?* p. 149.

45. Ibid., p. 150.

46. Ibid., passim, but esp. pp. 149–152, 156–160.

47. See, for example, ibid., p. 140.

48. Thomas S. Kuhn, *The Structure of Scientific Revolutions*, 2nd ed. (Chicago: University of Chicago, 1970).

49. Quine made this argument in many works, but I believe its first appearance was in "Two Dogmas of Empiricism," in *From a Logical Point of View*, rev. ed. (New York: Harper and Row, 1963), pp. 20–46.

50. The best thick book on this topic, in my opinion, is Philip Kitcher, *The Advancement of Science: Science Without Legend, Objectivity Without Illusions* (New York: Oxford University Press, 1963). I have no doubt that professional philosophers will regard my abbreviated discussion of the philosophical issues surrounding objectivity in science to be incomplete at best. But this book is not primarily directed at an academic audience. Anyway, for those who would want a fuller defense of my position, I direct them to Kitcher's book, with which I am in agreement, at least as to major theses.

51. Ibid., p. 247.

52. "Two Dogmas of Empiricism," p. 43.

53. For an overview of string theory, see Brian Greene, *The Elegant Universe: Superstrings, Hidden Dimensions, and the Quest for the Ultimate Reality* (New York: W.W. Norton, 2003). For a critique of string theory and a general discussion of the challenges of theory formation in physics, see Sabine Hossenfelder, *Lost in Math: How Beauty Leads Physics Astray* (New York: Basic Books, 2018).

54. The present lack of adequate empirical support for string theory is the inspiration for Prescod-Weinstein's impassioned indictment of "white empiricism." (See note 5.) In her view, "white empiricism" allows physicists to continue to advocate for string theory despite the absence of confirming empirical support while, at the same time, not offering "axiomatic acceptance of [Black women's] agency in discourses about race and gender." "White Empiricism," p. 430. It would take us too far afield to engage at length with Prescod-Weinstein on string theory, but I note in passing that string theory has many sharp critics and many of these critics, such as Lee Smolin, Peter Woit, and Sabine Hossenfelder, are white, so her claim that string theory is "given room to breathe in

professional spaces" because its advocates are white lacks support.

55. My discussion of the development of vaccines for Covid-19 relies principally on two sources: Elie Dolgin, "The Tangled History of mRNA Vaccines," *Nature* 597, no. 7876 (2021): 318–324 and Gina Koleta and Benjamin Mueller, "Halting Progress and Happy Accidents: How mRNA Vaccines Were Made," *New York Times*, January 15, 2022, www.nytimes.com/2022/01/15/health/mrna-vaccine.html.

56. In discussing the James Webb Telescope I have relied upon Joel Achenbach, "James Webb Telescope Will Open a New Window on the Cosmos—If Everything Goes Just Right," *Washington Post*, December 22, 2021, www.washingtonpost.com/science/interactive/2021/webb-space-telescope-launch/?itid=lk_inline_manual_2&itid=lk_inline_manual_8 and NASA, "Webb Space Telescope," www.jwst.nasa.gov/ (last accessed April 30, 2022).

57. Scott O. Lilienfeld, "Microaggressions: Strong Claims, Inadequate Evidence," *Perspectives on Psychological Science* 12(1) (2017): 138–169 (negligible support for claim of adverse impact on mental health).

58. Diana Kwon, "The Rise of Citational Injustice: How Scholars Are Making References Fairer," *Nature* 603, no. 7902 (2022): 568–571. See also Collins, "Intersectionality and Epistemic Injustice," p. 121 (contending that patterns of citation can manifest epistemic violence).

59. Kristie Dotson, "Conceptualizing Epistemic Oppression," *Social Epistemology* 28(2) (2014): 115–138, 115.

60. Briana Toole, "From Standpoint Theory to Epistemic Oppression," *Hypatia* 34(4) (2019): 598–618, 614.

61. Harding, "Standpoint Theories: Productively Controversial," p. 195. See also Toole, "From Standpoint Theory to Epistemic Oppression," p. 600 ("one is not epistemically privileged *in virtue* of occupying a particular social location," but rather "epistemic privilege may be *achieved* through the process of consciousness-raising")

62. Harding, *Whose Science?* pp. 124–125, 131–132.

63. Alison Wylie and Sergio Sismondo, "Standpoint Theory, in Science," in *International Encyclopedia of the Social and Behavioral Sciences*, ed. James D. Wright, 2nd ed. (New York: Elsevier, 2015), pp. 324–330, 326.

64. Harding, "Rethinking Standpoint Epistemology," p. 454.

65. Cassandra L. Pinnick, "Feminist Epistemology: Implications for Philosophy of Science," *Philosophy of Science* 61(4) (1994): 646–657, 656.

66. Kristina Rolin, "The Bias Paradox in Feminist Standpoint Epistemology," *Episteme* 3(1-2) (2006): 125-136, 130.

67. Wylie and Sismondo, "Standpoint Theory, in Science," p. 326.

68. Sagan apparently first uttered this dictum on the television series *Cos-*

mos. The eighteenth-century French scholar Pierre-Simon Laplace is often given credit for first formulating this principle, but it is now known popularly as the Sagan Standard. "Sagan Standard," *Wikipedia* en.wikipedia.org/wiki/Sagan_standard (accessed May 2, 2022).

69. Cassandra L. Pinnick, "Science Education for Women: Situated Cognition, Feminist Standpoint Theory, and The Status of Women in Science," *Science & Education* 17 (2008): 1055–1063, 1062.

70. Prescod-Weinstein, "White Empiricism," p. 421.

71. Ibid., p. 430.

72. Ibid., pp. 437–438.

73. Ibid., p. 440.

74. Wylie and Sismondo, "Standpoint Theory, in Science," p. 327.

75. This summary is largely based on Ruth B. Merkatz, "Inclusion of Women in Clinical Trials: A Historical Overview of Scientific, Ethical, and Legal Issues," *JOGNN* 27(1) (1998): 78–84.

76. The Belmont Report, National Commission for the Protection of Human Subjects of Biomedical and Behavioral Research, available at www.hhs.gov/ohrp/regulations-and-policy/belmont-report/index.html (accessed May 2, 2022).

77. John T. Jost et al., "Political Conservatism as Motivated Social Cognition," *Psychological Bulletin* 139(3) (2003): 339–375.

78. Wylie and Sismondo, "Standpoint Theory, in Science," p. 327.

79. Carol Gilligan, *In a Different Voice: Psychological Theory and Women's Development* (Cambridge, MA: Harvard University Press, 1982), p. 18.

80. Ibid., pp. 2-3.

81. Ibid., p. 19.

82. See, for example, James Rachels, *The Elements of Moral Philosophy* (San Francisco: McGraw-Hill, 1999).

83. *In a Different Voice*, p. 2.

84. Rolin, "The Bias Paradox in Feminist Standpoint Epistemology," p. 131.

85. Ibid.

86. Ibid., pp. 130–133. Jonathan Cole's book is *Fair Science: Women in the Scientific Community* (New York: Free Press, 1979). The paper by Katila and Merilainen is "A Serious Researcher or Just Another Nice Girl? Doing Gender in a Male-Dominated Scientific Community," *Gender Work and Organization* 6(3) (1999): 163–173.

87. For examples of the vast literature on this topic see National Academies of Sciences, Engineering, and Medicine, *Sexual Harassment of Women: Climate, Culture, and Consequences in Academic Sciences, Engineering, and Medi-*

cine (Washington, D.C.: National Academies Press, 2018) (finding widespread harassment) and Flamino Squazzoni et al. "Peer Review and Gender Bias: A Study on 145 Scholarly Journals," *Science Advances* 7 (January 6, 2021) (finding no evidence of bias in peer review).

88. In the United States, the first legal recognition of sexual harassment came in a 1976 U.S. District Court decision (issued by a male judge), *Williams v. Saxbe* (D.D.C.).

89. Rolin, "The Bias Paradox in Feminist Standpoint Epistemology," p. 132.

90. Katila and Merilainen, "A Serious Researcher or Just Another Nice Girl?" pp. 167–168.

91. Ibid., pp. 168–169.

92. Ibid., p. 165.

93. Ibid., p. 169.

94. For a concise summary of the issue, see Linda Chavez, "Comparable Worth," *Wall Street Journal*, August 24, 2005, www.wsj.com/articles/SB112484922678721494.

95. Biography of Elizabeth Anderson, website of Philosophy Department, University of Michigan, lsa.umich.edu/philosophy/people/faculty/elizabeth-anderson.html (accessed May 14, 2022).

96. Elizabeth Anderson, "Uses of Value Judgments in Science: A General Argument with Lessons from a Case Study of Feminist Research on Divorce," *Hypatia* 19(1) (2004): 1–24. Indeed, the focus of Anderson's article is less the benefit of research guided by feminist values than the legitimate role, as she sees it, of values in scientific research.

97. Abigail Stewart, et al., *Separating Together: How Divorce Transforms Families* (New York: Guilford Press, 1997).

98. "Uses of Value Judgments in Science," p. 20.

99. See David Neumark and William Wascher, *The Effect of New Jersey's Minimum Wage Increase on Fast-food Employment: A Re-evaluation Using Payroll Records* (Cambridge, MA: National Bureau of Economic Research, 1995).

100. "Uses of Value Judgments in Science," p. 23.

101. Richard Delgado and Jean Stefancic, *Critical Race Theory: An Introduction*, 3rd ed. (New York: New York University Press, 2017), p. 11.

102. Maria C. Malagon, Lindsay Perez Huber, and Veronica N. Velez, "Our Experiences, Our Methods: Using Grounded Theory to Inform a Critical Race Theory Methodology," *Seattle Journal for Social Justice* 8(1) (2009): 253–272, 257.

103. Patricia Hill Collins, *Black Feminist Thought: Knowledge, Consciousness, and the Politics of Empowerment*, 2nd ed. (New York: Routledge, 2000), pp. 257, 271.

104. Prescod-Weinstein, "White Empiricism," p. 430.

105. Lauren Farrell, Mel Langness, and Elsa Falkenburger, "Community Voice Is Expertise," Urban Institute, February 19, 2021, www.urban.org/urban-wire/community-voice-expertise.

106. The [Sewell] Report, [U.K.] Commission on Race and Ethnic Disparities, March 2021, p. 31, assets.publishing.service.gov.uk/government/uploads/system/uploads/attachment_data/file/974507/20210331_-_CRED_Report_-_FINAL_-_Web_Accessible.pdf.

107. Melina Abdullah, "Statement Regarding the Ongoing Trial of Jussie Smollett," December 7, 2021, blacklivesmatter.com/statement-regarding-the-ongoing-trial-of-jussie-smollett/.

108. Brendan O'Neill, "The Tyranny of Lived Experience," *Spiked*, March 19, 2021, www.spiked-online.com/2021/03/19/the-tyranny-of-lived-experience/.

109. Visitor Code of Conduct, Columbus Museum of Art (July 2022), www.columbusmuseum.org/wp-content/uploads/2022/07/UPDATED-Visitor-Code-of-Conduct.pdf.

110. University of Cincinnati Libraries, "Racial Gaslighting," *Racial Justice Resources for Activists, Advocates & Allies*, guides.libraries.uc.edu/racialjusticeresources/racialgaslighting (accessed May 6, 2022).

111. Cecilia Kersten, "8 Ways to Be a (Better) Ally," *The Peel* (Syracuse University), October 14, 2020, news.syr.edu/the-peel/2020/10/14/8-ways-to-be-a-better-ally/.

112. George Mason University, Counseling and Psychological Services, "Anti-Racism Resources," caps.gmu.edu/resources-and-self-help/anti-racism-resources/ (accessed May 2, 2022), citing Elly Belle, "How White People Can Hold Each Other Accountable to Stop Institutional Racism," August 2, 2019, www.teenvogue.com/story/white-people-can-hold-each-other-accountable-to-stop-institutional-racism. As another example, the University of Pennsylvania recommends an article in Sojourners magazine, which advises "Try just to listen and sit with someone else's experience." Courtney Ariel, "For Our White Friends Desiring to Be Allies, " August 16, 2017, sojo.net/articles/our-white-friends-desiring-be-allies, referenced by the university's Center for Social Impact Strategy csis.upenn.edu/independent-learning/for-our-white-friends-desiring-to-be-allies/ (accessed May 2, 2022).

113. Reni Eddo-Lodge, *Why I'm No Longer Talking to White People About Race* (London: Bloomsbury Publishing, 2017).

114. An audio recording of the talk, along with transcribed excerpts, is available at www.commonsense.news/p/the-psychopathic-problem-of-the-white#-details.

115. Kwame Anthony Appiah, "Why Are Politicians Suddenly Talking

About Their 'Lived Experience'?" *The Guardian*, November 14, 2020, www.theguardian.com/commentisfree/2020/nov/14/lived-experience-kamala-harris.

116. 1 Timothy 2: 11–12.

Chapter 2
The Unproven Claim of Systemic Racism

1. Julian M. Rucker and Jennifer A. Richeson, "Toward an Understanding of Structural Racism: Implications for Criminal Justice," *Science* 374(6565) (2021): 286–290, 288. The authors use the term "structural racism" instead of "systemic racism." In the literature, the terms are often used interchangeably, although systemic racism is considered the broader term. See Paula A. Braveman et al., "Systemic and Structural Racism: Definitions, Examples, Health Damages, and Approaches to Dismantling," *Health Affairs* 41(2) (2022): 171–178, 172.

2. Angela Hanks, Danyelle Solomon, and Christian E. Weller, "Systemic Inequality: How America's Structural Racism Helped Create the Black-White Wealth Gap," Center for American Progress, February 21, 2018, p. 4, www.americanprogress.org/article/systematic-inequality/. I should note that some proponents of the systemic racism doctrine hedge their bets by claiming that if intentional acts of discrimination are widespread enough then they can be considered "manifestations of systemic racism." Paula Braveman et al., "Systemic Racism and Health Equity," Robert Wood Johnson Foundation (2022), p. 9, www.rwjf.org/en/library/research/2021/12/systemic-racism-and-health-equity.html. Dylann Roof's horrific murders are mentioned as one such manifestation. Ibid. How Roof's despicable and idiotic homicides can be traced to allegedly racist policies and laws, such as higher interest rates charged to persons with bad credit, is left unexplained.

3. "Systemic Inequality: How America's Structural Racism Helped Create the Black-White Wealth Gap"; Emily Moss, et al., "The Black-White Wealth Gap Left Black Households More Vulnerable," Brookings Institution, December 8, 2020, www.brookings.edu/blog/up-front/2020/12/08/the-black-white-wealth-gap-left-black-households-more-vulnerable/; Sean Collins, "The Systemic Racism Black Americans Face, Explained in 9 Charts," *Vox*, June 17, 2020, www.vox.com/2020/6/17/21284527/systemic-racism-black-americans-9-charts-explained; Shayanne Gal et al., "26 Simple Charts to Show Friends and Family Who Aren't Convinced Racism Is Still a Problem in America," *Insider*, July 8, 2020, www.businessinsider.com/us-systemic-racism-in-charts-graphs-data-2020-6. A more comprehensive, and in many ways, better resource are various Stanford University websites that address systemic racism.

See news.stanford.edu/2022/02/01/examining-systemic-racism-advancing-ra-cial-equity/ and library.stanford.edu/blogs/stanford-libraries-blog/2021/08/introducing-know-systemic-racism-ksr-project. However, because the infor-mation is not organized in charts, it requires more effort to distill the crux of the arguments set forth there. That said, those with the time should review the significant volume of information set forth on these sites to ensure they are acquainted with the best arguments for systemic racism.

4. Richard E. Lapchick, "The 2020 Racial and Gender Report Card: Na-tional Basketball Association," The Institute for Diversity and Ethics in Sport, July 23, 2020, p. 6; Christina Gough, "Players in the NFL in 2021, by Ethnici-ty," *Statista*, March 18, 2022, www.statista.com/statistics/1167935/racial-diver-sity-nfl-players/.

5. Dimitrije Curcic, "NBA Salaries Analysis (1991–2022)," *RunRepeat*, November 10, 2021, runrepeat.com/salary-analysis-in-the-nba-1991-2019.

6. For a book-length discussion of the flaws and fallacies often encoun-tered in statistical arguments, see Thomas Sowell, *Discrimination and Dispari-ties*, rev. ed. (New York: Basic Books, 2019).

7. Title VII, in its current form, is codified at 42 U.S.C. § 2000e. Portions of this section of my argument borrow from my previously published article, "Should We Impose Quotas? Evaluating the 'Disparate Impact' Argument Against Legalization of Assisted Suicide," *Journal of Law, Medicine, & Ethics* 30(1) (2002): 6–16.

8. *Griggs v. Duke Power Co.*, 401 U.S. 424 (1971). See also *Albemarle Paper Co. v. Moody*, 422 U.S. 405 (1975).

9. *Griggs*, 401 U.S. at 431.

10. *Albemarle*, 422 U.S. at 425 (plaintiffs must show the test in question caused an adverse impact). See also *Wards Cove Packing Co. v. Antonio*. 490 US. 642, 656–657 (1989) *modified in part by statute* (specifically identified practices must be causally linked with disparate impact). This part of the holding in *Wards Cove* was modified by the Civil Rights Act of 1991, which provides that where "elements of a respondent's decisionmaking process are not capable of separa-tion for analysis, the decisionmaking process" may be analyzed globally. In other words, a specific practice need not be identified if it is impossible to do so. The requirement of a causal link remains. See 42 U.S.C. § 2000e-2(k)(1)(A)(i) and (B)(i). Subsection (A)(i) of the statute also codifies the business necessity test first set forth in *Griggs*. See *Griggs* 401 U. S. at 432.

11. *Texas Dept. of Housing and Community Affairs v. Inclusive Communities Project, Inc.*, No. 13-1371, slip op. at 18, 576 U.S. 519 (2015).

12. Ibid. at 19–20.

13. Allyson Chiu and Amber Ferguson, "The Troubled Legacy of Fem-

inine Care Products," *Washington Post*, May 31, 2022, www.washingtonpost. com/wellness/2022/05/31/feminine-wash-honey-pot-history/.

14. For a succinct disparate impact argument against the death penalty, see "Race and The Death Penalty," ACLU, www.aclu.org/other/race-and-death-penalty (accessed June 1, 2022). For examples of the disparate impact argument in the assisted suicide context, see the sources collected in note 2, "Should We Impose Quotas?" at 14.

15. Oregon Division of Public Health, *Twenty-Fourth Annual Report on Death with Dignity Act* (2022), p. 3 (95 percent of patients requesting assisted dying were white). The percentages are comparable in Washington and even California, which is a much more diverse state. Washington State Department of Health, *Death with Dignity Act Report* (2021), p. 9 (92.8 percent); California Department of Public Health, *California End of Life Option Act 2020 Data Report* (2021), p. 5 (87.4 percent).

16. *How To Be an Antiracist*, p. 117. I should note that although Kendi believes racism is systemic, he rejects use of the term; he prefers "racist policy." Ibid., p. 18.

17. Jenna Portnoy, "Youngkin Aide Balks at Racism as a Health Crisis," *Washington Post*, June 16, 2022, www.washingtonpost.com/dc-md-va/2022/06/15/racial-disparities-health-care-youngkin/.

18. *Buchanan v. Warley*, 245 U.S. 60 (1917) (unanimous decision).

19. *Shelley v. Kraemer*, 334 U.S. 1 (1948) (unanimous decision).

20. Guo Xu and Abhay Aneja, "Segregation Policies in Federal Government in Early 20th Century Harmed Backs for Decades," *The Conversation*, November 20, 2020, theconversation.com/segregation-policies-in-federal-government-in-early-20th-century-harmed-blacks-for-decades-145669.

21. Farrell Evans, "How Jim Crow Era Laws Suppressed the African American Vote for Generations," *History*, May 13, 2021, www.history.com/news/jim-crow-laws-black-vote.

22. Hilary Parkinson, "Executive Orders 9980 and 9981: Ending Segregation in the Armed Forces and the Federal Workforce," National Archives, May 19, 2014, prologue.blogs.archives.gov/2014/05/19/executive-orders-9980-and-9981-ending-segregation-in-the-armed-forces-and-the-federal-workforce/.

23. "New York State's Human Rights Law's 75th Anniversary," New York State Division of Human Rights dhr.ny.gov/75 (accessed June 4, 2022); "Connecticut Civil Rights Law Chronology," Commission on Human Rights and Opportunities, portal.ct.gov/CHRO/Legal/Legal/Connecticut-Civil-Rights-Law-Chronology (accessed June 4, 2022).

24. *Brown v. Board of Education*, 347 U.S. 483 (1954) (unanimous decision).

25. The text of the Civil Rights Act of 1957 may be found at: www.senate. gov/artandhistory/history/resources/pdf/Civil_Rights_Act_1957.pdf.

26. Executive Order 10925 (1961), available at: www.presidency.ucsb. edu/documents/executive-order-10925-establishing-the-presidents-committee-equal-employment-opportunity.

27. Executive Order 11063 (1962), available at: www.archives.gov/federal-register/codification/executive-order/11063.html.

28. The text of the Civil Rights Act of 1964 may be found at: www.senate. gov/artandhistory/history/resources/pdf/CivilRightsActOf1964.pdf.

29. The text of the Voting Rights Act of 1965 may be found at: catalog. archives.gov/id/299909.

30. The text of the Fair Housing Act of 1968 (Title VIII of the Civil Rights Act of 1968) may be found at: www.govinfo.gov/content/pkg/COMPS-343/pdf/COMPS-343.pdf.

31. The text of the Equal Credit Opportunity Act may be found at: http://uscode.house.gov/view.xhtml.

32. *Jones v. Alfred H. Mayer*, 392 U.S. 409 (1968).

33. *Johnson v. Railway Express Agency*, 421 U.S. 454 (1975).

34. See note 26 above.

35. *University of California v. Bakke*, 438 U.S. 265 (1978).

36. President Johnson outlined his ambitious civil rights and poverty agenda in his January 8, 1964 State of the Union address, which may be found at: www.presidency.ucsb.edu/documents/annual-message-the-congress-the-state-the-union-25.

37. A summary of the Social Security Amendments of 1965, including the provisions establishing Medicaid, may be found at: www.ssa.gov/policy/docs/ssb/v28n9/v28n9p3.pdf.

38. A history of food stamp programs may be found at: www.fns.usda.gov/snap/short-history-snap#1964.

39. The text of the Child Nutrition Act of 1966 may be found at: www.fns. usda.gov/cna-amended-pl-111-296.

40. This article provides an insightful analysis of the Economic Opportunity Act of 1964, including how it formed an integral part of the Johnson administration's efforts to improve conditions for needy black communities: Martha J. Bailey and Nicholas J. Duquette, "How Johnson Fought the War on Poverty: The Economics and Politics of Funding at the Office of Economic Opportunity," *Journal of Economic History* 74(2) (2014): 351–388.

41. Medicaid Coverage Rates for the Nonelderly by Race/Ethnicity, Kaiser Family Foundation, www.kff.org/medicaid/state-indicator/nonelderly-medicaid-rate-by-raceethnicity.

42. Characteristics of Supplemental Nutrition Program Households: Fiscal Year 2019, United States Department of Agriculture, Table B10, p. 92, fns-prod.azureedge.us/sites/default/files/resource-files/Characteristics2019.pdf.

43. Chuck Marr and Yixuan Huang, "Women of Color Especially Benefit from Working Family Tax Credits," Center on Budget and Policy Priorities, September 9, 2019, www.cbpp.org/research/federal-tax/women-of-color-especially-benefit-from-working-family-tax-credits#_ftn1.

44. Michael Tanner and Charles Hughes, "The War on Poverty Turns 50: Are We Winning Yet?" Cato Institute Policy Analysis No. 761 (2014), p.1.

45. John Donahue and James Heckman, "Continuous Versus Episodic Change: The Impact of Civil Rights Policy on the Economic Status of Blacks," *Journal of Economic Literature* 29(4) (1991): 1603–1643, 1607.

46. Ibid., p. 1641.

47. I have specifically stated there is no racism embedded in *civil* legal systems. I have yet to consider the criminal justice system. I will.

48. "Systemic Inequality: How America's Structural Racism Helped Create the Black-White Wealth Gap," p. 12.

49. Will Fischer and Chye-Ching Huang, "Mortgage Interest Deduction Is Ripe for Reform," Center for Budget and Policy Priorities, June 25, 2013, www.cbpp.org/research/mortgage-interest-deduction-is-ripe-for-reform.

50. "Systemic Inequality: How America's Structural Racism Helped Create the Black-White Wealth Gap," p. 26.

51. Walter E. Williams, *Race & Economics: How Much Can Be Blamed on Discrimination?* (Stanford CA: Hoover Institution Press, 2011), p. 39.

52. Sumit Argawal, et al., "Did the Community Reinvestment Act (CRA) Lead to Risky Lending?" Kreisman Working Paper Series in Housing Law and Policy No. 8 (2012), chicagounbound.uchicago.edu/housing_law_and_policy/9/.

53. *Race & Economics: How Much Can Be Blamed on Discrimination?* p. 131.

54. *Pigford v. Glickman,* 185 F.R.D. 82 (D.D.C. 1999), *aff'd,* 206 F.3d 212 (D.C. Cir. 2000).

55. Tadlock Cowan and Jody Feder," The *Pigford* Cases: USDA Settlement of Discrimination Suits by Black Farmers," Congressional Research Service, (May 29, 2013), nationalaglawcenter.org/wp-content/uploads/assets/crs/RS20430.pdf.

56. See, for example, Ta-Nehisi Coates, "The Case for Reparations," *The Atlantic* 313(5) (2014): 54–71.

57. "Systemic Inequality: How America's Structural Racism Helped Create the Black-White Wealth Gap," p. 1.

58. Board of Governors of the Federal Reserve System, "Changes in U.S. Family Finances from 2016 to 2019: Evidence from the Survey of Consumer

Finances," *Federal Reserve Bulletin*, vol. 16 (2020), Net Worth, Table 2, www. federalreserve.gov/publications/2020-bulletin-changes-in-us-family-financ-es-from-2016-to-2019.htm. Families can consist of one person; "family" in current Federal Reserve usage is equivalent to the previously utilized term "household."

59. Ibid.

60. "Systemic Inequality: How America's Structural Racism Helped Create the Black-White Wealth Gap," Table 1, p. 8.

61. "The Case for Reparations," p. 64.

62. Robert C. Lieberman, "Race, Institutions, and the Administration of Social Policy," *Social Science History* 19(4) (1995): 511–542, 514.

63. Zinzi D. Bailey et al., "Structural Racism and Health Inequities in the USA: Evidence and Interventions," *Lancet* 369 (April 8, 2017): 1453–1463, 1454–1455.

64. Larry DeWitt, "The Decision to Exclude Agricultural and Domestic Workers from the 1935 Social Security Act," *Social Security Bulletin* 70(4) (2010): 49–68.

65. Ibid., p. 59

66. Ibid., p. 64.

67. Ibid., p. 53.

68. Ibid., p. 65, n. 16.

69. Price V. Fishback, et al., "The HOLC Maps: How Race and Poverty Influenced Real Estate Professionals' Evaluation of Lending Risk in the 1930s," National Bureau of Economic Research, Working Paper 28146 (rev. 2021), p. 3 www.nber.org/papers/w28146.

70. Ibid., p. 8.

71. Ibid.

72. Ibid., pp. 9–11.

73. Ibid., p. 15.

74. Ibid., p. 23.

75. U.S. Bureau of the Census, *Fifteenth Census of the United States: 1930—Families, Vol. VI* (Washington, D.C.: USGPO, 1933), Table 23, p. 17; U.S. Bureau of the Census, *Sixteenth Census of the United States: 1940—Housing, Vol. II* (Washington, D.C.: USGPO, 1943), Table 16a, p. 48. The term "native" whites was used to distinguish this group from foreign-born whites.

76. "The HOLC Maps," p. 28.

77. Underwriting Manual, Federal Housing Administration, (1938), 937, available at: www.huduser.gov/portal/sites/default/files/pdf/Federal-Housing-Administration-Underwriting-Manual.pdf.

78. Ibid., 980(1).

79. Ibid., 980(3)g.

80. See, for example, Richard Rothstein, *The Color of Law* (New York: Liveright, 2017), esp. pp. 63–75.

81. Ibid., p. 66.

82. Fishback, et al., "The HOLC Maps," p. 9.

83. Underwriting Manual, 812–824, 1019–1066.

84. David Reiss, "The Federal Housing Administration and African-American Homeownership," *Journal of Affordable Housing and Community Development Law* 26(1) (2017): 123–150, 127.

85. George Streator, "Housing Bias Curb Called Minor Gain," *New York Times*, April 27, 1949, available at: timesmachine.nytimes.com/timesmachine/1949/04/27/84560798.html?pageNumber=23.

86. United States Commission on Civil Rights, 1961 Commission on Civil Rights Report, Book 4—Housing (Washington, D.C.: USGPO, 1961), p. 25.

87. Ibid.

88. Ibid.

89. John Kimble, "Insuring Inequality: The Role of the Federal Housing Administration in the Urban Ghettoization of African Americans," *Law & Social Inquiry* 32(2) (2007): 399–434, 403.

90. *Sixteenth Census of the United States: 1940—Housing, Vol. II*, Table 1, p. 7.

91. U.S. Bureau of the Census, *Seventeenth Census of the United States: 1950—Housing, Vol. I* (Washington, D.C.: USGPO, 1953), Table 3, pp. 1-2. In 1940, the census had separate categories for "Negro" and "other nonwhite" in reporting percent of owner occupancy, whereas in 1950 there was only a "nonwhite" category. Given the small number of "other nonwhite" occupied units compared to "Negro" occupied units in 1940 (56,133 versus 1,671,887 in urban areas), combing these two categories had little effect on the percentages for homeownership in 1950.

92. 1961 Commission on Civil Rights Report, Book 4—Housing, pp. 121–122.

93. Ibid., p. 25.

94. See note 27.

95. U.S. Bureau of the Census, *Eighteenth Census of the United States: 1960—Housing, Vol. I* (Washington, D.C.: USGPO, 1963), United States Summary, p. xxviii. What about the homeownership percentages in 1960? How do they compare to the 1950 percentages? One problem in carrying out a comparison is that the Bureau of the Census changed its categories in 1960. It no longer divided owners into urban, rural nonfarm, and farm categories. Instead, it divided owners into central city SMSAs (SMSA = standard metropolitan

statistical area), not central city SMSAs, and outside SMSAs. Taking these categories and contrasting them with 1950 or 1940 data would be an apples to oranges comparison. That said, with respect to central city ownership in 1960, the percentages were 31.4 percent homeownership among nonwhites versus 50.3 percent among whites, for a gap of 18.9 percent; outside central cities but within SMSAs, the percentages were 51.7 percent nonwhite versus 73.5 percent white, for a gap of 21.8 percent. Outside SMSAs, the gap was larger, with nonwhite ownership at 45.2 percent and white ownership at 69.2 percent, for a gap of 24 percent. Ibid., Table G, p. xxvii. The largest group number of owners, black and white, were in SMSAs. Even though no straightforward comparison can be made, it would be fair to say there was some increase in the gap between percent of black owners and percent of white owners.

96. Andre M. Perry and David Harshbarger, "America's Formerly Redlined Neighborhoods Have Changed, and So Must Solutions to Rectify Them," Brookings Institution (October 24, 2019), available at: www.brookings.edu/research/americas-formerly-redlines-areas-changed-so-must-solutions/.

97. Ibid., Table 1.

98. Ibid.

99. U. S. Bureau of the Census, *Quarterly Residential Vacancies and Homeownership, First Quarter 2022*, Table 7 (April 27, 2022), available at: www.census.gov/housing/hvs/files/currenthvspress.pdf .

100. "The Federal Housing Administration and African-American Homeownership," p. 131.

101. Ibid., p. 132.

102. *Fifteenth Census of the United States: 1930—Families, Vol. VI*, Table 18, p. 12.

103. Ellora Derenoncourt, et al., "The Racial Wealth Gap, 1860-2020," March 8, 2021, p. 11, available at: www.russellsage.org/sites/default/files/Derenoncourt.Proposal.pdf.

104. U.S. Equal Employment Opportunity Commission, *Race-Based Charges (Charges Filed With EEOC) FY 1997-FY2021*, available at: www.eeoc.gov/statistics/race-based-charges-charges-filed-eeoc-fy-1997-fy-2021.

105. Ibid.

106. Ibid. See also U. S. Equal Employment Opportunity Commission, *Data Visualization: All Charge Data* (FY 2016-FY2020) (providing definition of merit resolution), available at: www.eeoc.gov/statistics/data-visualizations-all-charge-data. These percentages add up to less than 100 percent because a number of charges are dismissed for administrative reasons.

107. Sara McLanahan, "Fragile Families and the Reproduction of Poverty," *Annals of the American Academy of Political and Social Science* 621(1) (2009):111–

131, 122.

108. Eva Sierminska, "The 'Wealth-Being' of Single Parents," in *The Triple Bind of Single-Parent Families*, ed. Rense Nieuwenhuis and Laurie C. Maldonado (Bristol, U.K.: Policy Press, 2018): 51–79, 52–53.

109. Ibid., p. 55.

110. "Changes in U.S. Family Finances from 2016 to 2019: Evidence from the Survey of Consumer Finances," Net Worth, Table 2; Ana Hernandez Kent, "Single Mothers Face Difficulties with Slim Financial Cushions," *Economy Blog* (Federal Reserve Bank of St. Louis), May 9, 2020 (author's calculations based on data from Survey of Consumer Finances), available at: www.stlouisfed.org/on-the-economy/2022/may/single-mothers-slim-financial-cushions.

111. Robert I. Lerman and W. Bradford Wilcox, "For Richer, For Poorer: How Family Structures Economic Success in America," American Enterprise Institute (2014), Figure 1, p. 10, www.aei.org/research-products/report/for-richer-for-poorer-how-family-structures-economic-success-in-america/.

112. U. S. Bureau of the Census, "Income and Poverty in the United States: 2020," (September 2021), Table B2, www.census.gov/data/tables/2021/demo/income-poverty/p60-273.html.

113. "For Richer, For Poorer: How Family Structures Economic Success in America," p. 38.

114. Ibid.

115. Ian V. Rowe, "Creating an Opportunity Society and Upward Mobility for the Black Community and People of All Races," in *The State of Black America: Progress, Pitfalls, and the Promise of the Republic*, ed. William B. Allen (New York: Encounter Books, 2022), p. 220, Figure 6.7.

116. Gretchen Livingston, "The Changing Profile of Unmarried Parents," Pew Research Center, April 25, 2018, www.pewresearch.org/social-trends/2018/04/25/the-changing-profile-of-unmarried-parents/; "For Richer, For Poorer: How Family Structures Economic Success in America," p. 38.

117. "For Richer, For Poorer: How Family Structures Economic Success in America," pp. 20, 23.

118. "Fragile Families and the Reproduction of Poverty," p. 122.

119. Julie DaVanzo and M. Omar Rahman, "American Families: Trends and Correlates," *Population Index* 59(3) (1993): 350–386, 375.

120. Sara McLanahan and Christopher Jencks, "Was Moynihan Right? What Happens to Children of Unmarried Mothers," *Education Next* (Spring 2015): 15–20, 19.

121. "American Families: Trends and Correlates," pp. 374–375. See also "Fragile Families and the Reproduction of Poverty," p. 122.

122. "American Families: Trends and Correlates," Figure 9, p. 360.

123. Michelle J.K. Osterman et al., "Births: Final Data for 2020," *National Vital Statistics Reports* 70(17) (February 7, 2022), Table 11, p. 28, www.cdc.gov/nchs/data/nvsr/nvsr70/nvsr70-17.pdf.

124. "Was Moynihan Right? What Happens to Children of Unmarried Mothers," p. 17. See also "Births: Final Data for 2020," Table 11, p. 28.

125. Annie E. Casey Foundation, "2021 Kids Count Data Book," Table 4, p. 15, www.aecf.org/resources/2021-kids-count-data-book.

126. An annotated copy of the Moynihan report may be found at: www.theatlantic.com/politics/archive/2015/09/the-moynihan-report-an-annotated-edition/404632/.

127. Ibid. See also "Fragile Families and the Reproduction of Poverty," pp. 111–112.

128. A 2014 study found that the family income premium for married black women was about $20,000 a year, certainly enough to allow for some savings after adjusting for additional expenses. "For Richer, For Poorer: How Family Structures Economic Success in America," Figure 21B, p. 36. See also "Creating an Opportunity Society and Upward Mobility for the Black Community and People of All Races," p. 220 (net worth of two-parent black families exceeds net worth of single-parent white families).

129. Glenn C. Loury, "Why Does Racial Inequality Persist? Culture, Causation and Responsibility," May 7, 2019, p. 1, available at: www.manhattan-institute.org/why-does-racial-inequality-persist.

130. Ibid., p. 1.

131. Ibid., p. 11.

132. "Creating an Opportunity Society and Upward Mobility for the Black Community and People of All Races," p. 220.

133. Is the unfavorable family composition of black families today itself a result of slavery, under which slaves could not even legally marry? Some have made this argument, but it lacks support. In the late nineteenth and early twentieth century the percentage of blacks in marital relationships was higher than the percentage of whites in such relationships, indicating that slavery did not lead to a breakdown in the black family. The trend toward black single-parent (single-mother) families did not begin until the mid-twentieth century and only started to accelerate after the mid-1960s. Some have blamed this trend on the unintended effects of welfare programs, but we do not have to resolve that claim here. See the discussion in *Race & Economics*, pp. 7–9.

134. Data for these disparities can be found in various sources. Here are a few: Liz Sablich, "7 Findings That Illustrate Racial Disparities in Education," Brookings Institution, June 6, 2016, www.brookings.edu/blog/brown-center-chalkboard/2016/06/06/7-findings-that-illustrate-racial-disparities-in-education/; "26 Simple Charts to Show Friends and Family Who Aren't Convinced Racism Is Still a Problem in America," (see note 3); "Why Does Racial Inequality Persist? Culture, Causation and Responsibility," pp. 8–12.

135. The Annie E. Casey Foundation, "Investing in Tomorrow: Helping Families Build Savings and Assets," January 2016, p. 2, www.aecf.org/resources/investing-in-tomorrow-helping-families-build-savings-and-assets.

136. Compare Raegen Miller and Diana Epstein, "There Still Be Dragons: Racial Disparity in School Funding Is No Myth," Center for American Progress (July 2011), www.americanprogress.org/article/there-still-be-dragons/ with Jason Richwine, "The Myth of Racial Disparities in Public School Funding," The Heritage Foundation (April 20, 2011), www.heritage.org/education/report/the-myth-racial-disparities-public-school-funding.

137. "There Still Be Dragons: Racial Disparity in School Funding Is No Myth," Table 2.

138. John U. Ogbu, *Black American Students in an Affluent Suburb: A Study in Academic Disengagement* (Mahwah, NJ: Lawrence Erlbaum Associates, 2003).

139. Ibid., p. 23.

140. Ibid., p. 259.

141. Ibid., p. 37.

142. Ibid., p. 211.

143. John McWhorter, *Woke Racism: How a New Religion Has Betrayed Black America* (New York: Portfolio/Penguin, 2021), p. 126.

144. U.S. Department of Education, Office for Civil Rights, and U.S. Department of Justice, Civil Rights Division, "Joint 'Dear Colleague' Letter on the Nondiscriminatory Administration of School Discipline," January 8, 2014, www2.ed.gov/about/offices/list/ocr/letters/colleague-201401-title-vi.html.

145. Veronique Irwin et al., "Report on Indicators of School Crime and Safety: 2021," National Center for Education Statistics, U.S. Department of Education (2022), p. 2 and Figure 5, nces.ed.gov/pubs2022/2022092.pdf.

146. Josh Kinsler, "School Discipline: A Source or Salve for the Racial Achievement Gap?" *International Economic Review* 54(1) (2013): 355–383, 382.

147. U. S. Commission on Civil Rights, "Beyond Suspensions: Examining School Discipline Policies and Connections to the School-to-Prison Pipeline for Students of Color with Disabilities," (July 2019), p. 161, www.usccr.gov/files/pubs/2019/07-23-Beyond-Suspensions.pdf.

148. Ibid., pp. 177, 180–182 (referencing p. 114, Figure 9).

149. Ibid., p. 184.

150. John Paul Wright, et al., "Prior Problem Behavior Accounts for the Racial Gap in School Suspensions," *Journal of Criminal Justice* 42(3) (2014):

257–266, 251.

151. "School Discipline: A Source or Salve for the Racial Achievement Gap?" p. 360.

152. Nora Gordon, "Disproportionality in Student Discipline: Connecting Policy to Research," Brookings Institution, January 18, 2018, www.brookings.edu/research/disproportionality-in-student-discipline-connecting-policy-to-research/.

153. Elizabeth Arias and Jiaquan Xu, "United States Life Tables, 2019," *National Vital Statistics Reports* 70(19) (2022), Table A, p. 3, www.cdc.gov/nchs/data/nvsr/nvsr70/nvsr70-19.pdf. The difference in life expectancy between black females and white females is about three years; that between black males and white males is over five years. For males, the significant difference in homicide rates for black males needs to be taken into account.

154. Jenna Portnoy, "Virginia Board of Health Reprimands Health Commissioner," *Washington Post*, June 23, 2022, www.washingtonpost.com/dc-md-va/2022/06/23/greene-disparities-health-youngkin/.

155. "Systemic Racism and Health Equity," p. 11.

156. Christen Linke Young, "There Are Clear Race-Based Inequalities in Health Insurance and Health Outcomes," Brookings Institution, February 19, 2020, www.brookings.edu/blog/usc-brookings-schaeffer-on-health-policy/2020/02/19/there-are-clear-race-based-inequalities-in-health-insurance-and-health-outcomes/.

157. Briand D. Smedley, Adrienne Y. Stith, and Alan R. Nelson, eds. *Unequal Treatment: Confronting Racial and Ethnic Disparities in Health Care* (Washington, D.C.: National Academies Press, 2003), p. 5. This study was requested by Congress, which expressed concern about healthcare disparities. Ibid., p. 3. I note how strange it is for a thoroughly racist system to have its principal legislative body request an inquiry into healthcare disparities.

158. Ibid., p. 5.

159. Ibid., p. 75.

160. Elizabeth A. Howell, "Reducing Disparities in Severe Maternal Morbidity and Mortality," *Clinical Obstetrics and Gynecology* 61(2) (2018): 387–399, 391.

161. David R. Williams, Naomi Priest, and Norman Anderson, "Understanding Associations Between Race, Socioeconomic Status and Health: Patterns and Prospects," *Health Psychology* 35(4) (2016): 407–411, 409.

162. Laura Dwyer-Lindgren et al., "Inequalities in Life Expectancy Among U.S. Counties, 1980 to 2014: Temporal Trends and Key Drivers," *JAMA Internal Medicine* 177(7) (2017): 1003–1011, 1008.

163. For behaviors related to cancer, at the global level, see GBD 2019

Cancer Risk Factor Collaborators, "The Global Burden of Cancer Attributable to Risk Factors, 2010-19: A Systematic Analysis for the Global Burden Disease Study 2019," *Lancet* 400 (2022): 563–91. For racial differences in the prevalence of certain conditions, see the following: Centers for Disease Control and Prevention, "National Diabetes Statistics Report 2020," Figure 2, Table 3, www.cdc.gov/diabetes/pdfs/data/statistics/national-diabetes-statistics-report. pdf; Craig M. Hales, et al. "Prevalence of Obesity and Severe Obesity Among Adults: United States 2017–2018," NCHS Data Brief no. 360 (2020), Figure 2, p.2, www.cdc.gov/nchs/data/databriefs/db360-h.pdf; "Reducing Disparities in Severe Maternal Morbidity and Mortality," p. 397; Kenneth D. Kochanek, Elizabeth Arias, and Robert N. Anderson, "How Did the Cause of Death Contribute to Racial Differences in Life Expectancy in the United States in 2010?" NCHS Data Brief no. 125 (2013), www.cdc.gov/nchs/data/databriefs/db125. pdf.

164. "How Did the Cause of Death Contribute to Racial Differences in Life Expectancy in the United States in 2010?" Figure 4, p. 4 and Figure 5, p. 5.

165. I will concede this statement lacks a firm empirical foundation, so in that sense it is speculative. But I believe it is a reasonable extrapolation from data currently available.

166. Joia Crear-Perry, "Social and Structural Determinants of Health Inequities in Maternal Health," *Journal of Women's Health* 30(2) (2021): 230–235; "Structural Racism and Health Inequities in the USA: Evidence and Interventions," *passim* (see note 63).

167. "Structural Racism and Health Inequities in the USA: Evidence and Interventions," p. 1456.

168. "Social and Structural Determinants of Health Inequities in Maternal Health," p. 231.

169. See, for example, Jeneen Interlandi, "Why Doesn't the United States Have Universal Health Care?" *New York Times Magazine*, August 14, 2019, www. nytimes.com/interactive/2019/08/14/magazine/universal-health-care-racism. html.

170. *Unequal Treatment: Confronting Racial and Ethnic Disparities in Health Care*, p. 79.

171. German Lopez, "The VA Scandal of 2014 Explained," *Vox*, May 13, 2015, www.vox.com/2014/9/26/18080592/va-scandal-explained.

172. See, for example, *Unequal Treatment: Confronting Racial and Ethnic Disparities in Health Care*, pp. 10–11.

173. Kelly Hoffman, et al., "Racial Bias in Pain Assessment and Treatment Recommendations, and False Beliefs About Biological Differences Between Blacks and Whites," *PNAS* 113(16) (2016): 4297–4301.

174. "How Did the Cause of Death Contribute to Racial Differences in Life Expectancy in the United States in 2010?" Figure 3, p. 3.

175. Austin Frakt, "What Can Be Learned from Differing Rates of Suicide Among Groups," *New York Times*, December 30, 2020, www.nytimes.com/2020/12/30/upshot/suicide-demographic-differences.html.

176. "How Did the Cause of Death Contribute to Racial Differences in Life Expectancy in the United States in 2010?" Figure 3, p. 3.

177. "Virginia Board of Health Reprimands Health Commissioner" (see note 154).

178. "Reducing Disparities in Severe Maternal Morbidity and Mortality," p. 393.

179. "Prevalence of Obesity and Severe Obesity Among Adults: United States 2017–2018," Figure 2, p.2.

180. Daniel B. Nelson, Michele H. Moniz, and Matthew M. Davis, "Population-Level Factors Associated with Maternal Mortality in the United States, 1997–2011," *BMC Public Health* 18 (2018): 1007–1014, 1012.

181. Ibid., p. 1011.

182. Monica Saucedo, et al., "Understanding Maternal Mortality in Women with Obesity and the Role of Care They Receive: A National Case-Control Study," *International Journal of Obesity* 45 (2021): 258–265, 260.

183. Monica F. MacDorman et al., "Racial and Ethnic Disparities in Maternal Mortality in the United States Using Enhanced Vital Records, 2016–2017," *American Journal of Public Health* 111(9) (2021): 1673–1681, 1676.

184. Ibid.

185. See, for example, Patricio Lopez-Jaramillo, et al., "Obesity and Preeclampsia: Common Pathophysiological Mechanisms," *Frontiers in Physiology* 9 (2018): 1838–1848.

186. Eric Kaufmann, "The Social Construction of Racism in the United States," Manhattan Institute, April 7, 2021, p. 15, www.manhattan-institute.org/social-construction-racism-united-states.

187. Benjamin Fearnow, "Ben Crump Says He Wants to End 'Legalized Genocide': 'They're killing African Americans'," *Newsweek*, May 16, 2021, www.newsweek.com/ben-crump-says-he-wants-end-legalized-genocide-they-re-killing-african-americans-1591937.

188. "Fatal Force," *Washington Post*, updated July 15, 2022, www.washingtonpost.com/graphics/investigations/police-shootings-database/.

189. Nicholas Jones, et al., "2020 Census Illuminates Racial and Ethnic Composition of the Country," U.S. Census Bureau, August 12, 2021, www.census.gov/library/stories/2021/08/improved-race-ethnicity-measures-reveal-united-states-population-much-more-multiracial.html.

190. Roland G. Fryer, Jr., "An Empirical Analysis of Racial Differences in Police Use of Force," *Journal of Political Economy* 127(3) (2019): 1210–1261.

191. Ibid., p. 1214.

192. Ibid.

193. Robert VerBruggen, "Fatal Police Shootings: A Review of the Evidence and Suggestions for Future Research," Manhattan Institute, March 9, 2022, p. 7, www.manhattan-institute.org/verbruggen-fatal-police-shootings.

194. Ibid., *passim*.

195. Ibid., pp. 3, 8–10.

196. Ibid., pp. 17–19, 21.

197. Roland G. Fryer, Jr., "What the Data Say About Police," *Wall Street Journal*, June 22, 2020, www.wsj.com/articles/what-the-data-say-about-police-11592845959.

198. "An Empirical Analysis of Racial Differences in Police Use of Force," p. 1213.

199. Ibid., p. 1239.

200. U.S. Department of Justice, Civil Rights Division, "Investigation of the Baltimore City Police Department," August 10, 2016, p. 98. See also pp. 129–136, www.justice.gov/crt/file/883296/download. To my knowledge, no study has questioned the core findings of this report, so I accept them as accurate even though the report's discussion of housing segregation resulting from New Deal policies is flawed for reasons discussed previously.

201. Federal Bureau of Prisons, "Inmate Statistics, Inmate Race," July 9, 2022, www.bop.gov/about/statistics/statistics_inmate_race.jsp.

202. John Gramlich, "Black Imprisonment Rate in the U.S. Has Fallen by a Third Since 2006," Pew Research Center, May 6, 2020, www.pewresearch.org/fact-tank/2020/05/06/share-of-black-white-hispanic-americans-in-prison-2018-vs-2006/. See also E. Ann Carson, "Prisoners in 2018," U.S Department of Justice, Bureau of Justice Statistics, April 2020, bjs.ojp.gov/content/pub/pdf/p18.pdf.

203. Ibid.

204. Federal Bureau of Investigation, "Crime in the United States, 2019," Table 43A, ucr.fbi.gov/crime-in-the-u.s/2019/crime-in-the-u.s.-2019/tables/table-43.

205. Mark Motivans, "Federal Justice Statistics, 2020," U.S. Department of Justice, Bureau of Justice Statistics, May 2022, Table 4, p. 7 and Table 7, p. 11, bjs.ojp.gov/content/pub/pdf/fjs20.pdf.

206. Colleen Chien, "America's Paper Prisons: The Second Chance Gap," *Michigan Law Review* 119(3) (2020): 519–612, Appendix, Table A-2.

207. American Civil Liberties Union, "A Tale of Two Countries: Racially

Targeted Arrests in the Era of Marijuana Reform," 2020, p. 5, www.aclu.org/sites/default/files/field_document/marijuanareport_03232021.pdf.

208. "Prisoners in 2018," Table 13, p. 21 and Table 15, note g, p. 23

209. See, for example, Radley Balko, "There Is Overwhelming Evidence That the Criminal Justice System Is Racist. Here's the Proof," *Washington Post*, June 10, 2020, www.washingtonpost.com/graphics/2020/opinions/systemic-racism-police-evidence-criminal-justice-system/.

210. Traci Burch, "Skin Color and the Criminal Justice System: Beyond Black-White Disparities in Sentencing," *Journal of Empirical Legal Studies* 12(3) (2015): 395–420, 411. As indicated by the article's title, the author undertook a study of how skin color, in addition to race, affected sentence length, with the working theory being that darker skin color translated into longer sentences. The author claims her study supports that conclusion. As skin color issues are beyond the scope of my critique, I will not comment other than to note that judgments of skin color reflect a substantial element of subjectivity.

211. Emily Owens, Erin M. Kerrison, and Bernardo Santos Da Silveira, "Examining Racial Disparities in Criminal Case Outcomes Among Indigent Defendants in San Francisco," Quattrone Center for the Fair Administration of Justice, University of Pennsylvania Law School (2017), p. 22, www.law.upenn.edu/live/files/6791-examining-racial-disparities-may-2017combinedpdf. The authors speculate that disparities in initial booking charges may have downstream effects on sentencing, but concede that "there may be unobserved, legally relevant factors other than bias (e.g., actual criminal conduct, or how particular individuals interact with officers) that ... explain the observed disparities" in booked charges. Ibid., p. 8.

212. Thomas F. Pettigrew, *A Profile of the Negro American* (Princeton, NJ: D. Van Nostrand, 1964), pp. 144, 146.

213. For an illuminating discussion of the genesis and content of the Rockefeller Drug Laws, see Michael Javen Fortner, "The Carceral State and the Crucible of Black Politics: An Urban History of the Rockefeller Drug Laws," *Studies in American Political Development* 27 (April 2013): 14–35.

214. Jeremy W. Peters, "Albany Reaches Deal to Repeal '70s Drug Laws," *New York Times*, March 25, 2009, www.nytimes.com/2009/03/26/nyregion/26rockefeller.html.

215. "The Carceral State," p. 27.

216. Ibid., p. 29.

217. Ibid., p. 35.

218. A concise and informative summary of the key provisions of this act, and of the law's evolution over the decades, may be found at: Families Against Mandatory Minimums, "A Brief History of Crack Cocaine Sentencing Laws,"

2012, famm.org/wp-content/uploads/FS-Brief-History-of-Crack-Laws.pdf.

219. Ibid.

220. Ibid.

221. Ibid.

222. A summary of the House of Representatives version of the Equal Act of 2021 may be found at: www.congress.gov/bill/117th-congress/house-bill/1693 (accessed August 10, 2022).

223. A summary of black support for the Anti-Drug Abuse Act of 1986 may be found in the majority opinion of the Supreme Court in *Terry v. United States*, Case No. 20-5904, slip. op. at 2, n. 2 (June 14, 2021) (considering petitioner's request for a reduction of sentence).

224. John Hope Franklin, *Reconstruction: After the Civil War* (Chicago: University of Chicago Press, 1961), esp. pp. 36–39, 108–109, 194–202.

225. A summary of the Civil Liberties Act of 1988, which provided for reparations to interned Japanese Americans, may be found at: Anti-Defamation League, "Understanding the Civil Liberties Act of 1988," 2013, www.adl.org/sites/default/files/Understanding-the-Civil-Liberties-Act-of-1988.pdf.

226. Annie E. Casey Foundation, "Will Asset-Building Policies Lead to Equity? Applying the Racial Wealth Audit," February 15, 2016, www.aecf.org/blog/will-asset-building-policies-lead-to-equity-applying-the-racial-wealth-audi.

Chapter 3

The Misguided, Dystopian Goal of Equity

1. Biden-Harris 2020 Campaign Ad, "Equality vs. Equity," available at: www.youtube.com/watch?v=w4kowE_YIVw.

2. Ibram X. Kendi, "We Still Don't Know Who the Coronavirus's Victims Were," *The Atlantic*, May 2, 2021, www.theatlantic.com/ideas/archive/2021/05/we-still-dont-know-who-the-coronaviruss-victims-were/618776/. Interestingly, even though Kendi asserts that we lack sufficient information to determine the identity of coronavirus victims, he is certain there were significant racial disparities in rates of death, rates of hospitalization, etc.

3. Ibid.

4. Ibid.

5. Executive Order no. 13985 of January 20, 2021, "Executive Order on Advancing Racial Equity and Support for Underserved Communities Through the Federal Government," *Federal Register* 86 (January 25, 2021): 7009–7013.

6. Ibid.

7. "We Still Don't Know Who the Coronavirus's Victims Were."

8. Liz Hamel, et al., "KFF COVID-19 Vaccine Monitor: May, 2021," Kaiser Family Foundation, May 28, 2021, Figure 1, www.kff.org/coronavirus-covid-19/poll-finding/kff-covid-19-vaccine-monitor-may-2021/.

9. In stating that the vaccination program was a success, I am not asserting that the federal government's response to the COVID-19 outbreak as a whole was a success. The federal government's response was plagued by mixed messages and indecisiveness, especially in the early stages of the pandemic.

10. "KFF COVID-19 Vaccine Monitor: May, 2021," Table 1 and Figure 2.

11. Ibid. ("Younger adults and Black adults remain disproportionately likely to say they will wait and see before getting a vaccine, while Republicans, rural residents, and White Evangelical Christians are disproportionately likely to say they will definitely not get vaccinated."). See also Joseph Goldstein and Matthew Sedacca, "Why Only 28 Percent of Young Black New Yorkers Are Vaccinated," *New York Times*, August 12, 2021, www.nytimes.com/2021/08/12/nyregion/covid-vaccine-black-young-new-yorkers.html.

12. Lucas A. Berenbrok, et al., "Access to Potential COVID-19 Vaccine Administration Facilities: A Geographic Information Systems Analysis," University of Pittsburgh and West Health Policy Center, February 2, 2021, Figure 6, p.17, s8637.pcdn.co/wp-content/uploads/2021/02/Access-to-Potential-COVID-19-Vaccine-Administration-Facilities-2-2-2021.pdf.

13. Abby Goodnough and Jan Hoffman, "The Elderly vs. Essential Workers: Who Should Get the Coronavirus Vaccine First?" *New York Times*, December 5, 2020, www.nytimes.com/2020/12/05/health/covid-vaccine-first.html.

14. Ibid.

15. Ibram X. Kendi, *How To Be an Antiracist* (New York: One World, 2019), p. 18.

16. Ibid., pp. 18, 19.

17. Sydney Johnson, "California Math Curriculum Spurs New Controversy About Accelerated Learning," *EdSource*, May 20, 2021, edsource.org/2021/california-math-guidance-sparks-new-curriculum-controversy-among-parents/655272.

18. Ibid. The accusation was made by Education Trust-West. See "A Pathway to Equitable Math Instruction," 2021, esp. Stride 1, "Dismantling Racism in Mathematics Instruction," equitablemath.org/. The "Dismantling Racism" handbook contains helpful hints on how to spot white supremacist thinking at work, e.g., when there is an emphasis on objectivity, urgency, perfectionism, or worship of the written word.

19. Brian Conrad, "Public Comments on the CMF," 2022, sites.google.com/view/publiccommentsonthecmf/#h.ns5n6hdqa4x8. Professor Conrad is director of the undergraduate studies program in mathematics at Stanford University.

20. California Department of Education, "Mathematics Framework Revision Timetable," 2022, www.cde.ca.gov/ci/ma/cf/mathfwrevtimeline2021.asp.

21. Ashley Gross, "Seattle Public Schools Says It Will No Longer Offer Separate Honors Classes in Middle School," KNKX Public Radio, February 18, 2020, www.knkx.org/youth-education/2020-02-18/seattle-public-schools-says-it-will-no-longer-offer-separate-honors-classes-in-middle-school.

22. Donna St. George, "Honors Classes for All Leave Some Parents Asking: Is It Really Honors?" *Washington Post*, August 7, 2019, www.washingtonpost.com/local/education/honors-classes-for-all-leave-some-parents-asking-is-it-really-honors/2019/08/03/f3adef36-a1a6-11e9-b8c8-75dae2607e60_story.html.

23. Rachel Blustain, "Gifted Programs Worsen Inequality. Here's What Happens When Schools Try to Get Rid of Them," *The Hechinger Report*, October 14, 2020, available at: www.nbcnews.com/news/education/gifted-programs-worsen-inequality-here-s-what-happens-when-schools-n1243147.

24. Rich Lowry, "The War on Gifted-and-Talented Programs," *National Review*, October 12, 2021, www.nationalreview.com/2021/10/the-war-on-gifted-and-talented-programs/.

25. Robby Soave, "An Elite Public High School Changed Its Admissions Standards to Reduce the Asian-American Student Population," *Reason*, April 2, 2021, reason.com/2021/04/02/thomas-jefferson-asian-admissions-plf-lawsuit/.

26. Ibid. See also Margaret Barthel, "Supreme Court Lets Thomas Jefferson High Admissions Policy Stand—For Now," *dcist*, April 26, 2022, dcist.com/story/22/04/26/supreme-court-thomas-jefferson-lawsuit/.

27. "Supreme Court Lets Thomas Jefferson High Admissions Policy Stand—For Now."

28. Ellen Barry, "Boston Overhauls Admissions to Exclusive Exam Schools," *New York Times*, July 15, 2021, www.nytimes.com/2021/07/15/us/boston-schools-entrance-exams-admissions.html.

29. Chicago Public Schools Policy Manual, "Admissions Policy for Magnet, Selective Enrollment and Other GoCPS Schools and Programs," July 27, 2022, policy.cps.edu/download.aspx?ID=82. See also Mauricio Pena, "Chicago Aims to Revamp Its Admissions Policy for Selective Enrollment Schools, *Chalkbeat Chicago*, March 10, 2002, chicago.chalkbeat.org/2022/3/10/22971778/chicago-aims-to-revamp-its-admissions-policy-for-selective-enrollment-schools.

30. "Gifted Programs Worsen Inequality."

31. Ibid.

32. Perry Stein, "Literacy Scores Show Widening Achievement Gap in

D.C. During Pandemic," *Washington Post*, March 17, 2022, www.washing-tonpost.com/education/2022/03/17/dc-schools-achievement-gap-pandemic-reading/.

33. Joseph Cast and Erin Wilcox, "Thomas Jefferson High School Becomes an Arena for the Battle Between Parents and Policy," Pacific Legal Foundation, January 24, 2022, pacificlegal.org/thomas-jefferson-high-school-battle-between-parents-and-policy/.

34. College Board, "National SAT Validity Study," 2019, satsuite.college-board.org/media/pdf/national-sat-validity-study-overview-admissions-enroll-ment-leaders.pdf.

35. Worcester Polytechnic Institute, "Test-Blind Admissions," www.wpi.edu/admissions/undergraduate/apply/how-to/test-blind-admissions.

36. Ibid.

37. Ember Smith and Richard V. Reeves, "SAT Math Scores Mirror and Maintain Racial Inequity," Brookings Institution, December 1, 2020, www.brookings.edu/blog/up-front/2020/12/01/sat-math-scores-mirror-and-main-tain-racial-inequity/.

38. *How to Be an Antiracist*, p. 101.

39. "SAT Math Scores Mirror and Maintain Racial Inequity."

40. Ibid.

41. Mark Huelsman, "The Debt Divide: The Racial and Class Bias Behind the 'New Normal' of Student Borrowing," Demos, 2015, esp. p. 16, Figure 7, www.demos.org/sites/default/files/publications/Mark-Debt%20divide%20Final%20(SF).pdf.

42. Michael T. Nietzel, "Remedial Education: Escaping Higher Education's Hotel California," *Forbes*, October 22, 2018, www.forbes.com/sites/michaeltnietzel/2018/10/22/remedial-education-escaping-higher-educa-tions-hotel-california/?sh=34aa68795f20.

43. I note that the Brookings study agrees that if "we want a true merito-cratic admissions process, we need to give all children the chance to compete by addressing inequity early in life." "SAT Math Scores Mirror and Maintain Racial Inequity."

44. Fitchburg State University, "Policy Review with an Equity Lens," 2022, p. 4, www.fitchburgstate.edu/sites/default/files/documents/2022-03/Eq-uity%20Lens%20Guide.pdf.

45. The American Bar Association (ABA), the organization responsible for accrediting law schools, has for years pushed law schools to increase the rate of admissions for blacks and other minorities. This drive culminated in a proposed standard for accreditation which would have explicitly tied accredita-tion to a school's admission rates for "underrepresented groups related to race and ethnicity" as well as the presence of an "inclusive and equitable environment for students, faculty, and staff with respect to race, color, ethnicity, religion, national origin, gender, gender identity or expression, sexual orientation, age, disability, and military status." After significant criticism, the proposed standard was withdrawn at the ABA meeting in August 2022. Stephanie Francis Ward, "Legal Ed Pulls Back HOD Diversity Resolution, Saying More Discussion Is Needed," *ABA Journal*, August 8, 2022, www.abajournal.com/web/article/legal-ed-pulls-back-hod-diversity-resolution-saying-more-discussion-is-needed.

46. My summary of this incident is based primarily on Robert Shipley, "One Georgetown Law Professor Fired, One Resigns After Conversation About Black Students' Academic Performance Accidentally Recorded," FIRE, March 18, 2021, www.thefire.org/one-georgetown-law-professor-fired-one-resigns-after-conversation-about-black-students-academic-performance-accidentally-recorded/. This online essay contains a transcript of the conversation.

47. Bill Treanor, "A Message to the Georgetown Law Community (Updated)," Georgetown Law, March 21, 2021, www.law.georgetown.edu/news/a-message-to-the-georgetown-law-community/.

48. Yonat Shimron, "Study: Girls Raised Jewish Outperform Christian Girls Academically," *Washington Post*, May 13, 2022, www.washingtonpost.com/religion/2022/05/13/study-girls-raised-jewish-outperform-christian-girls-academically/.

49. Ibid.

50. GBD 2019 Cancer Risk Factor Collaborators, "The Global Burden of Cancer Attributable to Risk Factors, 2010-19: A Systematic Analysis for the Global Burden Disease Study 2019," *Lancet* 400 (2022): 563–91.

51. American Medical Association, "Organizational Strategic Plan to Embed Racial Justice and Advance Health Equity, 2021-2023," 2021, p. 18, Figure 3, www.ama-assn.org/system/files/2021-05/ama-equity-strategic-plan.pdf.

52. Ibid., pp. 9, 20.

53. Ibid., p. 20. The AMA plan states the quote from Kendi is from his book *How To Be an Antiracist*.

54. A description of the projects of the NIMHD may be found at www.nih.gov/about-nih/what-we-do/nih-almanac/national-institute-minority-health-health-disparities-nimhd (accessed September 1, 2022).

55. Minnesota Department of Health, Center for Health Equity, "Eliminating Health Disparities Initiative," 2020, www.health.state.mn.us/communities/equity/ehdi/handout.pdf.

56. "Organizational Strategic Plan to Embed Racial Justice and Advance Health Equity, 2021-2023," p. 4. England's American colonies first used slaves in 1619. 400 years takes us to 2019. The Thirteenth Amendment abolished slavery as of 1865. The AMA does not explain its arithmetic, leaving us to wonder whether in the AMA's estimation the labor of blacks was "forced" until a few years ago.

57. Ibid., pp. 2, 5, 13, 14, 18, 37, 38.

58. Ibid., p. 13.

59. Ibid., pp. 14, 22.

60. Ibid., p. 37.

61. Ibid., pp. 6, 12, 16, 17, 18, 20, 37, 39.

62. Ibid., p. 37.

63. Ibid.

64. American Medical Association and Association of American Medical Colleges, "Advancing Health Equity: A Guide to Language, Narrative and Concepts," 2021, www.ama-assn.org/about/ama-center-health-equity/advancing-health-equity-guide-language-narrative-and-concepts-0.

65. "Organizational Strategic Plan to Embed Racial Justice and Advance Health Equity, 2021-2023," p. 48.

66. Ibid.

67. Ibid., p. 62.

68. Alec Schemmel, "Med School Has Students Pledge To Fight 'Gender Binary' and 'Colonialism,' Honor 'Indigenous' Healing," WCTI, October 14, 2022, wcti12.com/news/nation-world/universitys-pledge-has-students-swear-to-honor-indigenous-healing-fight-gender-binary-and-colonialism-minnesota-critical-race-theory-white-coat-ceremony-medical-supremacy.

69. "Advancing Health Equity: A Guide to Language, Narrative and Concepts," p. 2.

70. Ibid., p. 5.

71. Ibid., p. 8.

72. Ibid.

73. Ibid.

74. Ibid., p. 13.

75. Ibid., p. 15.

76. Ibid., p. 30.

77. Ibid., p. 38.

78. Ibid., p. 42.

79. AMA Ed Hub, AMA Center for Health Equity, "Prioritizing Equity: Narratives and Language," June 16, 2022, available at: edhub.ama-assn.org/ama-center-health-equity/video-player/18703007?resultClick=1&bypassSolrId=M_18703007.

80. Ibid.

81. Ibid.

82. Bram Wispelwey and Michelle Morse, "An Antiracist Agenda for Medicine," *Boston Review*, March 17, 2021, bostonreview.net/articles/michelle-morsebram-wispelwey-what-we-owe-patients-case-medical-reparations/.

83. Ibid.

84. Ibid.

85. Usha Lee McFarling, " 'So Much More To Do': A Hospital System's Campaign To Confront Racism—And Resistance to Change—Makes Early Strides," *STAT*, August 25, 2022, www.statnews.com/2022/08/25/mass-general-brigham-campaign-confront-racism-early-progress/.

86. Brigham and Women's Hospital, "Addressing Disparities in Heart Failure Admissions," www.brighamandwomens.org/about-bwh/newsroom/addressing-heart-admission-disparities (accessed September 7, 2022).

87. Ibid.

88. Lauren A. Eberly, et al., "Identification of Racial Inequities in Access to Specialized Inpatient Heart Failure Care at an Academic Medical Center," *Circulation: Heart Failure*, November 2019, www.ahajournals.org/doi/10.1161/CIRCHEARTFAILURE.119.006214.

89. Ibid., Table 2, p. 6.

90. Ibid., p. 5.

91. Ibid.

92. Ibid., p. 7.

93. Ibid., p. 4.

94. Xander Landen, "Utah, Minnesota Back Down on Race-Based COVID Care as New York Faces Lawsuit," *Newsweek*, January 23, 2022, www.newsweek.com/utah-minnesota-back-down-race-based-covid-care-new-york-faces-lawsuit-1672011.

95. John B. Judis and Ruy Teixeira, "New York's Race-Based Preferential Covid Treatments," *Wall Street Journal*, January 7, 2022, www.wsj.com/articles/new-york-race-based-covid-treatment-white-hispanic-inequity-monoclonal-antibodies-antiviral-pfizer-omicron-11641573991.

96. National Kidney Foundation, "Understanding African American and Non-African American eGFR Laboratory Results," 2022, www.kidney.org/atoz/content/race-and-egfr-what-controversy.

97. Salvador Rizzo, "Former Trump Adviser Falsely Claims States Are Rationing Scarce Covid Treatments Based Largely on Race," *Washington Post*, February 10, 2022, www.washingtonpost.com/health/2022/02/10/conservatives-covid-treatments-race/.

98. "The Elderly vs. Essential Workers: Who Should Get the Coronavirus

Vaccine First?"

99. "Advancing Health Equity: A Guide to Language, Narrative and Concepts," p. 2.

100. *How To Be an Antiracist*, p. 19.

101. Annie McGown, Vice President and Associate Provost for Diversity, Office of Diversity, Texas A&M University, E-Mail to Deans re "New ACES Plus Fellowship," July 8, 2022, available at: wordpress.aflegal.org/wp-content/uploads/2022/09/1-1.pdf.

102. Karra McCray, "Black Representation Among Commissioned Officers in the Biden White House," Joint Center for Political and Economic Studies, September 12, 2022, jointcenter.org/black-representation-among-commissioned-officers-in-the-biden-white-house/.

103. Ibid.

104. Jeff Lawson, "A Message from Twilio CEO Jeff Lawson," Twilio Blog, September 14, 2022, www.twilio.com/blog/a-message-from-twilio-ceo-jeff-lawson.

105. Amanda Su and Deena Zaru, "Minneapolis Public Schools Defends Policy To Prioritize Retaining Educators of Color When Determining Layoffs," ABC News, August 19, 2022, abcnews.go.com/US/minneapolis-public-schools-defends-policy-prioritize-retaining-educators/story?id=88491641.

106. Angela D. Alsobrooks, "The New FBI Site Is a Matter of Equity," *Washington Post*, November 4, 2022, www.washingtonpost.com/opinions/2022/11/04/maryland-most-equitable-spot-new-fbi-headquarters/.

107. Financial Services Racial Equity, Inclusion, and Economic Justice Act, HR 2543, 117th Cong., 2nd sess., referred in Senate, June 21, 2022, www.congress.gov/bill/117th-congress/house-bill/2543/text.

108. Oscar Perry Abello, "The Federal Reserve's Reckoning on Racial Equity," *Next City*, November 22, 2021, nextcity.org/features/the-federal-reserves-reckoning-on-racial-equity/Resources

109. Ibid.

110. Board of Governors of the Federal Reserve System, "The Federal Reserve System Purposes & Functions-Section 5," 2022, www.federalreserve.gov/aboutthefed/files/pf_5.pdf.

111. "Executive Order on Advancing Racial Equity and Support for Underserved Communities Through the Federal Government."

112. Michael Levenson, "Judge Blocks $4 Billion U.S. Debt Relief Program for Minority Farmers," *New York Times*, June 23, 2021, www.nytimes.com/2021/06/23/us/politics/biden-debt-relief-black-farmers.html.

113. Alan Rappeport, "Climate and Tax Bill Rewrites Embattled Black Farmer Relief Program," *New York Times*, August 12, 2022, www.nytimes.

com/2022/08/12/business/economy/inflation-reduction-act-black-farmers.html.

114. Adrian Florido, "Debt Relief for Black Farmers Shows Challenges of Pursuing Racial Equity with Policy," National Public Radio, August 31, 2022, www.npr.org/2022/08/31/1120126881/debt-relief-for-black-farmers-shows-challenges-of-pursuing-racial-equity-with-po.

115. Ibid.

116. Staff writer, "Where Are America's Women Engineers?" *Thomas Insights*, November 16, 2021, www.thomasnet.com/insights/where-are-america-s-women-engineers/.

117. Earl Ofari Hutchinson, "The Black-Latino Blame Game," *Los Angeles Times*, November 25, 2007, www.latimes.com/la-op-hutchinson25nov25-story.html.

118. Shawn Huber and Jill Cowan, "Here's What Was Said on the Leaked Recording of L.A. City Council Members," *New York Times*, October 12, 2022, www.nytimes.com/2022/10/11/us/la-city-council-audio-recording-leaked.html. See also Sandy Banks, "Lessons of the Audio Leak: Solidarity Is Dead. Let's Ditch the Label 'People of Color'," *Los Angeles Times*, November 21, 2022, www.latimes.com/california/story/2022-11-21/lessons-of-the-audio-leak-solidarity-is-dead-lets-ditch-the-label-people-of-color.

119. Universal Declaration of Human Rights (adopted by the General Assembly of the United Nations, December 10, 1948), available at: www.un.org/en/about-us/universal-declaration-of-human-rights.

120. Karl Marx, "Critique of the Gotha Program," in *Marx & Engels: Basic Writings on Politics & Philosophy*, ed. Lewis S. Feuer (Garden City, NY: Anchor Books, 1959), p. 119.

121. PR Newswire, "With Global Spending Projected To Reach $15.4 Billion by 2026, Diversity, Equity & Inclusion Takes the Lead Role in the Creation of Stronger Businesses," November 3, 2021, www.prnewswire.com/news-releases/with-global-spending-projected-to-reach-15-4-billion-by-2026--diversity-equity--inclusion-takes-the-lead-role-in-the-creation-of-stronger-businesses-301413808.html.

122. See, for example, Quillette Podcast #196, "When Workplace Anti-Racism Training Goes off the Rails," August 29, 2022 (discussing experience of employee of Philadelphia nonprofit), quillette.com/2022/08/29/when-workplace-anti-racism-training-goes-off-the-rails/.

123. The experiences of Jodi Shaw, a white employee at Smith College, who resigned after being humiliated at a mandatory DEI session, are not uncommon. See Bari Weiss, "Whistleblower at Smith College Resigns over Racism," *Common Sense*, February 19, 2021, www.commonsense.news/p/whistleblower-at-smith-college-resigns.

124. Some incidents are summarized in Joseph H. Manson, "Why I'm Leaving the University," July 4, 2022, josephhmanson.com/2022/07/04/why-im-leaving-the-university/. One other notable incident was the compelled, groveling apology of the president of the American Historical Association, James H. Sweet, who had the temerity to mention in a blog post that many African slaves who were transported to the Western Hemisphere were first enslaved by other Africans before they were sold to Europeans. See Bret Stephens, "This Is the Other Way That History Ends," *New York Times*, August 30, 2022, www.nytimes.com/2022/08/30/opinion/history-sweet-aha-academia.html.

125. Editorial, "Science Must Respect the Dignity and Rights of All Humans," *Nature Human Behavior* 6 (2022): 1029–1031, 1030, www.nature.com/articles/s41562-022-01443-2.

126. Ibid.

127. Ibid., p. 1029.

128. Society for Personality and Social Psychology, "Demonstrating Our Commitment to Anti-Racism Through Programming and Events," 2023, spsp.org/events/demonstrating-our-commitment-anti-racism-through-programming-and-events (accessed January 15, 2023).

129. For an overview of bodily integrity identity disorder, and a comparison with gender dysphoria, see Antonia Ostgathe, Thomas Schnell, and Erich Kasten, "Bodily Integrity Disorder and Gender Dysphoria: A Pilot Study to Investigate Similarities and Differences," *American Journal of Applied Psychology* 3(6) (2014): 138–143.

130. Some may dispute this conclusion, pointing out that the medical treatment transitioning individuals often request, especially surgery, is not inexpensive. True, but because these costs are spread out over millions of people, the increase in health insurance premiums or taxes that results is minimal.

131. Conor Friedersdorf, "What to Teach Young Kids About Gender," *The Atlantic*, September 16, 2022, www.theatlantic.com/ideas/archive/2022/09/how-to-teach-gender-identity-in-schools/671422/.

132. LGBTQIA Resource Center, University of California at Davis, "Pronouns and Inclusive Language," 2021, lgbtqia.ucdavis.edu/educated/pronouns-inclusive-language. This website notes that the chart does not provide an exhaustive list, stating "Any combination is possible!" Great.

133. Robby Soave, "Conservatives Wrongly Portrayed the Loudoun County Sexual Assault as a Transgender Bathroom Issue," *Reason*, November 1, 2021, reason.com/2021/11/01/conservatives-wrongly-portrayed-the-loudoun-county-sexual-assault-as-a-transgender-bathroom-issue/.

134. Federal Bureau of Prisons, U.S. Department of Justice, "Transgender

Offender Manual," January 18, 2017, esp. p. 5 ("the agency shall consider [placement] on a case-by-case basis" in light of security and safety concerns), www.bop.gov/policy/progstat/5200.04.pdf.

135. *Diagnostic and Statistical Manual of Mental Disorders*, 5th ed. (Washington, D.C.: American Psychiatric Association, 2013).

136. Emily Lefroy, "4-Year-Old Announces 'I'm a Boy!' in Transgender Gender Reveal at Parade," *New York Post*, August 8, 2022, nypost.com/2022/08/08/4-year-old-announces-hes-a-boy-in-transgender-gender-reveal/.

137. See, e.g., Lisa Littman, "Individuals treated for Gender Dysphoria with Medical and/or Surgical Transition Who Subsequently Detransitioned: A Survey of 100 Detransitioners," *Archives of Sexual Behavior* 50 (2021): 3353–3369.

138. Michael Biggs, "Estrogen Is Associated with Greater Suicidality Among Transgender Males, and Puberty Suppression Is Not Associated with Better Mental Health Outcomes for Either Sex," Reader Comment to Jack L. Turban, et al. "Access to Gender-Affirming Hormones During Adolescence and Mental Health Outcomes Among Transgender Adults," PLOS ONE 17(1) (2022), journals.plos.org/plosone/article/comment?id=10.1371/annotation/dcc6a58e-592a-49d4-9b65-ff65df2aa8f6.

139. Madison Aitken, et al. "Self-Harm and Suicidality in Children Referred for Gender Dysphoria," *Journal of the American Academy of Child and Adolescent Psychiatry* 55(6) (2016): 513–520.

140. Azeen Ghorayshi, "Report Reveals Sharp Rise in Transgender Youth in the U.S.," *New York Times*, June 10, 2022, www.nytimes.com/2022/06/10/science/transgender-teenagers-national-survey.html.

141. See, for example, discussion of some of these books in Andrew Sullivan, "Who Is Looking Out for Gay Kids?" *Substack*, April 8, 2022, andrewsullivan.substack.com/p/who-is-looking-out-for-gay-kids-a19.

142. Jodie Patterson, *Born Ready: The True Story of a Boy Named Penelope* (New York: Crown Books for Young Readers, 2021).

143. Some of the material in this section is borrowed from blog posts I authored that appeared on the website for the Center for Inquiry, principally the blog post entitled "Transgender Athletes and Justice in an Imperfect World," August 2, 2021, centerforinquiry.org/blog/transgender-athletes-and-justice-in-an-imperfect-world/.

144. Christophe Saudan et al. "Testosterone and Doping Control," *British Journal of Sports Medicine* 40 (Suppl. 1) (2006): i21–i24, bjsm.bmj.com/content/40/suppl_1/i21.

145. Cyd Zeigler and Karleigh Webb, "These 32 Trans Athletes Have Competed Openly in College," *Outsports*, April 6, 2022, www.outsports.com/trans/2022/1/7/22850789/trans-athletes-college-ncaa-lia-thomas. Trans men compete in men's sports also. No one has made an objection regarding their participation because their biological history does not place them at a competitive advantage.

146. Megan McArdle, "Don't Forget the Other Women in the Pool," *Washington Post*, February 25, 2022, www.washingtonpost.com/opinions/2022/02/24/lia-thomas-ivy-league-swimming-championships/.

147. "These 32 Trans Athletes Have Competed Openly in College."

148. Larry Strauss, "In Real Life, Transgender Girls in Sports Are a Non-Controversy: Retired High School Coach," *USA Today*, April 19, 2021, www.usatoday.com/story/opinion/voices/2021/04/09/transgender-girls-sports-reality-not-controversial-column/7088759002/.

149. American Civil Liberties Union, "Four Myths about Trans Athletes, Debunked," April 30, 2020, www.aclu.org/news/lgbtq-rights/four-myths-about-trans-athletes-debunked.

150. Roman Stubbs, "Conn. High School Girls File Federal Suit To Prevent Transgender Athletes from Competing," *Washington Post*, February 12, 2020, www.washingtonpost.com/sports/2020/02/12/conn-high-school-girls-file-federal-suit-prevent-transgender-athletes-competing/.

Chapter 4

Christian Nationalism: Imposing a Religious Identity on the United States

1. See, e.g., Remarks of Rep. Michele Bachmann, Thanksgiving Family Forum, Des Moines, Iowa, November 19, 2011, available at: www.youtube.com/watch?v=aY8Zw5NzUXQ (minute 1:01:00) ("American exceptionalism is grounded on the Judeo-Christian ethic, which is really based upon the Ten Commandments. The Ten Commandments were the foundation for our law.").

2. Andrew Torba and Andrew Isker, *Christian Nationalism: A Biblical Guide to Taking Dominion & Disciplining Nations* (Middletown, DE: Gab AI, 2022), pp. 19, 20.

3. Ibid., p. xxvi.

4. S. Jonathan O'Donnell, "Unipolar Dispensations: Exceptionalism, Empire, and the End of One America," *Political Theology* 20(1) (2019): 66–84, esp. pp. 68–69. See also Tara Isabella Burton, "Understanding the Christian Broadcasting Network, the Force Behind the Latest Pro-Trump Newscast," *Vox*, August 5, 2017, www.vox.com/identities/2017/8/5/16091740/christian-broadcasting-network-cbn-pat-robertson-trump.

5. Bradley Onishi and Annika Brockschmidt, "Michael Flynn, Donald

Trump, and the Ascendance of Spiritual Warfare in America," *Think* (NBC News opinion blog), October 2, 2022, www.nbcnews.com/think/opinion/michael-flynn-trump-americas-christian-nationalism-threat-rcna50289. See also Thomas D. Ice, "What Is Dominion Theology?" Liberty University Digital Commons (May 2009), available at: core.ac.uk/download/pdf/58821994.pdf.

6. Pew Research Center, "Beyond Red vs. Blue: The Political Typology," November 9, 2021, www.pewresearch.org/politics/2021/11/09/beyond-red-vs-blue-the-political-typology-2/ (23 percent of Republicans are "faith and flag" conservatives who believe government should promote religious values). Although the estimate of a quarter of Republicans being hard-core Christian nationalists is probably more or less correct, many more Republicans sympathize with some of the Christian nationalists' positions, if not their entire ideology. See University of Maryland Critical Issues Poll, "American Attitudes on Race, Ethnicity, and Religion," May 2022, Q. 21, criticalissues.umd.edu/sites/criticalissues.umd.edu/files/American%20Attitudes%20on%20Race%2CEthnicity%2CReligion.pdf. (43 percent of Republicans believe the Constitution would allow the government to declare the United States a Christian nation).

7. Samuel L. Perry et al., "The Devil That You Know: Christian Nationalism and Intent To Change One's Voting Behavior for or Against Trump in 2020," *Politics and Religion* 15 (2022): 229–246.

8. Jack Jenkins, "Republicans Mostly Mum on Calls To Make GOP 'Party of Christian Nationalists'," *Washington Post*, August 19, 2022, www.washingtonpost.com/religion/2022/08/19/republicans-mostly-mum-calls-make-gop-party-christian-nationalism/.

9. Kelsey Vlamis, "Trump Says 'Americans Kneel to God and God Alone' as Support for Christian Nationalism Grows Among Republicans," *Insider*, July 24, 2022, www.businessinsider.com/trump-americans-kneel-to-god-christian-nationalism-grows-in-gop-2022.

10. National Archives, Declaration of Independence, available at: www.archives.gov/founding-docs/declaration-transcript.

11. Perhaps Barton's best book is *Original Intent: The Courts, the Constitution, & Religion*, 6th ed. (Aledo, TX: Wallbuilder Press, 2011). Other Christian nationalist authors who rely heavily on quotations from some of the Founders include Gary DeMar, *America's Christian History: The Untold Story* (Powder Springs, GA: American Visions, 1995); John Eidsmoe, *Christianity and the Constitution: The Faith of Our Founding Fathers* (Grand Rapids, MI: Baker Academic, 1995); and Tim LaHaye, *Faith of Our Founding Fathers: A Comprehensive Study of America's Christian Foundations* (Green Forest, AR: Master Books, 1994).

12. Wallbuilders, "The Founders as Christians," wallbuilders.com/the-

founders-as-christians/.

13. Barton, *Original Intent*, p. 152.

14. For a book length treatment of religion in the colonies, the classic work is William Warren Sweet, *Religion in Colonial America* (New York: Charles Scribner's Sons, 1942).

15. Frank Lambert, *The Founding Fathers and the Place of Religion in America* (Princeton: Princeton University Press, 2003), pp. 161–162, 178. See also Steven K. Green, *Inventing a Christian America: The Myth of the Religious Founding* (New York: Oxford University Press, 2015), esp. pp. 130–153.

16. Brooke Allen, *Moral Minority: Our Skeptical Founding Fathers* (Chicago: Ivan R. Dee, 2006). For Washington in particular, see also Joseph J. Ellis, *His Excellency: George Washington* (New York: Vintage Books, 2005). For Franklin in particular, see also H.W. Brands, *The First American: The Life and Times of Benjamin Franklin* (New York: Doubleday, 2000), esp. pp. 94–95, 657–658. I list Jefferson as a Founder even though he was in France at the time of the Constitutional Convention and the adoption of the Bill of Rights. He corresponded with Madison during this time and scholars agree he influenced Madison on various issues, including the necessity for a Bill of Rights. See Leonard W. Levy, *Origins of the Bill of Rights* (New Haven: Yale University Press, 1999), pp. 32–34. In any event, Christian nationalists usually include Jefferson among the Founders because he authored the draft of the Declaration of Independence.

17. Gordon S. Wood, *Revolutionary Characters: What Made the Founders Different* (New York: Penguin, 2007), p. 15.

18. Jennifer Schuessler, "For Richard Dawkins, Traditional Christmas Carols Trump Atheism," *New York Times*, December 16, 2011, archive.nytimes.com/artsbeat.blogs.nytimes.com/2011/12/16/for-richard-dawkins-traditional-christmas-carols-trump-atheism/.

19. Wallbuilders, "Benjamin Franklin's Letter to Thomas Paine," wallbuilders.com/benjamin-franklins-letter-thomas-paine/.

20. Anson Phelps Stokes, *Church and State in the United States*, vol. 1 (New York, Harper & Bros., 1950), p. 392.

21. Forrest Church, *The Separation of Church and State: Writings on a Fundamental Freedom by America's Founders* (Boston: Beacon Press, 2004), pp. 56–59.

22. Ibid.

23. Stokes, *Church and State in the United States*, p. 394.

24. National Archives, Articles of Confederation, available at: www.archives.gov/milestone-documents/articles-of-confederation.

25. Ibid.

26. National Archives, The Constitution of the United States, available at:

www.archives.gov/founding-docs/constitution-transcript.

27. In this paragraph and at various other points in this chapter I borrow from my prior book, *The Necessity of Secularism: Why God Can't Tell Us What To Do* (Durham, NC: Pitchstone, 2014), esp. chapter 2.

28. Edwin S. Gaustad, *Faith of Our Fathers: Religion and the New Nation* (San Francisco: Harper & Row, 1987), p. 113.

29. Isaac Kramnick and R. Laurence Moore, *The Godless Constitution: A Moral Defense of the Secular State* (New York: W.W. Norton & Co., 2005), p. 37.

30. Morton Borden, *Jews, Turks, and Infidels* (Chapel Hill, NC: University of North Carolina Press, 1984), p. 16.

31. Kramnick and Moore, *The Godless Constitution*, p. 37.

32. Gaustad, *Faith of Our Fathers*, p. 118.

33. Kramnick and Moore, *The Godless Constitution*, pp. 105–106.

34. Ibid., p. 146.

35. National Reform Association, "Mission Statement," nationalreformassociation.weebly.com/.

36. The letter is reproduced in Church, *The Separation of Church and State*, pp. 129–130.

37. For a summary and analysis of the debate in Congress over the religion clauses of the First Amendment, see Douglas Laycock, "Nonreferential Aid to Religion: A False Claim About Original Intent," *William and Mary Law Review* 27 (1986): 875–923; Leonard W. Levy, *The Establishment Clause: Religion and the First Amendment* (New York: Macmillan, 1986), esp. pp. 75–84.

38. Laycock, "Nonpreferential Aid to Religion," pp. 882–883.

39. See, for example, the majority opinion in *Locke v. Davey*, 540 U.S. 712, 718 (2004) (stating that the establishment clause and the free exercise clause are "frequently in tension").

40. See, e.g., *Carson v. Makin*, No. 20-1088 (June 21, 2022) (Supreme Court holds Maine must provide tuition assistance to religious schools if it provides such assistance to secular private schools).

41. See, e.g., Barton, *Original Intent*, pp. 27–37.

42. Commonwealth of Massachusetts, "Massachusetts Declaration of Rights – Article 3 (1780)," www.mass.gov/news/massachusetts-declaration-of-rights-article-3.

43. See, e.g., *Cantwell v. Connecticut*, 310 U.S. 296 (1940) (ruling free exercise clause of First Amendment is incorporated via the due process clause of the Fourteenth Amendment and, therefore, applicable to state governments).

44. Benjamin Franklin Letter to Ricard Price, 1780, quoted in Alexander H. Bullock, "The Centennial of the Massachusetts Constitution," *Proceedings of the Antiquarian Society* 1 (1882): 189, 229–230, available at: www.mass.gov/

news/massachusetts-declaration-of-rights-article-3.

45. Joseph Story, *Commentaries on the Constitution of the United States*, 4th ed. (Boston: Little, Brown & Co., 1873), §1871.

46. Ibid., §1877.

47. Barton, *Original Intent*, pp. 37, 170, 173.

48. A summary of Story's correspondence setting forth his disagreement with Jefferson can be found in Green, *Inventing a Christian America*, p. 225.

49. *Vidal v. Girard's Executors*, 2 How. (43 U.S.) 127, 198 (1844).

50. Barton, *Original Intent*, p. 254.

51. Ibid.

52. Barton, *Original Intent*, p. 286.

53. Green, *Inventing a Christian America*, esp. pp. 163–170; Matthew Stewart, *Nature's God: The Heretical Origins of the American Republic* (New York: W.W. Norton & Co., 2014).

54. Some may argue that natural law is perfectly compatible with Christianity, and that many Christian theologians, such as Thomas Aquinas, have argued that humans can use reason to discern the natural law undergirding much of morality. However, Christians also claim that revelation is superior to reason and that various fundamental truths exceed the reach of reason and can be known only through revelation. Thomas Aquinas, *Summa Theologica*, I, question 1, art.1.

55. A classic contemporary work by a Loyalist minister is Jonathan Boucher, *A View of the Causes and Consequences of the American Revolution* (London: G.G. and J. Robinson, 1797), reprint available at: www.forgottenbooks.com/en/books/AViewoftheCausesandConsequencesoftheAmericanRevolution_10150428.

56. See, e.g., Barton, *Original Intent*, pp. 81–86; Torba and Isker, *Christian Nationalism*, pp. 57–66.

57. The text of the Mayflower Compact can be found at the website of Yale Law School's Avalon Project, avalon.law.yale.edu/17th_century/mayflower.asp.

58. The text of the Fundamental Orders of 1639 can be found at the website of Yale Law School's Avalon Project, avalon.law.yale.edu/17th_century/order.asp.

59. Torba and Isker, *Christian Nationalism*, pp. 57–58.

60. Kramnick and Moore, *The Godless Constitution*, p. 72.

61. *Two Treatises of Government*, ed. Thomas L. Cook (1690; New York: Hafner Publishing Company, 1947).

62. *A Letter Concerning Toleration* (1689; Amherst, NY: Prometheus Books, 1990).

63. Ibid., pp. 18, 19.

64. Ibid., p. 20.

65. Lambert, *The Founding Fathers and the Place of Religion in America*, p. 75.

66. Ibid., p. 92.

67. Phyllis Schafly and George Neumayr, *No Higher Power: Obama's War on Religious Freedom* (Washington, DC: Regnery, 2012), esp. p. 149 (Constitution is designed for people shaped by Golden Rule and Ten Commandments).

68. Barton, *Original Intent*, pp. 247–252.

69. Torba and Isker, *Christian Nationalism*, p. 32.

70. S. Harrison Thomson, *Europe in Renaissance and Reformation* (New York: Harcourt, Brace & World, 1963), p. 491.

71. Ibid.

72. Mark David Hall, *Did America Have a Christian Founding? Separating Modern Myth from Historical Truth* (Nashville: Nelson Books, 2019), pp. 36–41.

73. Alexander Hamilton, James Madison, and John Jay, *The Federalist Papers*, ed. Clinton Rossiter (New York: New American Library, 1961), p. 57 (Federalist No. 6; Hamilton).

74. Ibid., p. 301 ("The oracle who is always consulted and cited on this subject is the celebrated Montesquieu.") (Federalist No. 47; Madison).

75. *Summa Theologica*, II-II, question 11, art. 3.

76. Perry G. E. Miller, "The Contribution of Protestant Churches to Religious Liberty in Colonial America," in *American Civilization: Readings in the Cultural and Intellectual History of the United States*, ed. Eugene C. Drozdowski (Glenview, IL: Scott, Foresman and Company, 1972), pp. 51–52.

77. Ibid., p. 52.

78. Lambert, *The Founding Fathers and the Place of Religion in America*, p. 75.

79. Ibid.

80. Stephen Wolfe, *The Case for Christian Nationalism* (Moscow, ID: Canon Press, 2022), p. 358.

81. Ibid., pp. 354–357.

82. Deborah A. Schwartz and Jay Wishingrad, "The Eighth Amendment, Beccaria, and the Enlightenment: An Historical Justification for the Weems v. United States Excessive Punishment Doctrine," *Buffalo Law Review* 24 (3) (1975): 783–838.

83. Details of these punishments may be found in Michel Foucault, *Discipline and Punish: The Birth of the Prison* (New York: Vintage Books, 1979), esp. pp. 3–69.

84. The placard is quoted in the Supreme Court's decision in *McCreary County v. ACLU*, 545 U.S. 844 (2005).

85. See, e.g., H.R. 31, 105th Cong., 1st sess., available at: www.congress. gov/105/bills/hconres31/BILLS-105hconres31rfs.pdf (declaring Ten Commandments as significant for development of fundamental legal principles of Western civilization); J. Res. Kentucky General Assembly, SJR 18 (2003 session), available at: apps.legislature.ky.gov/law/acts/03RS/documents/0032.pdf (declaring, inter alia, that Ten Commandments provide foundation for many civil and criminal laws in Kentucky).

86. Barton, *Original Intent*, pp. 55–80.

87. Augustine, "Questions on Exodus," trans. John Litteral, chap. 20, question 71, sites.google.com/site/aquinasstudybible/home/exodus/questions-on-exodus-by-augustine-of-hippo.

88. For academic discussion of the common morality, see Tom L. Beauchamp and James F. Childress, *Principles of Biomedical Ethics*, 6th ed. (New York: Oxford University Press, 2009), pp. 2–5, 387–397; Ronald A. Lindsay, "Slaves, Embryos, and Nonhuman Animals: Moral Status and the Limitations of Common Morality Theory," *Kennedy Institute of Ethics Journal* 15 (4) (2005): 323–346.

89. Sissela Bok, *Common Values* (Columbia, MO: University of Missouri Press, 1995), p. 15.

90. On this point, see Lynn Hunt, *Inventing Human Rights* (New York: W. W. Norton & Company, 2007).

91. The text of the Code of Hammurabi can be found at the website of Yale Law School's Avalon Project: avalon.law.yale.edu/ancient/hamframe.asp.

92. Oliver Wendell Holmes, *The Common Law* (Boston: Little, Brown and Company, 1923), pp. 1–38.

93. W. L. Warren, *Henry II* (Berkeley, CA: University of California Press, 1973), pp. 317–361.

94. Jeremy D. Weinstein, "Adultery, Law, and the State: A History," *Hasting Law Journal* 38(1) (1986): 195–238, 208–210.

95. Ibid., pp. 211–212. See also Warren, *Henry II*, pp. 462–465.

96. F. W. Maitland, "The Growth of Statute and Common Law and the Rise of The Court of Chancery, 1307–1600," in F.C. Montague and F.W. Maitland, *A Sketch of English Legal History* (New York: F. P. Putnam's Sons, 1915).

97. Julius Goebel, Jr., "King's Law and Local Custom in Seventeenth Century New England," *Columbia Law Review* 31(3) (1931): 416–448, 423 n. 14.

98. A summary of this seminal case can be found in Mark Fortier, "Coke, Ellesmere, and James I," *Renaissance Quarterly* 51(4) (1998): 1255–1281, 1259–1262.

99. Ibid.

100. Ibid., pp. 1277–1279.

101. The Federal Judiciary Act of 1789, 1 Statutes at Large 73 (1845), available at: www.archivesfoundation.org/documents/judiciary-act-1789/.

102. J. Michael Medina, "The Bible Annotated: Use of the Bible in Reported American Decisions," *Northern Illinois University Law Review* 12 (1991): 187–254.

103. Goebel, Jr., "King's Law and Local Custom in Seventeenth Century New England," pp. 422–423.

104. *Vidal v. Girard's Executors*, 2 How. (43 U.S.) at 198.

105. *Rex v. Taylor,* 3 Keble 607 (1675). A summary of the case can be found in A. H. Wintersteen, "Christianity and the Common Law," *University of Pennsylvania Law Review* 38 (1890): 273–285.

106. Wintersteen, "Christianity and the Common Law," p. 273.

107. *Vidal v. Girard's Executors*, 2 How. (43 U.S.) at 198.

108. Wintersteen, "Christianity and the Common Law."

109. *Gitlow v. New York*, 268 U.S. 652 (1925).

110. *McGowan v. Maryland*, 366 U.S. 420, 473 (1961).

111. Michael C. McGarrity and Calvin A. Shivers, Federal Bureau of Investigation, "Confronting White Supremacy," June 4, 2019 (Statement before the House Oversight and Reform Committee, Subcommittee on Civil Rights and Civil Liberties), www.fbi.gov/news/testimony/confronting-white-supremacy.

112. Wolfe, *The Case for Christian Nationalism*, pp. 464–465.

CONCLUSION

1. For an overview of the Enlightenment, I recommend Peter Gay, *The Enlightenment: An Interpretation* (New York: Alfred A. Knopf, 1973).

2. Jamelle Bouie, "The Enlightenment's Dark Side," *Slate*, June 5, 2018, slate.com/news-and-politics/2018/06/taking-the-enlightenment-seriously-requires-talking-about-race.html.

3. Hugh Thomas, *The Slave Trade* (New York: Simon & Schuster, 1997), esp. pp. 488–511.

4. Dana Adams Schmidt, "Saudi Arabian Slavery Persists Despite Ban by Faisal in 1962," *New York Times*, March 28, 1967, www.nytimes.com/1967/03/28/archives/saudi-arabian-slavery-persists-despite-ban-by-faisal-in-1962.html.

5. Samantha Lock, "'To Kill a Mockingbird,' Other Books Banned from California Schools over Racism Concerns," *Newsweek*, November 13, 2020, www.newsweek.com/kill-mockingbird-other-books-banned-california-schools-over-racism-concerns-1547241.

6. Claire Moses, "The Spread of Book Banning," *New York Times*, July 31, 2022, www.nytimes.com/2022/07/31/briefing/book-banning-debate.html.

7. Cristina Beltran, "To Understand Trump's Support, We Must Think in Terms of Multiracial Whiteness," *Washington Post*, January 15, 2021, www.washingtonpost.com/opinions/2021/01/15/understand-trumps-support-we-must-think-terms-multiracial-whiteness/.

8. Wolfe, *The Case for Christian Nationalism*, pp. 384–385.

ACKNOWLEDGMENTS

David Kadue read almost the entire manuscript and provided many helpful comments, editorial observations, and substantive suggestions. The work has been much improved as a result. I am deeply indebted to him.

Russell Blackford read a draft of the Introduction and Chapter 1. His insightful critique saved me from some errors, and I am very grateful for his advice.

Justin Vacula read portions of the draft and made thoughtful suggestions for which I owe him thanks.

Jonathan Field challenged me on the topic of systemic racism, and my arguments in Chapter 2 have been sharpened thanks to him.

I am thankful to Kurt Volkan, publisher at Pitchstone Publishing, for encouraging me to pursue this work. I am pleased to be associated with Pitchstone, which has an enviable track record of publishing works that engage the mind and rely on argument, not rhetoric.

Writing a book, at least the way I do it, is an enterprise that requires solitude and quiet for extended periods of time. My love and gratitude to Debra, my wife, for her patience, understanding, and support.

ABOUT THE AUTHOR

Ronald A. Lindsay, a philosopher (PhD, Georgetown University) and lawyer (JD, University of Virginia) was an attorney with the international law firm of Seyfarth LLP for twenty-six years before joining the Center for Inquiry, where he served as president and CEO from 2008 through 2016. He is the author of two prior nonfiction books, *The Necessity of Secularism* (Pitchstone 2014) and *Future Bioethics* (Prometheus 2008), and the novel *The Lost Song of Goliath* (Nineteenth Street Publishers 2019). He has also written numerous philosophical and legal essays, including the entry on "Euthanasia" in the *International Encyclopedia of Ethics* (Wiley Blackwell 2013). He may be found on Twitter @ RALindsay. A native of Boston, he currently lives in Loudoun County, Virginia, with his wife, Debra, where their presence is usually tolerated by their cat.